# Marriage, Money and Divorce in Medieval Islamic Society

High rates of divorce, often taken to be a modern and western phenomenon, were also typical of medieval Islamic societies. By pitting these high rates of divorce against the Islamic ideal of marriage, Yossef Rapoport radically challenges the usual assumptions about the legal inferiority of Muslim women and their economic dependence on men. He argues that marriages in late medieval Cairo, Damascus and Jerusalem had little in common with the patriarchal models advocated by jurists and moralists. The transmission of dowries, women's access to waged labour, and the strict separation of property between spouses made divorce easy and normative, initiated by wives as often as by their husbands. This carefully researched work of social history is interwoven with intimate accounts of individual medieval lives, making for a truly compelling read. It will be of interest to scholars of all disciplines concerned with the history of women and gender in Islam.

YOSSEF RAPOPORT is an associated member of the Faculty of Oriental Studies, University of Oxford.

**Cambridge Studies in Islamic Civilisation**



*Published titles in the series are listed at the back of the book*

# Marriage, Money and Divorce in Medieval Islamic Society

YOSSEF RAPOPORT

*University of Oxford*

CAMBRIDGE
UNIVERSITY PRESS

CAMBRIDGE UNIVERSITY PRESS
Cambridge, New York, Melbourne, Madrid, Cape Town, Singapore, São Paulo

Cambridge University Press
The Edinburgh Building, Cambridge CB2 8RU, UK

Published in the United States of America by Cambridge University Press, New York

www.cambridge.org
Information on this title: www.cambridge.org/9780521847155



First published 2005
This digitally printed version 2007

*A catalogue record for this publication is available from the British Library*

*Library of Congress Cataloguing in Publication data*
Rapoport, Yossef, 1968–
Marriage, money and divorce in medieval Islamic society / Yossef Rapoport.
p. cm. – (Cambridge studies in Islamic civilization)
Includes bibliographical references and index.
ISBN 0-521-84715-X
1. Marriage – Egypt – Cairo – History – To 1500. 2. Marriage – Syria – Damascus – History – To 1500. 3. Marriage – Jerusalem – History – To 1500. 4. Divorce – Egypt – Cairo – History – To 1500. 5. Divorce – Syria – Damascus – History – To 1500. 6. Divorce – Jerusalem – History – To 1500. 7. Marriage (Islamic law) 8. Divorce (Islamic law) 9. Islamic countries – Social conditions. I. Title. II. Cambridge studies in Islamic civilization.
HQ525.I8R36 2005
306′.0917′67 – dc22 2004058573

ISBN 978-0-521-84715-5 hardback
ISBN 978-0-521-04580-3 paperback

To my parents, with love

# Contents

# Acknowledgments

This book grew out of my doctoral dissertation in the Department of Near Eastern Studies at Princeton University, and I am grateful to my advisors there, A. L. Udovitch, Michael Cook and William C. Jordan, for both their criticisms and for enduring support.

I was also fortunate to be able to draw on the wisdom and knowledge of many former students at Princeton – more than I could mention here. In particular, I would like to thank Shahab Ahmed, Nenad Filipoviç, Roxani Margariti, Christine Philliou and Baki Tezcan for their friendship and insights. Adam Sabra first introduced me to the field of Mamluk studies. His rigorous approach to social history has been an example I have striven to follow. Tamer el-Leithy shared my fascination with everything Mamluk, from queer anecdotes to coned hats, and his original and sensitive mind has been a constant source of inspiration.

Many colleagues offered their help at particular junctures. I would like to acknowledge the kind advice and assistance I received from Maristella Botticini, Mark Cohen, Shaun Marmon, Donald Little, Christian Müller, Giovanni Oppenheim, David Powers, Yusuf Ragib, Amy Singer, Daniella Talmon-Heller, Bethany J. Walker, Michael Winter and Amalia Zomeño. I am obliged to Rifaat Ebou-el-Hajj for reminding me of the reason for embarking on this project in the first place.

The Graduate School of Princeton University helped with financial support throughout the course of my doctoral studies. The Department of Middle Eastern History at Tel Aviv University provided a timely post-doctoral scholarship during the later stages of the work. The librarians of the Chester Beatty Collection made my stay in Dublin both highly enjoyable and extremely useful.

An earlier version of chapter 5 was published as "Ibn Taymiyya on Divorce Oaths," in A. Levanoni and M. Winter (eds.), *The Mamluks in Egyptian and Syrian Politics and Society* (Leiden: Brill, 2004), 191–217. An earlier version of part of chapter 4 was published as "Divorce and the Elite Household in Late Medieval Cairo," *Continuity and Change* 16/2 (August 2001), 201–18.

Gilat Levy, truly my better half, saw this book through from its conception. Her sharp logic and her feminism were as precious to me as her encouragement and patience. She is also a living testimony to the little we learn from history; despite her intense involvement with this book and its contents, she still agreed to be my wife.

# Glossary

| | |
|---|---|
| *awlād al-nās* | collective term for the children of the *mamlūk* military elite. |
| *faskh* | judicial divorce, or annulment of marriage, by an Islamic court. |
| *fatwā*, pl. *fatāwā* | legal opinion issued by a *muftī*, often as a result of a petition or enquiry. |
| *ḥilf bi'l-ṭalāq* | oath on pain of repudiation; divorce oath. |
| *iqṭā'* | a right to land revenue held in return for military service. |
| *jihāz* | dowry or trousseau, the property brought by the bride into a marriage. |
| *khānqāh* | a Sufi lodge, often associated with prayers for the dead. |
| *khul'* | consensual separation, in which a husband grants a divorce in return for monetary compensation. |
| *mamlūk* | a slave, member of the military elite. |
| *muftī* | a jurisconsult, a learned man who delivers legal responsa (*fatāwā*). |
| *mut'a* | compensation sometimes paid to a divorcée following unilateral repudiation. |
| *nuzūl* | the practice of handing down an office or position, usually from father to son. |
| *qāḍī* | a judge in an Islamic court. |
| *qasāma* | a sworn undertaking registered in court at the instigation of the authorities. |
| *ribāṭ* | a Sufi lodge, often reserved for female mystics. |
| *ṣadāq* | dower; the groom's marriage gift, usually divided into advance and deferred payments. Also called *mahr*. |
| *taḥlīl* | making permissible; marriage with the intention of permitting the bride to a husband from a previous marriage. |
| *ṭalāq* | divorce achieved through unilateral repudiation by the husband. |
| *ta'wīḍ* | compensation for a widow in lieu of a deferred marriage gift. |
| *zāwiya* | a Sufi lodge, often associated with male followers of a mystical order. |

# Abbreviations

| | |
|---|---|
| *AI* | *Annales Islamologiques* |
| *BSOAS* | *Bulletin of the School of Oriental and African Studies* |
| *EI*[2] | *Encyclopedia of Islam*, 2nd edition (Leiden, 1960) |
| *IJMES* | *International Journal of Middle Eastern Studies* |
| *ILS* | *Islamic Law and Society* |
| *JAOS* | *Journal of the American Oriental Society* |
| *JESHO* | *Journal of the Economic and Social History of the Orient* |
| *MSR* | *Mamlūk Studies Review* |
| *SI* | *Studia Islamica* |

# Introduction

Shihāb al-Dīn Aḥmad Ibn Ṭawq, a notary in late fifteenth-century Damascus, liked to keep a detailed record of his transactions and other memorable events. This is what he wrote in his diary on Ṣafar 19, 890 (March 7, 1485):

> Monday the 19th. In the last few days the weather was very windy. The gusts broke in half an almond tree in the garden, one of the big ones. The tree fell on a heavy pear tree and trimmed its upper half. Many trees were lost. Let us seek refuge in Allāh from the wickedness of our souls and our evil deeds.
>
> I divorced my wife at her request, by mutual consent, after being accused of repudiating her and for doing things and not doing others. The witnesses were Ibn Nūr al-Dīn al-Khaṭṭābī and his colleague Ibn al-Dayrī. She became unlawful to me.
>
> In the afternoon we witnessed the remarriage of Yūsuf ibn Khālid and his divorcee, the manumitted slave-girl of Amat Sulṭān, in the Mosque of Manjak. The marriage gift was 10 Ashrafī gold coins, which remain a due debt upon the groom. The witnesses were the writer of these lines and Ibn Nūr al-Dīn al-Khaṭṭābī. Shaykh Muhannā presided, and Ibn al-Dayrī accepted the marriage on behalf of the groom.[1]

Divorce was pervasive in late medieval Damascus. As a notary, Ibn Ṭawq made his living out of witnessing the divorce deeds and the subsequent marriages of other Damascene couples, many of which he then recorded in his diary. Squeezed between the storm that swept through his backyard and his afternoon business in the mosque, Ibn Ṭawq's own divorce has an almost casual air to it. The reasons for the divorce remain obscure. The relations between the long-time spouses appear to have been good. The only mention of a row came three years earlier, when the two quarreled over the bracelets worn by their daughter Fāṭima, and Ibn Ṭawq threatened to divorce his wife if she let Fāṭima wear them again.[2] More recently, there was some domestic tension on account of the slave maid, whom Ibn Ṭawq felt showed him disrespect. He even records beating the slave-girl with a stick, something for which he felt deeply ashamed.[3] There was also the matter of Ibn Ṭawq's

[1] Shihāb al-Dīn Aḥmad Ibn Ṭawq, *Al-Ta'līq. Yawmiyyāt Shihāb al-Dīn Aḥmad Ibn Ṭawq (834/1430–915/1509): Mudhakkirāt Kutibat bi-Dimashq fī Awākhir al-'Ahd al-Mamlūkī, 885/1480–908/1502*, ed. Ja'far al-Muhājir, vol. I (885/1480–890/1485) (Damascus: Institut Français de Damas, 2000), 449.

[2] *Ibid.*, 153. [3] *Ibid.*, 431.

outstanding debt to a textile merchant called Zayn al-Dīn. At the beginning of the month Ibn Ṭawq swore to repudiate his wife three times if he were to ask Zayn al-Dīn for another loan as long as the existing debt was not paid.[4] While the diary has no mention of a remarriage, two-and-a-half months later Ibn Ṭawq's wife gave birth to their third child, a daughter called 'Ā'isha.[5] Only then do we learn that she was in her seventh month when the consensual divorce took place.

The dramatic increase in the rates of divorce over the past several decades has changed the fabric of Western societies: it is associated with breaking away from traditional meanings of family and marriage, of gender relations, and of religion. Most of all, divorce is associated, for good and for bad, with modernity. The rise of divorce is attributed to diverse facets of modern life: decline in belief, breakdown in family values, unadulterated individualism and pursuit of self-interest, rising expectations about marriage, rising life expectancy, increasing economic independence of women and the empowering effect of feminism. The link between modernity and soaring divorce rates has led many to question the future viability of marriage as a social institution.[6]

This has been a Eurocentric debate if there ever was one. The outpouring of scholarly and popular works dealing with the rise of divorce in the West all but disregards the historical examples of past societies in which divorce rates have been consistently high. Two major examples are pre-modern Japan and Islamic Southeast Asia. In nineteenth-century Japan at least one in eight marriages ended in divorce.[7] In West Java and the Malay Peninsula divorce rates were even higher, reaching 70 percent in some villages, as late as the middle of the twentieth century.[8] In these societies divorce was part and parcel of tradition; it was frequent and normative, and did not involve any stigma that would hinder the remarriage of divorced persons. In direct opposition to developments in the West, modernity brought with it greater stability in marriage and a sharp decline in divorce rates.[9]

The pre-modern Middle East was another traditional society that had consistently high rates of divorce over long periods of time. Despite some current misgivings over the imminent disintegration of the Muslim family as a result of frequent divorces, the fact is that divorce rates were higher in Ottoman or medieval Muslim societies than they are today.[10] A decade of research on the history of Ottoman families, mostly drawing on the abundant court registers, has shown that divorce was a

[4] *Ibid.*, 442. [5] *Ibid.*, 472.

[6] On divorce in Western societies, see R. Phillips, *Untying the Knot. A Short History of Divorce* (Cambridge: Cambridge University Press, 1991); L. Stone. *Road to Divorce: England 1530–1987* (Oxford: Clarendon Press, 1990).

[7] Laurel L. Cornell, "Peasant Women and Divorce in Pre-industrial Japan," *Signs* 15 (1990), 710–32.

[8] Gavin W. Jones, "Modernization and Divorce: Contrasting Trends in Islamic Southeast Asia and the West," *Population and Development Review* 23 (1997), 95–114.

[9] William J. Goode, *World Changes in Divorce Patterns* (New Haven: Yale University Press, 1993), 214–49.

[10] On the current debate on divorce in the Middle East, see M. Zilfi, "'We Don't Get Along': Women and *Hul* Divorce in the Eighteenth Century," in M. Zilfi (ed.), *Women in the Ottoman Empire: Middle Eastern Women in the Early Modern Era* (Leiden: E. J. Brill, 1997), 264–5. On the current rates of divorce in Middle Eastern countries, see Goode, *World Changes*, 270.

common feature of family life. In eighteenth-century Aleppo divorce was a "fairly common occurrence," with at least 300 divorces registered annually, and many more going on unregistered.[11] The court of Ottoman Nablus recorded as many marriages as divorces, which shows "relatively high rates of divorce."[12] A similar picture of high divorce rates and a normative attitude to divorce emerges from studies of Ottoman court records in Istanbul, Cairo, Cyprus, Sofia and ʿAyntab.[13]

Divorce in medieval Middle East societies appears to have been just as common. Due to the general absence of pre-Ottoman court records, the evidence tends to be qualitative rather than quantitative, but several studies based on legal opinions (*fatwās*) from medieval North Africa and al-Andalus give the impression of a pattern of frequent and normative divorce.[14] The prevalence of divorce among the non-Muslim minorities in medieval Islam is an indirect testimony to the frequency of divorce among the Muslim majority. In the thirteenth century the Coptic Church of Egypt, which originally regarded marriage as a holy and unbreakable sacrament, was forced to legalize limited forms of divorce. This legal change allowed the ecclesiastical law to follow the practice of the Coptic community, undoubtedly influenced by its Muslim neighbors.[15] Similarly, the papers of the Cairo Geniza, relating to the Jewish community of medieval Cairo, show that

[11] A. Marcus, *The Middle East on the Eve of Modernity: Aleppo in the Eighteenth Century* (New York: Columbia University Press, 1989), 206.

[12] J. Tucker, "Ties that Bound: Women and Family in Eighteenth and Nineteenth-Century Nablus," in N. Keddie and B. Baron (eds.), *Women in Middle Eastern History: Shifting Boundaries in Sex and Gender* (New Haven: Yale University Press, 1992), 241. See also J. Tucker, *In the House of the Law: Gender and Islamic Law in Ottoman Syria and Palestine* (Berkeley: University of California Press, 1998).

[13] R. Jennings, "Divorce in the Ottoman Sharia Court of Cyprus, 1580–1640," *SI* 77–78 (1993), 155–68; A. A. Abdal-Rehim, "The Family and Gender Laws in Egypt during the Ottoman Period," in A. El-Azhary Sonbol (ed.), *Women, Family and Divorce Laws in Islamic History* (Syracuse: Syracuse University Press, 1996), 96–111; S. Ivanova, "The Divorce between Zubaida Hatun and Essaied Osman Aga: Women in the Eighteenth-Century Shariʿa Court of Rumelia," in El-Azhary Sonbol (ed.), *Women, Family and Divorce Laws*, 112–25; Zilfi, "'We Don't Get Along'"; L. Peirce, "'She is Trouble and I Will Divorce Her': Orality, Honor and Divorce in the Ottoman Court of ʿAintab," in G. Hambly (ed.), *Women in the Medieval Islamic World: Power, Patronage, Piety* (London: Curzon Press, 1999), 269–300. The following studies play down the incidence of divorce in Ottoman society, but without, I believe, due critical approach to their sources: M. Meriwether, *The Kin Who Count. Family and Society in Ottoman Aleppo, 1770–1840* (Austin: University of Texas Press, 1999), 130; F. Zarinebaf-Shahr, "Women, Law and Imperial Justice in Ottoman Istanbul in the late Seventeenth Century," in El-Azhary Sonbol (ed.), *Women, Family and Divorce Laws*, 87.

[14] D. Powers, "Women and Divorce in the Islamic West: Three Cases," *Hawwa* 1 (2003), 29–45; D. Powers, "Women and Courts in the Maghrib, 1300–1500," in M. Khalid Masud, Rudolf Peters and David S. Powers (eds.), *Dispensing Justice in Muslim Courts: Qadis, Procedures and Judgments* (forthcoming); H. R. Idris, "Le mariage en Occident musulman d'après un choix de fatwàs médiévales extraites du Miʿyār d'al-Wanšarīsī," *SI* 32 (1970), 157–67; H. R. Idris, "Le mariage en Occident musulman. Analyse de fatwàs médiévales extraites du Miʿyār d'al-Wanšarīsī," *Revue de l'Occident Musulman et de la Méditerranée* 12 (1972), 45–62; 17 (1974), 71–105; 25 (1978), 119–38; A. Zomeño, *Dote y matrimonio en al-Andalus y el norte de África. Estudio de la jurisprudencia islámica medieval* (Madrid: Consejo Superior de Investigationes Cientificas, 2000).

[15] Mohamed Afifi, "Reflections on the Personal Laws of Egyptian Copts," in el-Azhary Sonbol (ed.), *Women, Family and Divorce Laws*, 202–15; Jacques Masson, "Histoire des causes du divorce dans le tradition canonique copte (des origines au XIIIe siècle)," *Studia Orientalia Christiana. Collectanea* 14 (1970–1), 163–250; 15 (1972–3), 181–294.

divorce was "abundantly practiced," with divorce "much more common in these times and places than [it was amongst] the Jewish families of Europe and America until the last generation." In fact, the earliest fragment of paper found in the Geniza is a divorce deed.[16]

Yet, despite the acknowledged prevalence of divorce in pre-modern Muslim societies, historians have still to problematize divorce as a social institution. In most accounts, divorces simply happen, like an act of God. In his study of Ottoman Aleppo, Marcus highlights the way divorce and high mortality rates broke up households and dispersed parents and children; but he overlooks the dissimilarity between man-made divorce and the natural causes of high mortality.[17] Other historians, also drawing on Ottoman court records, outlined the common legal causes for divorces, noting that consensual separation (*khulʿ*) appears to have been as common as unilateral repudiation by the husband (*ṭalāq*).[18] But few have asked why divorces were so common, or attempted to identify what social forces made couples separate from each other so frequently, or suggested what it all tells us about pre-modern Muslim societies in general – and in particular about the nature of marriage, family and patriarchy.

However, in a patriarchal society, divorce appears to be a paradox. Though inscribed in Islamic law as a patriarchal privilege, divorce undermines the patriarchal social order by destabilizing households, increasing the number of female-headed households and debasing the ideal of marriage. If the family was indeed the central building block of pre-modern Muslim society, and an institution that was to be protected from the penetrating eyes of the public gaze, then we would expect the incidence of divorce to be as low as possible. Indeed, if the ideal family of medieval Muslim societies was the patriarchal household, frequent divorce would surely have resulted in the creation of familial institutions that were less than ideal, as many more women would have had to make a living on their own. Moreover, if medieval Muslim societies looked upon the unattached young female as a threat to morality, and if marriage was so highly prized for both men and women, we would expect to find divorce being used only as a last resort. This was clearly not the case for much of the history of the Islamic Middle East.

This book sets out to explain the economic, legal and social causes of Muslim divorce in the Middle Eastern cities of Cairo, Damascus and Jerusalem in the Mamluk period (1250–1517). The starting point is the emergence of the Mamluk state in Egypt, Syria and Palestine, and the consolidation of a distinct military elite largely composed of ex-slaves (*mamlūks*), divided by any number of military households, and headed by a sultan residing in the capital, Cairo. The end point is the demise of this state at the hands of the Ottomans, an event that also marked the end of the medieval political and social order. These two-and-a-half centuries

16 S. D. Goitein, *A Mediterranean Society. The Jewish Communities of the Arab World as Portrayed in the Documents of the Geniza*, 6 vols. (Berkeley: University of California Press, 1967–93), vol. III, 260–72.

17 Marcus, *On the Eve of Modernity*, 198.

18 See in particular Zilfi, "'We Don't Get Along'"; Peirce, "'She is Trouble and I Will Divorce Her.'"

of Mamluk rule are unified by enduring political and legal institutions, many of which can be attributed to the first Mamluk sultans. But this was also a period of radical changes. From the viewpoint of family history, the period should be divided along the fault-line of the first outbreak of the Black Death in 749/1348. The plague, which was to recur at periodic intervals of ten to fifteen years, inflicted a staggering death toll of up to a third of the urban population. The demographic disaster, alongside its traumatic economic repercussions, indirectly triggered a transformation in gender relationships within families.

The population of Mamluk Cairo, Damascus and Jerusalem was cross-cut by sharp distinctions of wealth and rank, language and religion. The ruling horse-riding military elite, whose members mostly spoke to each other in Turkish or Circassian, was assisted by an indigenous Arabic-speaking scholarly elite, who filled the ranks of the state bureaucracy and judiciary. This state apparatus straddled some of the largest metropolises in the medieval world, most notably the capital, Cairo, which may have had up to a quarter of a million inhabitants. The population of these cities was a hotchpotch of different ethnic groups, including sizable Christian and Jewish minorities, who were autonomous in applying their own family law. While the main focus of this book is the application of Islamic family law among the Muslim Sunni majority, it will become evident that, despite the differences in legal frameworks, Muslims, Jews and Christians shared broadly similar family structures, as well as fairly similar notions of the ideal family. The Jewish family of the Geniza and the Muslim family of the Mamluk period were not very far apart.

The incidence of divorce in Mamluk society was remarkably high. The diary of the notary Shihāb al-Dīn Ibn Ṭawq gives ample testimony to the pervasiveness of divorce in late fifteenth-century Damascus, and the work of the contemporary Egyptian scholar Muḥammad b. ʿAbd al-Raḥmān al-Sakhāwī (d. 902/1497) does the same for Cairo. In his mammoth centennial biographical dictionary, containing 12,000 entries for notable men and women, al-Sakhāwī recorded information on the marital history of about 500 women.[19] This sample, the largest we have for any period of medieval Islam (and the subject of a more detailed analysis later in this book), shows a pattern of repeated divorces and remarriages by Mamluk women. At least a third of all the women mentioned by al-Sakhāwī married more than once, with many marrying three times or more. The reason for the high rates of remarriage was mainly the frequency of divorce; according to al-Sakhāwī's records, three out of ten marriages in fifteenth-century Cairo ended in divorce.[20]

[19] Muḥammad b. ʿAbd al-Raḥmān al-Sakhāwī, *al-Ḍawʾal-Lāmiʿ li-Ahl al-Qarn al-Tāsiʿ*, ed. Ḥusām al-Qudsī, 12 vols. (Cairo: Maṭbaʿat al-Quds, 1934–6).

[20] B. Musallam, "The Ordering of Muslim Societies," in F. Robinson (ed.), *The Cambridge Illustrated History of the Islamic World* (Cambridge: Cambridge University Press, 1996), 186–97; Y. Rapoport, "Divorce and the Elite Household in Late Medieval Cairo," *Continuity and Change* 16/2 (August 2001), 201–18. See also H. Lutfi, "Al-Sakhāwī's *Kitāb al-Nisāʾ* as a Source for the Social and Economic History of Muslim Women during the Fifteenth Century AD," *Muslim World* 71 (1981), 104–24; R. Roded, *Women in the Islamic Biographical Dictionaries: From Ibn Saʿd to Who's Who* (Boulder: Lynne Rienner, 1994).

The frequency of divorce in Mamluk society forces a re-thinking of gender relations in medieval Muslim societies, and in particular their economic and legal dimensions. From an economic perspective, we need to reconsider women's economic independence within and outside marriage. Since divorce was so common, and sometimes perhaps arbitrary, women could not have been as dependent on their husbands as Muslim jurists would have us believe. Frequent divorce suggests that marriage was not a promise of financial security, and that alternative sources of revenue must have been available to divorced (as well as widowed) women.

From a legal perspective, the notion of divorce as a patriarchal privilege needs to be put in a social context. Was the frequency of divorce a simple result of the easy repudiation allowed by Islamic law? Should the history of divorce, as one scholar put it, be part of the "histories of distress," alongside domestic violence?[21] In part, the questions appear to be: Did men or women initiate the majority of divorces, and what were the most common reasons underlying divorce? But the frequency of divorce and its value as a symbol of patriarchy require us to broach a larger question, which is, like divorce itself, at the intersection of law and society: How did Islamic family law translate into the reality of medieval marriage?

The economic causes and implications of frequent divorces, and in particular women's financial independence, are the subject of the first three chapters of this book. The first chapter focuses on the dowries brought by Mamluk brides. The dowry, almost always in the form of a trousseau, was a major factor determining the degree of women's economic independence, especially among the Mamluk elites. Far from being token gifts, dowries functioned as a form of pre-mortem inheritance reserved exclusively for daughters. Once the dowry was donated by the bride's parents, it remained under the woman's exclusive ownership and control throughout marriage, and then again through widowhood and divorce.

The second chapter focuses on the majority of working women, for whom dowries were of lesser value. That remunerative work was undertaken by women, both within and outside marriage, is crucial for an understanding of the balance of power that existed between husbands and wives, as well as for a comprehension of the phenomenon of frequent divorce. Wages, mostly from work in the manufacture of textiles, allowed many women to remain single for long periods of time, so forming a sizable and often unacknowledged minority in medieval Muslim societies.

The third chapter examines the economics of marriage itself. A striking characteristic of Mamluk marriages is the way in which husbands and wives attached a cash value to various aspects of their relationships. The intrusion of cash contracts typical of the marketplace challenged the ideal of the autonomous and hierarchical patriarchal household, and the monetization of marriage was a major factor determining the rates and patterns of divorce in Mamluk society.

[21] Dalenda Largueche, "Confined, Battered and Repudiated Women in Tunis since the Eighteenth Century," in El-Azhary Sonbol (ed.), *Women, Family and Divorce Laws*, 259.

The basic inequality of Islamic law, whereby a husband can divorce his wife at will, has been one of the major sources of a husband's power over his wife. The absolute right of husbands to dissolve the marriage contract at will, like the absolute right of a master to manumit his slave, was the ultimate symbol of patriarchal authority. Yet divorce was rarely a one-sided affair. The fourth chapter shows how some women manipulated patriarchal ideals in order to initiate divorce, or used their financial leverage power to force their husbands to grant them a divorce.

The paradoxical role of divorce in simultaneously upholding and undermining patriarchy is at the core of the fifth chapter, which considers the use of oaths on pain of divorce. Repudiation was the ultimate symbol of patriarchy, and therefore the basis for the most solemn and binding type of oath in the Mamluk period – and also the cause of many unwanted divorces. The main focus of the chapter is the attempt of the religious reformer Taqī al-Dīn Ibn Taymiyya (d. 728/1328) to change the Sunni law regarding divorce oaths, an attempt which landed him and his followers in jail.

A study of Mamluk divorce provides, almost by necessity, a gendered perspective on Mamluk history. An analysis of the relations of power within households can contribute to Mamluk political and economic history in ways that go beyond a simplistic equation of a political patriarchal order and a domestic one. The extraordinary power accorded to oaths on pain of divorce reveals how marital authority was both evoked and pawned in order to bolster social commitments that went far beyond the domestic sphere. Our understanding of the medieval Near Eastern textile industry becomes richer and more complex after considering the contribution of female spinners, embroiderers and seamstresses. When viewed through the lenses of gender, the grant of fiefs (*iqṭāʿ*) to the sons of the military appears to stem from the same domestic logic as the inheritance of office in religious institutions. The increasing intervention of the judicial system in conjugal life, coupled with the increasing monetization of marriage, tell us a great deal about the role of the law and, by implication, about the power of the state.

But anyone who seeks in this book a grand narrative about patriarchy and Islam should be advised to look elsewhere. I have tried, as Lila Abu Lughod advised, "to specify, to particularize and to ground in practice, place, class and time the experiences of women and the dynamics of gender."[22] Coming dangerously close to being anecdotal, this book attempts to individualize these experiences. I have sought to rescue from the historical texts and documents a sense of the humanity of the people whose lives – the very intimate and personal aspects of their lives – I am recounting in this book. I purposefully elaborated and extended the sections dealing with individuals like the seamstress Ḍayfa or the slave-girl Zumurrud and her consecutive marriages. These are not merely case studies illustrating a point; I hope they acquired a life of their own.

[22] L. Abu Lughod, "Feminist Longings and Postcolonial Conditions," in L. Abu Lughod (ed.), *Remaking Women. Feminism and Modernity in the Middle East* (Princeton: Princeton University Press, 1998), 22.

## Sources

More is probably known about women in Mamluk society than in any other medieval Muslim milieu.[23] Mamluk society left us a wealth of legal and literary sources pertaining to the private or domestic life of its members, and these sources compensate for the almost complete absence of court archives. As is true for other periods of medieval Islam, very few Mamluk documents survived in their original form. The Ḥaram collection, consisting of about a thousand documents mostly emanating from the court of a late fourteenth-century *qāḍī*, is the only Mamluk court archive in our possession. It has been catalogued by Donald Little, and was the subject of a monograph by Huda Lutfi, who paid unusual attention to questions of gender.[24] Hundreds of endowment deeds, mainly originating in late fifteenth-century Cairo, have also survived. Their contribution to our understanding of gender relations in Mamluk society has been highlighted by Carl Petry.[25] More directly relevant to the study of divorce are about a dozen Muslim marriage contracts from the Mamluk period unearthed during archaeological excavations in Egypt. The Geniza adds a few documents relating to Jewish marriage and divorce, although most of the Geniza material dates from the Fatimid period.

While the documentary evidence is thin, there is a wealth of other types of legal sources from the Mamluk period. These include legal manuals that reproduce models of common documents for the use of notaries; compilations of *responsa* by contemporary *muftī*s, mostly dealing with real-life cases; and descriptions of judicial proceedings in chronicles, some of which were composed by court officials. Legal matters are also discussed by the authors of prescriptive treatises, primarily because judicial practice tended to deviate from proper moral behavior. The *Madkhal* of the Cairene Mālikī jurist Ibn al-Ḥājj (d. 737/1336–7) is the most well-known example of this kind of Mamluk moralistic literature.[26] In all these types of legal sources divorce occupies a prominent place. Since criminal law was mainly handled by the lay courts headed by military officials, family law and commercial law were the primary responsibilities of *qāḍī*s and *muftī*s.

While using Mamluk legal sources, one has to keep in mind the pluralism of the Mamluk legal system, a pluralism that allowed individuals to approach the law in a strategic manner. The Mamluk judicial system allowed litigants to choose

Pluralism of Mamluk legal system

[23] Aḥmad ʿAbd al-Rāziq, *La femme au temps des Mamlouks en Egypte* (Cairo: Institut français d'archéologie orientale, 1973), is a useful introduction, even though largely anecdotal and with a heavy emphasis on the military elite. For a review, see N. Keddie, "Problems in the Study of Middle Eastern Women," *IJMES* 10 (1979), 225–40.

[24] D. Little, *A Catalogue of the Islamic Documents from al-Ḥaram aš-Šarīf in Jerusalem* (Beirut and Wiesbaden: F. Steiner, 1984); H. Lutfi, *Al-Quds al-Mamlûkiyya: A History of Mamlûk Jerusalem Based on the Ḥaram Documents* (Berlin: K. Schwarz, 1985); H. Lutfi, "A Study of Six Fourteenth-Century *Iqrārs* from al-Quds Relating to Muslim Women," *JESHO* 26 (1983), 246–94.

[25] C. Petry, "Class Solidarity Versus Gender Gain: Women as Custodians of Property in Later Medieval Egypt," in Keddie and Baron (eds.), *Women in Middle Eastern History*, 122–42.

[26] H. Lutfi, "Manners and Customs of Fourteenth-Century Cairene Women: Female Anarchy Versus Male Sharʿī Order in Muslim Prescriptive Treatises," in Keddie and Baron (eds.), *Women in Middle Eastern History*, 99–121.

the school doctrine they found most suitable to the case in hand. Chief *qāḍī*s representing all four Sunni schools of law presided in Cairo and Damascus, and during the fourteenth and fifteenth centuries the model was extended to include most other Mamluk urban centers.[27] The differences between the doctrines of the four schools allowed litigants a considerable room for maneuver. For example, a bride who wished to insert stipulations into her marriage contract could appeal to a Ḥanbalī judge, since only the Ḥanbalīs affirmed the validity of such stipulations. The school affiliation of the litigants appears to have been irrelevant.[28]

Another feature of the pluralism of the legal system were the *fatwās*, or legal *responsa*, issued by *muftī*s. Instead of appearing before a *qāḍī*, litigants could put their case to a *muftī*, whose ruling would be authoritative but not enforceable. The authority of *muftī*s did not derive from any official appointment, although most were either employed in the judiciary or given positions in educational institutions. Rather, the *muftī* and the *qāḍī* filled complementary functions. First, a favorable answer from a *muftī* was sought prior to court litigation before the *qāḍī*. Second, while the *qāḍī* had to follow the established orthodoxy, a *muftī* (even if it was the same man) was able to challenge the school doctrine. By virtue of the respect they commanded, distinguished *muftī*s were able to perform the functions of the "author-jurist," with responsibility for articulating, legitimizing and ultimately effecting legal change.[29] The most influential author-jurists of the Mamluk period were the above-mentioned Ibn Taymiyya, a Ḥanbalī jurist with no official position, and his contemporary, the chief Shāfiʿī *qāḍī* Taqī al-Dīn al-Subkī (d. 756/1355).

But the study of Mamluk marriage and divorce is made possible, first and foremost, by the autobiographical bent of much of Mamluk historiography. In the Mamluk period we find an unusual production of overtly autobiographical works, i.e., works devoted explicitly to the self-representation of the author.[30] Autobiographical material was often also inserted within the annalistic form of historical works. Many Mamluk chronicles and biographical dictionaries can be read like memoirs in which medieval historians talk about their families – children and female relatives included. They also furnish us with intimate information on friends or acquaintances, who had hoped to be immortalized through the text.[31]

[27] J. Escovitz, "The Establishment of Four Chief Judgeships in the Mamluk Empire," *JAOS* 102 (1982), 529–31; J. Nielsen, "Sultan al-Ẓāhir Baybars and the Appointment of Four Chief Qāḍīs, 663/1265," *SI* 60 (1984), 167–76; S. Jackson, "The Primacy of Domestic Politics: Ibn Bint al-Aʿazz and the Establishment of the Four Chief Judgeships in Mamluk Egypt," *JAOS* 115 (1995), 52–65; Y. Rapoport, "Legal Diversity in the Age of *Taqlīd*: The Four Chief Qadis under the Mamluks," *ILS* 10/2 (2003), 210–28.

[28] The possibility of choosing the most suitable doctrine from among the four legal schools is well attested in Ottoman court records. See, with regard to family law, Abdal-Rehim, "The Family and Gender Laws in Egypt"; Tucker, *In the House of the Law*, 83 ff.

[29] W. Hallaq, *Authority, Continuity and Change in Islamic Law* (Cambridge: Cambridge University Press, 2001), 166–235.

[30] Dwight F. Reynolds, *Interpreting the Self. Autobiography in the Arabic Literary Tradition* (Berkeley: University of California Press, 2001), 52–71.

[31] Reynolds, *Interpreting the Self*, 44–45; Nuha N. Khoury, "The Autobiography of Ibn al-ʿAdīm as Told to Yāqūt al-Rūmī," *Edebiyât: Special Issue – Arabic Autobiography* 7/2 (1997), 289–311.

While earlier historical writing had also dealt with these topics, it was usually in the framework of a political history where marriage was first and foremost an alliance between two households or dynasties. In the Mamluk period, on the other hand, we can look beyond the ruler's palace. When contemporary authors write about their own lives, they shed light on the families of the predominantly civilian upper and middle classes to which they belonged.

Generally speaking, we can expect more intimate details about family life from a late fifteenth-century author than from a historian writing in the thirteenth century. It is possible to speak of two stages in Mamluk historiography. The first can be identified with a group of thirteenth- and fourteenth-century Syrian historians. Authors like Abū Shāma (d. 665/1268), al-Yūnīnī (d. 726/1326), al-Jazarī (d. 739/1338) and al-Ṣafadī (d. 764/1363) introduced a more literary style of historical writing by incorporating a large number of anecdotes, poetry, and a certain degree of colloquialism. They also tended to include more autobiographical elements than their predecessors or their Egyptian contemporaries. A group of fifteenth-century historians, many of them students or associates of the Egyptian *qāḍī*, historian and traditionist Ibn Ḥajar al-ʿAsqalānī (d. 852/1449), introduced a second phase in Mamluk historiography. Al-Sakhāwī, the most prolific historian of the late fifteenth century, devoted much space to his personal affairs, and was unusually gossipy when writing biographies of women. Historians like al-Biqāʿī (d. 885/1480), Ibn Iyās (d. 930/1524) or Ibn Ṭūlūn (d. 953/1546) composed chronicles that are also semi-memoirs, and the work of Ibn Ṭawq is, for all practices and purposes, a diary.[32]

Women are well represented in Mamluk historiography, but they do not represent themselves. Mamluk women did not leave us chronicles and biographical dictionaries, nor, for that matter, almost any other form of literary production. Why this is so is not self-evident. We know that families of the educated classes took pride in teaching their daughters to read and write. In the Geniza we find private letters written by Jewish women.[33] Nuḍār (d. 730/1330), the daughter of the Muslim philologist Ibn Ḥayyān, copied her father's works in several volumes, and so did Fāṭima (d. 731/1331), daughter of the historian al-Birzālī.[34] Several literate elite

32 Li Guo, "Mamluk Historiographic Studies: The State of the Art," *MSR* 1 (1997), 15–43; D. Little, "Historiography of the Ayyūbid and the Mamlūk Epochs," in C. Petry (ed.), *The Cambridge History of Egypt*, vol. I: *Islamic Egypt, 640–1517* (Cambridge: Cambridge University Press, 1998), 421–32.

33 J. Kramer, "Women's Letters from the Cairo Genizah: A Preliminary Study" (in Hebrew), in Yael Atzmon (ed.), *Eshnav le-Ḥayehen shel Nashīm be-Ḥevrōt Yehūdiyōt* (Jerusalem: Merkaz Zalman Shazar, 1995), 161–81.

34 Both died in the prime of their youth, and we owe their biographies to their mourning fathers. On Nuḍār see al-Jazarī, *Taʾrīkh Ḥawādith al-Zamān wa-Anbāʾihi wa-Wafayāt al-Akābir waʾl-Aʿyān min Abnāʾihi. Al-Maʿrūf bi-Tāʾrīkh Ibn al-Jazarī*, ed. ʿUmar ʿAbd al-Salām Tadmurī, 3 vols. (Sayda: al-Maktabah al-ʿAṣriyya, 1998), vol. II, 240; Th. Emil Homerin, "'I've stayed by the Grave'. A Nasīb for Nuḍār," in Mustansir Mir (ed.), *Literary Heritage of Classical Islam. Arabic and Islamic Studies in Honor of James A. Bellamy* (Princeton: Princeton University Press, 1993), 107–18; Reynolds, *Interpreting the Self*, 77. On Fāṭima bt. ʿAlam al-Dīn al-Birzālī, see al-Jazarī, *Taʾrīkh*, vol. II, 477; Khalīl b. Aybak al-Ṣafadī, *Aʿyān al-ʿAṣr wa-Aʿwān al-Naṣr*, ed. ʿAlī Abū Zayd, Nabīl Abū ʿAmasha, Muḥammad al-Mawʿid and Maḥmūd Sālim Muḥammad, 6 vols. (Damascus: Dār al-Fikr, 1998), vol. IV, 30. See also the biography of Fāṭima bt. Kamāl al-Dīn al-Maghribī (d. 728/1328), who was known for her superb handwriting (al-Jazarī, *Taʾrīkh*, vol. II, 297).

women are mentioned by al-Sakhāwī in his biographical dictionary.[35] And yet, all that these women have left us are several poems composed by a single woman, ʿĀ'isha al-Bāʿūniyya (d. 922/1516), as well as a few verse fragments scattered in historical works.[36] The relative absence of female authors was not simply for want of literate women; rather, the forms and the extent of female literary expression were subject to social restrictions. In a society that attached high value to texts, authorship was an empowering act.[37] In the last instance, in spite of the wealth of the material, we are forced to read divorce through the prism of husbands.

Finally, many issues of marriage and family life have been left out. There is hardly any discussion of the choice of spouses. Polygamy and concubinage are touched upon indirectly as causes of divorces; but they deserve a monograph of their own. Another lacuna is the conspicuous rarity of the word "love." This is not to deny the existence of such emotions between medieval husbands and wives. On the contrary, I take my lead from Goitein, who, after pointing out differences between a medieval marriage and what we would like to see in a modern one, still pleads with us: "When Geniza husbands speak of love, we should take them seriously."[38] A history of love – and of sexuality – in the medieval Near East is both doable and important. But it deserves a separate study based on a wider range of sources. In particular, the evidence of popular literature and of poetry, hardly used in this work, promises to reveal much that we still do not know about the lives of medieval men and women.[39]

35 J. Berkey, "Women and Islamic Education in the Mamluk Period," in Keddie and Baron (eds.), *Women in Middle Eastern History*, 147–9; Lutfi, "al-Sakhāwī's *Kitāb al-Nisā'*," 119–21; Roded, *Women in the Islamic Biographical Dictionaries*, 69.

36 For ʿĀ'isha al-Bāʿūniyya and her poetry, see Reynolds, *Interpreting the Self*, 8; Najm al-Dīn al-Ghazzī, *al-Kawākib al-Sā'ira bi-A'yān al-Mi'ah al-ʿĀshirah*, ed. Jibrīl Sulaymān Jabbūr, 3 vols. (Beirut: American University Press, 1945–59), vol. I, 287–92. For al-Sakhāwī's correspondence in verse with his neighbor Sutayta bt. Kamāl al-Dīn Ibn Shīrīn (b. 855/1451), see al-Sakhāwī *Ḍaw'*, vol. XII, 107–12 (no. 674). Al-Suyūṭī, who compiled a collection of women's poetry from the classical sources, fails to mention even one poetess from the Mamluk period (Jalāl al-Dīn al-Suyūṭī, *Nuzhat al-Julasā' fī Ashʿār al-Nisā'*, ed. Ṣalāḥ al-Dīn al-Munajjid (Beirut: Dār al-Makshūf, 1958)).

37 Dana al-Sajdi, "Trespassing the Male Domain: The Qaṣīdah of Laylā al-Akhyaliyya," *Journal of Arabic Literature* 31 (2000), 121–46. In Sung China one finds a similar gap between the spread of literacy among elite women and the scanty remains of their literary production (P. Ebrey, *The Inner Quarters. Marriage and the Lives of Chinese Women in the Sung Period* [Berkeley: University of California Press, 1993], 120–24).

38 Goitein, *A Mediterranean Society*, vol. III, 165.

39 On how one may proceed on the subject of sexuality, see R. Irwin, "ʿAlī al-Baghdādī and the Joy of Mamluk Sex," in H. Kennedy (ed.), *The Historiography of Islamic Egypt (c. 950–1800)* (Leiden: Brill, 2000), 45–57; E. Rowson, "Two Homoerotic Narratives from Mamluk Literature: al-Ṣafadī's *Lawʿat al-shākī* and Ibn Dāniyāl's *Mutayyam*," in J. W. Wright and E. Rowson (eds.), *Homoeroticism in Classical Arabic Literature* (New York: Columbia University Press, 1997), 158–91. On the potential of Mamluk poetry for social history, see E. Homerin, "Reflections on Arabic Poetry in the Mamluk Age," *MSR* 1 (1997), 63–85.

CHAPTER 1

# Marriage, divorce and the gender division of property

In 732/1332, the Syrian historian Khalīl b. Aybak al-Ṣafadī happened to be in Cairo to witness the wedding celebrations of Ānūk, son and designated heir to Sultan al-Nāṣir Muḥammad. The bride – an amir's daughter – was accompanied by a trousseau that was carried over to the Citadel by 800 porters and 100 mules. Al-Ṣafadī, like many others who came to watch the public procession, saw all kinds of pillows, cushions, stools, chairs, silver and copper utensils, trays, bowls, rugs, earthenware pots, blankets and mattresses.[1] The more precious items, such as clothing and jewelry, were concealed inside hundreds of *dikka*s – multipurpose wooden chests.[2] A secretary in the entourage of the bride's father informed al-Ṣafadī that the gold alone weighed 80 Egyptian *qinṭār*s, that is, about 800,000 dinars. Another observer claimed that the total value of the dowry was closer to one million.[3] The monetary value cited was merely an estimate, for there was no official record of the value of the trousseau. While the gifts the groom gave his bride were required by Islamic law and therefore recorded, dowries were *not* registered in Muslim marriage contracts.

A prince, like any other groom, was required to pledge a marriage gift (*ṣadāq*) at the time of the marriage contract, part of which was paid at marriage and the remainder deferred. In this marriage contract, concluded some time before the wedding procession, Ānūk promised a marriage gift of 12,000 dinars, of which he paid 10,000 at marriage.[4] Compared with the size of the dowry brought by his

[1] Al-Ṣafadī, *A'yān*, vol. I, 713–14; Taqī al-Dīn al-Maqrīzī, *Kitāb al-Sulūk li-Ma'rifat al-Duwal wa'l-Mulūk*, ed. Muḥammad Muṣṭafā Ziyādah and Sa'īd 'Abd al-Fattāḥ 'Āshūr, 4 vols. (Cairo: Dār al-Kutub al-Miṣriyya, 1934–72), vol. II, 346. See also 'Abd al-Rāziq, *La femme*, 141–42.

[2] On the different functions of the *dikka* (or *dakka*) in medieval Near Eastern houses, see Goitein, *A Mediterranean Society*, vol. IV, 114; J. Sadan, *Le mobilier au Proche-Orient médiéval* (Leiden: E. J. Brill, 1976), 123–24. Al-Maqrīzī describes the *dikka* as something "like a bed" (*shibhu al-sarīr*) (*Kitāb al-Mawā'iẓ wa'l-I'tibār fī Dhikr al-Khiṭaṭ wa'l-Āthār al-ma'rūf bi'l-Khiṭaṭ al-Maqrīziyya*, ed. Muḥammad Zaynhum and Madīḥa al-Sharqāwī, 3 vols. [Cairo: Maktabat al-Madbūlī, 1998], vol. II, 606).

[3] Ismā'īl b. 'Umar Ibn Kathīr, *al-Bidāya wa'l-Nihāya*, ed. Aḥmad Abū Mulḥim et al., 14 vols. (Beirut: Dār al-Kutub al-'Ilmiyya, 1994), vol. XIV, 165; Jamāl al-Dīn Yūsuf Ibn Taghrī Birdī, *al-Nujūm al-Zāhira fī Mulūk Miṣr wa'l-Qāhirah*, 16 vols. (Cairo: [various publishers], 1929–72), vol. IX, 103. See also 'Abd al-Rāziq, *La femme*, 150.

[4] Ibn Taghrī Birdī, *Nujūm*, vol. IX, 100; al-Maqrīzī, *Sulūk*, vol. II, 343. The marriage contract is preserved in an administrative manual, but the amount of the *ṣadāq* is missing (Aḥmad b. 'Abdallāh

bride, however, this was pitiful. Even if we allow for considerable exaggeration in the valuation of the trousseau, the difference in value between the marriage gift of the groom and the bride's dowry was a difference of scale. It was the father of the bride who bore the lion's share of the matrimonial gifts, and this was a heavy burden even for the sultan's coffers. Al-Ṣafadī was informed that the current deficit in the royal accounts was partly a result of excessive spending on marrying off the sultan's daughters.[5] Al-Nāṣir Muḥammad endowed each of his eleven daughters, as well as his favorite slave-girls and concubines, with a large dowry. One daughter received a trousseau worth 800,000 dinars, consisting of bedclothes, textiles, and jewelry.[6] One of the sultan's manumitted slave-girls brought to her marriage a trousseau of jewelry and brocades worth 100,000 dinars.[7] Clearly, the deficit in the sultan's budget was caused by the weddings of his daughters, not by the marriages of his sons.[8]

Contrary to popular conceptions of marriage in traditional Muslim societies, and in spite of the emphasis placed in Islamic law on the gifts of the groom, Mamluk society was a dotal society, i.e., a society where the dowry brought by the bride was the substantial gift at marriage.[9] Grooms were required to pledge marriage gifts, but they were much smaller than the dowries, and for the most part deferred as a security for divorcées and widows. Generally speaking, a bride's dowry consisted of her trousseau – textiles, household utensils and, among the upper classes, jewelry. Cash and land, on the other hand, were very rarely included in brides' dowries. Property was gendered; daughters received trousseaux while being denied direct access to other types of property, especially land. The lines separating specifically male and specifically female assets became blurred only towards the end of the fifteenth century.

The dowry was a major factor determining the degree of Mamluk women's economic independence, especially among the elite. Dowries functioned as a form of pre-mortem inheritance reserved exclusively for daughters. Once the dowry was donated by the bride's parents, it remained under the woman's exclusive ownership and control throughout marriage, and then again through widowhood and

al-Qalqashandī, *Ṣubḥ al-Aʿshā fī Ṣināʿat al-Inshāʾ*, 14 vols. [Cairo: Dār al-Kutub al-Miṣriyya, 1913–18], vol. XIV, 303–08).

5 Al-Ṣafadī, *Aʿyān*, vol. III, 202; cf. Shihāb al-Dīn Aḥmad Ibn Ḥajar al-ʿAsqalānī, *al-Durar al-Kāmina fī Aʿyān al-Miʾah al-Thāminah*, 4 vols. (Hyderabad: Dāʾirat al-Maʿārif, 1929–32), vol. II, 430. See also D. Little, "Notes on the Early *Naẓar al-khāṣṣ*," in Thomas Phillip and Ulrich Haarmann (eds.), *The Mamluks in Egyptian Politics and Society* (Cambridge: Cambridge University Press, 1998), 235–53.

6 Ibn Taghrī Birdī, *Nujūm*, vol. IX, 175; al-Maqrīzī, *Sulūk*, vol. II, 249, 536. See also ʿAbd al-Rāziq, *La femme*, 140.

7 Mūsā b. Muḥammad al-Yūsufī, *Nuzhat al-Nāẓir fī Sīrat al-Malik al-Nāṣir*, ed. Aḥmad Ḥuṭayṭ (Beirut: ʿĀlam al-Kutub, 1986), 284.

8 On the sultan's descendants, see P. M. Holt, "An-Nāṣir Muḥammad b. Qalāwūn (684–741/1285–1341): His Ancestry, Kindred and Affinity," in U. Vermeulen and D. De Smet (eds.), *Egypt and Syria in the Fatimid, Ayyubid and Mamluk Eras* (Leuven: Uitgeverij Peeters, 1995), 313–24.

9 For dotal regimes in medieval Europe, see Martha Howell, *The Marriage Exchange. Property, Social Place and Gender in Cities of the Low Countries, 1300–1500* (Chicago: University of Chicago Press, 1998), 197–212, and the references cited there.

divorce. The absolute separation of property between husbands and wives meant that husbands had no formal right over their wives' dowries. This does not mean that women always had the access to markets that would allow them to freely trade their property. The economy, like property, was gendered. Up until the end of the fifteenth century women of property were much more likely to lend their money as creditors rather than to invest it in agricultural land. But the value of dowries should not be underestimated. For many elite women large dowries did mean financial security; and in some cases it was the husband who depended on a dowry rather than the other way around.

## The dowry

The prominence of the dowry in the marriage alliances of the elite is evident from the beginning of the fourteenth century. While dowries often amounted to hundreds of thousands of dinars, the marriage gift in royal marriage contracts was usually no more than several thousands.[10] A similar gap between the dowry and the marriage gift was a common feature of other elite marriages. An upper-class groom in late thirteenth-century Damascus expected his bride to bring a dowry worth 50,000 silver dirhams (about 2,500 dinars at the prevailing exchange rate).[11] In the middle of the fourteenth century, a Cairene merchant's daughter used 100,000 dirhams of pure silver for her trousseau.[12] One orphan girl in fourteenth-century Damascus had a dowry of 60,000 dirhams, as well as an annual income of 7,000 dirhams from a family endowment.[13] Badr al-Dīn al-Armawī, a senior bureaucrat in Cairo at the beginning of the fifteenth century, requested a 100,000-dirham loan towards an adequate trousseau for his daughter.[14] In comparison, marriage gifts in the marriages of top government officials and other members of the elite were rarely more than several hundred dinars.[15] The highest marriage gift recorded in marriage

[10] Compare a list of royal dowries (ʿAbd al-Rāziq, *La femme*, 150–51) with a list of the *ṣadāq* paid in royal marriages (Aḥmad ʿAbd al-Rāziq, "ʿAqdā Nikāḥ min ʿAṣr al-Mamālīk al-Baḥriyya," *al-Majallah al-ʿArabiyya li'l-ʿUlūm al-Insāniyya* [Kuwait] 6 [1986], 76; also a less reliable list in ʿAbd al-Rāziq, *La femme*, 132–33).

[11] ʿAbd al-Raḥmān b. Ibrāhīm b. al-Firkāḥ al-Fazārī (d. 690/1291), "Fatāwā al-Fazārī," Chester Beatty Collection, Dublin (hereafter Chester Beatty), MS 3330, fol. 14a. For exchange rates, see E. Ashtor-Strauss, *Les metaux précieux et la balance des payements du Proche-Orient à la basse époque* (Paris: SEVPEN, 1971), 48–49.

[12] Al-Maqrīzī, *Khiṭaṭ*, vol. II, 607.

[13] Najm al-Dīn al-Ṭarsūsī, *Kitāb Tuḥfat al-Turk*, ed. M. Minasri (Damascus: Institut Français de Damas, 1997), 20.

[14] Al-Sakhāwī, *Ḍaw'*, vol. III, 105.

[15] On the amounts of *ṣadāq* in the late fourteenth-century Jerusalem, see Lutfi, *al-Quds*, 289. For fifteenth-century examples, see Muḥammad b. ʿAbd al-Raḥmān al-Sakhāwī, *al-Jawāhir wa'l-Durar fī Tarjamat Shaykh al-Islām Ibn Ḥajar*, ed. Ibrāhīm Bājis ʿAbd al-Majīd, 3 vols. (Beirut: Dār Ibn Ḥazm, 1999), vol. I, 500, 505, 543; Muḥammad b. ʿAlī Ibn Ṭūlūn, *al-Thaghr al-Bassām fī Dhikr Man Wuliyya Qaḍā' al-Shām*, ed. Ṣalāḥ al-Dīn al-Munajjid (Damascus: Maṭbūʿāt al-Majmaʿ al-ʿIlmī al-ʿArabī, 1956), 158; Muḥammad b. ʿAlī Ibn Ṭūlūn, *Mufākahat al-Khilān fī Ḥawādith al-Zamān*, ed. Muḥammad Muṣṭafā, 2 vols. (Cairo: al-Mu'assasah al-Miṣriyyah al-ʿĀmmah lil-Ta'līf

contracts of non-royalty was pledged by an amir from Aswan in 734/1334. He offered his bride 500 dinars as her marriage gift, of which he paid only 100 at marriage.[16]

Dowry was important in the marriages of all urban classes. The North African traveler Ibn Baṭṭūṭa, visiting Syria in 726/1326, found that "it is the custom in that country that a girl's father gives her a dowry, the greater part of it consists in copper utensils. They contract [their marriages] according to it, and regard it with great pride."[17] His contemporary the moralist Ibn al-Ḥājj remarked that the trousseaux of every Cairene bride consisted of three *dikka* chests, one coated with silver, one with copper and one with brass.[18] Al-Maqrīzī, writing in the beginning of the fifteenth century and describing the practices of previous generations, reports that a standard trousseau consisted of at least one copper-coated *dikka*, worth 200 dinars, accompanied by a set of drinking vessels (*ṭāsāt*) made of brass and coated with silver, a set of platters, lamps, jewel boxes, a soda-ash container, a fumigator, a basin and a ewer.[19] The trousseaux of the daughters of amirs, wealthy bureaucrats or merchants consisted of seven *dikka* chests, each inlaid with costly materials.[20] In fifteenth-century Cairo, wealthy founders of religious institutions sometimes stipulated that their daughters' dowries should be paid from the endowed revenue.[21]

Occasionally we hear about the struggles of lower-class families to raise dowries for their daughters. One pious woman asked Ibn Taymiyya whether she should use all her property, consisting of clothes worth 1,000 silver dirhams (about 50 gold dinars), as dowry for her daughter, or, alternatively, sell the clothes and make the pilgrimage to Mecca.[22] A substantial part of most dowries must have been heirlooms given by the bride's mother out of her own trousseau.[23] An orphan girl's

wa'l-Tarjamah wa'l-Ṭibā'ah wa'l-Nashr, 1962–64), vol. I, 21; Aḥmad b. Muḥammad Ibn al-Ḥimṣī, *Ḥawādith al-Zamān wa-Wafayāt al-Shuyūkh wa'l-Aqrān*, ed. 'Umar 'Abd al-Salām al-Tadmurī, 3 vols. (Sayda: al-Maktaba al-'Aṣriyya, 1999), vol. I, 176, vol. II, 275; B. Martel-Thoumian, *Les civils et l'administration dans l'état militaire mamlūk (ix^e/xv^e siècle)* (Damascus: Institut Français de Damas, 1991), 370.

16 Su'ād Māhir, "'Uqūd al-Zawāj 'alā al-Mansūjāt al-Athariyya," in *al-Kitāb al-Dhahabī li'l-Iḥtifāl al-Khamsīnī bi'l-Dirāsāt al-Athariyya bi-Jāmi'at al-Qāhira*, 3 vols. (Cairo: al-Jihāz al-Markazī li'l-Kutub al-Jāmi'iyya wa'l-Madrasiyya wa'l-Wasā'il al-Ta'līmiyya, 1978), vol. I, 39–54. See also Ḥaram document no. 47 (brief summary in Little, *Catalogue*, 302).

17 Text: *wa-bihi yatabāya'ūna wa-bihi yatafākharūna* (Ibn Baṭṭūṭa, *Riḥlat Ibn Baṭṭūṭa al-Musammā Tuḥfat al-Nuẓẓār fī Gharā'ib al-Amṣār wa-'Ajā'ib al-Asfār*, ed. 'Abd al-Hādī al-Tāzī, 5 vols. [Rabat: Akādimiyat al-Mamlaka al-Maghribiyya, 1997], vol. I, 264).

18 Muḥammad b. Muḥammad Ibn al-Ḥājj, *al-Madkhal ilā Tanmiyat al-A'māl bi-Taḥsīn al-Niyyāt*, 4 vols. (Cairo: al-Maṭbā 'ah al-Miṣriyyah, 1929–32), vol. II, 167.

19 Al-Maqrīzī, *Khiṭaṭ*, vol. II, 606–07. All these items appear regularly in the contemporary trousseau lists of Jewish brides preserved in the Cairo Geniza (Goitein, *A Mediterranean Society*, vol. IV, 132–47, 430).

20 For discussion of the materials mentioned in this paragraph, see M. Milwright, "Pottery in the Written Sources of the Ayyubid–Mamluk Period (c. 567–923/1171–1517)," *BSOAS* 62 (1999), 515.

21 L. Fernandes, *The Evolution of a Sufi Institution in Mamluk Egypt: The Khânqâh* (Berlin: K. Schwarz, 1988), 68.

22 Taqī al-Dīn Ibn Taymiyya, *Fatāwā al-Nisā'*, ed. Ibrāhīm Muḥammad al-Jamal (Cairo: Maktabat al-Qur'ān, 1987), 89.

23 As was the case in the Geniza (Goitein, *A Mediterranean Society*, vol. IV, 130, 139, 143).

guardian was expected to provide her with a dowry by selling off some of her assets. Ibn Taymiyya allowed one such guardian to sell real estate so as to buy a dowry consisting of textiles and jewelry appropriate to the orphan girl's class.[24] When parents were unable to afford an adequate dowry, they could appeal for charity. Ibn Baṭṭūṭa reported that some of Damascus' endowments were dedicated to providing dowries to the daughters of the poor.[25]

Supplying a poor bride with a dowry is also a common topos in contemporary hagiographical literature. In one anecdote a poor widow begs a merchant to help her raise a dowry for her daughter, who is to marry in three days. The merchant helps her out, and in return only asks that the poor girl pray for his salvation.[26] Another generous merchant provided trousseaux for twelve hundred brides; indigent boys, on the other hand, he helped by paying for their circumcision expenses.[27] In a thirteenth-century anecdote, a wealthy merchant left 200 dinars with an old shaykh for safekeeping. The shaykh's wife took the money and used it towards the trousseau of her daughter. When the merchant learned what had happened, he was pleased that the money was spent on a good cause.[28]

The documents of the Cairo Geniza provide us with plenty of data regarding dowries in the marriages of the Jewish community in medieval Cairo. Under Jewish law, and in contrast to Islamic law, the groom acquires a right of usufruct over his bride's dowry. Therefore, Jewish marriage contracts include a detailed evaluation and itemization of the assets brought by the bride and handed over to the husband.[29] In spite of the difference in the formalities of the marriage contract, a similar pattern of matrimonial gifts prevailed among the Jewish and the Muslim communities. The trousseau lists of the Geniza enumerate copper utensils and bedding, as well as the bride's clothing and jewelry.[30] Among the very wealthy, parts of houses are sometimes included. But, as was the case among the Muslim majority, the dowry almost never included cash or land.[31]

The Geniza documents also give us a clearer idea about the value of dowries in urban society. During the thirteenth and fourteenth centuries upper-class Jewish families endowed their daughters with trousseaux worth several hundred dinars. The Jewish groom's marriage gifts, like the Muslim *ṣadāq*, were usually much

[24] Ibn Taymiyya, *Fatāwā al-Nisā'*, 202. For more examples, see al-Fazārī, "Fatāwā," fol. 81a; Abū 'Abdallāh Muḥammad b. 'Abdallāh al-Ḥasanī al-Jarawānī (d. 813/1410–11), "al-Mawāhib al-Ilāhiyya wa'l-Qawā'id al-Mālikiyya," Chester Beatty MS 3401, fol. 77a.

[25] Ibn Baṭṭūṭa, *The Travels of Ibn Baṭṭūṭa, A.D. 1325–1354*, trans. H. A. R. Gibb, 2 vols. (Cambridge: Hakluyt Society, 1958–62), vol. I, 149.

[26] C. Taylor, *In the Vicinity of the Righteous: Ziyāra and the Veneration of Muslim Saints in Late Medieval Egypt* (Leiden: Brill, 1998), 103–04.

[27] *Ibid.*, 104.

[28] A fifteenth-century version of the same story was adapted to inflation. Here, the shaykh had four daughters, and each received a share in a deposit of 10,000 dinars (*ibid.*, 145, and the sources cited there).

[29] Goitein, *A Mediterranean Society*, vol. III, 125–26.

[30] *Ibid.*, 128–29.

[31] The only two examples of dowries consisting of cash come from marriage contracts of Spanish immigrants, dated 1499 and 1510 (*ibid.*, vol. III, 123–31).

smaller. In one marriage contract, dated from the latter half of the thirteenth century, the bride brought a dowry worth 230 dinars. The groom delivered an advance payment of 15 dinars, and pledged an additional 35 dinars as a deferred marriage gift.[32] Lower on the social ladder were dowries of less than 100 dinars. In a marriage contract dated 1301, the bride brought with her a trousseau worth 59 dinars. The groom paid 10 dinars in advance and pledged another 20 dinars as a deferred marriage gift.[33] Poor Jewish brides brought trousseaux worth 10 dinars, and some brought nothing at all.[34]

When the dowry was substantial, the potential for friction was great, among both Muslims and Jews. In particular, disputes over the dowry occurred after the wife died childless. According to Islamic law, the widower of a childless wife is entitled to a half of her estate, but parents wanted to reclaim the entire dowries of their deceased daughters.[35] The author of a fifteenth-century legal manual recommends parents to testify that they have given the trousseau as a loan, for the purpose of beautification (*li-tatajammala bihā*). According to the author, this was a popular legal subterfuge designed to prevent the dowry from passing to the husband.[36] Despite the careful itemization of the trousseau in Jewish marriages, the Geniza papers reveal constant haggling over the dowry. In the Jewish community the problem was accentuated, since under Jewish law the husband is the sole heir of a childless wife. For this reason, special stipulations in rabbinic marriage contracts assured that half of a childless wife's dowry would return to her natal kin, and Karaites even allowed the natal family to inherit the entire dowry.[37]

Disputes could also occur between a father and his married daughter. In a case from late thirteenth-century Damascus, a father transferred the title of a house to his daughter, but she soon re-sold the property to her husband. The father then testified in court that he gave the property as a revocable gift.[38] Another father

[32] E. Ashtor-Strauss, *Tōldōt ha-Yehūdīm be-Mitzrayim ve-Sūryah taḥat Shilṭōn ha-Mamlūkīm*, 3 vols. (Jerusalem: Mossad ha-Rav Kuk, 1944–70), vol. III, 32–37 (no. 19).

[33] J. Mann, *Texts and Studies in Jewish History and Literature*, 2 vols. (Cincinnati: Hebrew Union College Press, 1931–35), vol. I, 429–31. For more examples from the Mamluk period, see Ashtor-Strauss, *Tōldōt*, vol. III, 67–70 (no. 39), 72–74 (no. 41).

[34] For examples from the Mamluk period, see the lists in Goitein, *A Mediterranean Society*, vol. III, 410 (no. 259), 415 (no. 331). When dowries are completely absent from Geniza marriage contracts it is difficult to know whether the bride was actually penniless or whether the dowry was written separately and was subsequently lost.

[35] Ibn Taymiyya, *Fatāwā al-Nisā'*, 195, 203; ʿUmar b. ʿAlī al-Qaṭṭānī Qāri' al-Hidāya, "al-Fatāwā al-Sirājiyya," MS British Library Or. 5781, fol. 14b.

[36] Al-Jarawānī, "Mawāhib," fols. 30b–31a. See also Zakariyā' al-Anṣārī (d. ca. 1520), *al-Iʿlām wa'l-Ihtimām bi-Jamʿ Fatāwā Shaykh al-Islām Abī Yaḥyā Zakariyā al-Anṣārī*, ed. Aḥmad ʿUbayd (Beirut: ʿĀlam al-Kutub, 1984), 312; ʿAbd al-Wahhāb al-Shaʿrānī, *al-Baḥr al-Mawrūd fī al-Mawāthīq wa'l-ʿUhūd*, on the margins of *Lawāqiḥ al-Anwār al-Qudsiyya fī Bayān al-ʿUhūd al-Muḥammadiyya* (Cairo, 1308/1890–1), 217–18 (cited by Qāsim Darāwsheh, "Celebrations and Social Ceremonies in Egypt during the Mamluk Period, 648/1250–923/1517" [in Hebrew] [MA dissertation, Hebrew University, 1986], 51).

[37] On this stipulation in rabbinic marriage contracts, see Goitein, *A Mediterranean Society*, vol. III, 104, 139. For Karaite marriage contracts, see Judith Olsowy-Schlanger, *Karaite Marriage Documents from the Cairo Geniza. Legal Tradition and Community Life in Mediaeval Egypt and Palestine* (Leiden: Brill, 1998), 241–45.

[38] Al-Fazārī, "Fatāwā," fol. 78b.

attempted to recover textiles he had given to his daughter at her wedding. He claimed that he had given the dowry to his daughter as a loan, while the daughter argued that the property had originally belonged to her mother, and that her father had no right over it. In his response, al-Subkī ruled that after a father had declared a certain property to be his daughter's dowry, bought it specifically for her wedding or presented it in the bridal procession, he could no longer revoke his gift.[39]

Medieval marriages were a gradual process, in which the transfer of property was done in several stages. In a study of matrimonial gifts in medieval North Africa and al-Andalus, Amalia Zomeňo noted that each stage of marriage, beginning with the search for a suitable match, was accompanied by the giving of gifts. The dowry was promised during the premarital negotiations and delivered to the groom's house before consummation, but the bride did not acquire full ownership over her dowry until the marriage was considered to be stable. This stage was reached only several years after the wedding, when the parents were sufficiently certain of the success of the match. Until then, the natal family retained the option of taking the dowry back.[40] As a result, the vast majority of disputes over dowries were intergenerational rather than conjugal. In the legal literature the question is almost never usurpation of the dowry by the husband, but rather the parents' attempt to revoke the gift. This intergenerational aspect of dowries was related to their function in Mamluk society.

## Dowry and inheritance

Broadly speaking, dowries can be viewed either as transfer of property from one household to another (an economic–demographic model) or as transfer of property from one generation to another (a devolutionist model). According to the economic model, the demographics of supply and demand in the marriage market determine the direction of matrimonial gifts. When the number of eligible grooms exceeds the number of marriageable brides, men have to pay for a suitable match. When the demographic balance is reversed it is the women who have to come up with dowries in order to clear the marriage market.[41] As we shall see in the next chapter, there are indeed indications of a surplus of women in the urban centers of the late medieval Near East, at least in some periods. However, the economic–demographic model cannot explain the prominence of the dowry in Mamluk society. First, the matrimonial gifts were reciprocal rather than unidirectional. Even though the dowry was the financially larger gift, the groom's marriage gift never disappeared.

[39] Taqī al-Dīn al-Subkī, *Kitāb al-Fatāwā*, 2 vols. (Cairo: Maṭbaʿat al-Qudsī, 1937), vol. I, 347. For similar views, al-Fazārī, "Fatāwā," fol. 78b; Ibn Taymiyya, *Fatāwā al-Nisā'*, 195, 203; Zakariyā al-Anṣārī, "'Imād al-Riḍā bi-Bayān Adab al-Qaḍā'," Chester Beatty MS 3420 (1), fol. 50b; Qāri' al-Hidāya, "al-Fatāwā al-Sirājiyya," fols. 8a, 14b.

[40] Zomeňo, *Dote y matrimonio*.

[41] For the theoretical foundations of this model, see G. Becker, *A Treatise on the Family* (Cambridge, MA: Harvard University Press, 1981), 84–87. For applicability in medieval Europe, see D. Herlihy, "The Medieval Marriage Market," *Medieval and Renaissance Studies* 6 (1976), 1–27.

Second, the market in eligible men and women was not symmetric, for men could and did marry several wives and take concubines. In fact, the demographic model predicts that the incidence of polygamy is incompatible with a dotal regime. Third, Muslim brides retained full ownership over their dowries. If the primary function of the dowry was as a market price for a suitable match, it should have been handed over to the groom.

The devolutionist model offers a more suitable explanation for the prominence of dowries in Mamluk society.[42] In this model, parents prefer to transfer wealth to their daughters in the form of dowries, while sons receive property through other mechanisms. The coexistence of the groom's marriage gift and the dowry poses no problem, since the two institutions had different purposes. The marriage gifts protected the bride against unilateral divorce and abuse by her husband, while the dowry was her share in her natal patrimony. As in Islamic law, the devolutionist model primarily regards the dowry as a transaction between parents and daughters, not between bride and groom. It fully accounts for the preoccupation of Mamluk society with intergenerational conflicts over the dowry and the corresponding marginalization of the husband's interests in this property.

The correspondence between the devolutionist model and actual practice in Mamluk society can be illustrated by the following example from the documents of the Ḥaram. Nāṣir al-Dīn al-Ḥamawī, a merchant from Jerusalem who mainly traded in olive oil and wool bought in the surrounding towns and villages, became terminally ill in 788/1386, towards the end of the fast of Ramaḍān.[43] He made three deathbed declarations on 1 Shawwāl (26 October). In one, he appointed the deputy preacher of the al-Aqṣā Mosque as the executor of his estate.[44] In another, he acknowledged holding in his possession 10,000 dirhams that legally belonged to his adolescent son, Muḥammad. Most probably, the source of this money was a gift from Nāṣir al-Dīn to his son.[45] In the third deed, Nāṣir al-Dīn acknowledged that he had endowed his daughter Fāṭima with a dowry, also in the value of 10,000 dirhams. Nāṣir al-Dīn noted that the money was spent on personal effects, as is the custom in giving a dowry (*dhālika ḥawā'ij 'alā 'ādat al-jihāz*). At the time the document was drawn, Fāṭima was already married to one Kamāl al-Dīn Aḥmad b. Sa'd al-Dīn Muḥammad, about whom nothing else is known.[46]

When Nāṣir al-Dīn died, Fāṭima was required to produce an itemization of her possessions in order to confirm her legal right over her dowry. The list is barely

42 J. Goody, "Bridewealth and Dowry in Africa and Euroasia", in J. Goody and S. J. Tambiah (eds.), *Bridewealth and Dowry* (Cambridge: Cambridge University Press, 1973). See also M. Botticini and Aloysius Siow, "Why Dowries?" *American Economic Review* 93/4 (2003), 1385–98.

43 For an assessment of the documents relating to Nāṣir al-Dīn and his financial affairs, see Little, *Catalogue*, 18; Donald P. Little, "Six Fourteenth Century Purchase Deeds for Slaves from al-Ḥaram Aš-Šarīf," *Zeitschrift der Deutschen Morgenländischen Gesellschaft* 131 (1981), 297–337, reprinted in his *History and Historiography of the Mamlūks* (London: Variorum, 1986).

44 Ḥaram document no. 717; Little, *Catalogue*, 309.

45 Ḥaram document no. 211, recto; published in K. al-'Aṣalī, *Wathā'iq Maqdisiyya Ta'rīkhiyya*, 3 vols. (Amman n.p., 1983–85), vol. II, 83 (no. 25).

46 Ḥaram document no. 209, recto; published in al-'Aṣalī, *Wathā'iq*, vol. II, 120 (no. 44).

legible, but among the items of Fāṭima's trousseau one can identify three tunics of varying colors, a Venetian chemise, kerchiefs, a couple of pillows and several cushions, a carpet, mats and rugs, and several pieces of silk. Fāṭima also brought with her lamps, a fumigator, a basin and a ewer, and at least one gold ring. Some of the items are designated as "new," indicating that they were purchased specifically for Fāṭima, while others are described as "old," probably indicating that they were handed over by her mother.[47] Unlike the trousseau lists preserved in the Geniza, there is no separate monetary evaluation for each item. The list was nevertheless sufficiently detailed to convince the court that Fāṭima's possessions were worth 10,000 dirhams. The *qāḍī* certified Nāṣir al-Dīn's acknowledgment concerning Fāṭima's dowry on the following day, 7 Dhū al-Qaʿdā (30 November).[48] Earlier, on 2 Dhū al-Qaʿdā (25 November) the *qāḍī* had certified the deathbed acknowledgment made by the late Nāṣir al-Dīn in favor of his son.[49]

The case of Fāṭima bt. Nāṣir al-Dīn al-Ḥamawī demonstrates the functions of dowries in Mamluk society. First, the dowry was the financially significant gift at marriage. Fāṭima received a dowry worth 10,000 dirhams, equivalent to about 400 dinars, much more than the average marriage gift in the city. No information is available on the marriage gift paid by Fāṭima's husband, but we know that her father Nāṣir al-Dīn pledged only 40 dinars as the deferred marriage gift of his own wife. This sum was above the average marriage gift encountered in the Ḥaram documents, which range from 5 to 20 dinars (or their equivalent in dirhams).[50] Second, Fāṭima received her dowry in the form of a trousseau – that is, a gender-specific type of property. Fāṭima's father supplied her with "personal effects," such as copper utensils, furniture and clothing. As far as we can tell, Fāṭima's dowry did not include cash or real estate. Third, the transfer of ownership did not take place at the time of the wedding. The dowry was already in Fāṭima's possession, probably since her relocation to her husband's house, but she did not acquire formal ownership until her father's death. On his deathbed Nāṣir al-Dīn still found it necessary to affirm his daughter's right to her dowry.

Most important, Fāṭima's dowry represented her share of her father's patrimony. Under Sunni inheritance law, daughters receive half the share of their brothers, and, when no brothers survive, only a half or two-thirds of the estate. There is little doubt that, at least in the urban centers, Islamic law was carefully followed when the estates of deceased persons were divided.[51] But the application of Islamic inheritance law did not exclude other means of handing down property from one generation to another. One way was gifts *inter vivos*, such as the dowry. It is surely

[47] Ḥaram document no. 830. [48] Ḥaram document no. 209, verso.

[49] Ḥaram document no. 211, verso; published in al-ʿAṣalī, *Wathāʾiq*, vol. II, 84 (no. 26).

[50] Ḥaram document no. 287; published in al-ʿAṣalī, *Wathāʾiq*, vol. II, 111 (no. 39). For the common amounts of *ṣadāq* found in the Ḥaram documents, see Little, *Catalogue*, 300–06; Lutfi, *al-Quds*, 285–90.

[51] When contemporary authors encountered the disinheritance of daughters in Bedouin tribes, they regarded the practice as uncivilized and un-Islamic. Tāj al-Dīn al-Subkī criticizes Bedouin amirs for not allowing daughters to inherit property (*Kitāb Muʿīd al-Niʿam wa-Mubīd al-Niqam* [Beirut: Dār al-Ḥadāthah, 1983], 55). Ibn Baṭṭūṭa noted that the Beja tribes near the Red Sea port of ʿAydhāb disinherit their daughters (*Riḥla*, vol. I, 230).

not a coincidence that Nāṣir al-Dīn has given his daughter a trousseau equal in value to the gift her brother received in cash; he must have wanted his wealth to be divided equally between his two adult children. Yet, he still divided the property along gender lines. Fāṭima received hers at marriage, while the marital situation of her brother appears to have been immaterial to the timing of the gift; she received a trousseau, while he received cash. Although it was equal in value, Muḥammad and Fāṭima still received gendered property.

This pattern of dividing the patrimony along gender lines between daughters and sons was common in Mamluk urban elites. Giving a trousseau to a daughter was one side of the coin, for at the same time daughters were not allowed to inherit other parts of a family's patrimony, reserved exclusively for sons. Among the religious elite, this meant the exclusive right of sons – and not of daughters – to inherit office from their fathers. The law recognized the right of professors in madrasas, preachers and other endowed office-holders to appoint their successors, subject to confirmation by the administrator of the endowment. This right was known as *nuzūl* or "handing down."[52] Examples of "handing down" positions from father to son abound in Mamluk chronicles, and the Ḥaram documents demonstrate that the nomination of a son as a successor was formally recognized in judicial practice. In one estate inventory a shaykh hands down to his son ten different appointments as teacher, administrator and an official witness in various institutions in Jerusalem. In another estate inventory a glassmaker hands down his appointment as the attendant (*farrāsh*) in the Madrasa al-Tankiziyya in favor of his son.[53] Holding office was gender-specific. While the dowry was, by definition, reserved exclusively for daughters, the right to hold office was fundamentally the prerogative of sons.

The *iqṭāʿ* of a member of the military elite – that is, the right of usufruct of land in return for military service – was similarly seen as part of one's patrimony, and attempts were made to pass it from father to son, or to other members of the extended household. While *iqṭāʿ* was in principle revocable, and its inheritance supposedly prohibited, there were many exceptions to the rule.[54] D. S. Richards found several hundred examples of fourteenth-century *awlād al-nās* (sons of *mamlūk* soldiers) appointed as amirs. In some cases, there is clear indication that they inherited the *iqṭāʿ*s of their fathers or other male relatives.[55] Again, as with civilian

[52] Al-Subkī, *Fatāwā*, vol. II, 224. See also the discussion in M. Chamberlain, *Knowledge and Social Practice in Medieval Damascus, 1190–1350* (Cambridge: Cambridge University Press, 1994), 94 ff.

[53] Lutfi, *al-Quds*, 309–11 (Ḥaram documents nos. 161, 347). For the handing down of menial positions, such as that of a janitor or a gatekeeper, see also al-Sakhāwī, *Ḍaw'*, vol. I, 247, vol. III, 79, 305, vol. VI, 295.

[54] For a recent overview of the literature on the inheritance of *iqṭāʿ*, and on the one-generation Mamluk aristocracy in general, see U. Haarmann, "Joseph's Law – the Careers and Activities of Mamluk Descendants before the Ottoman Conquest of Egypt," in Phillip and Haarmann (eds.), *The Mamluks in Egyptian Politics and Society*, 55–84.

[55] D. S. Richards, "Mamluk Amirs and their Families and Households," in Phillip and Haarmann (eds.), *The Mamluks in Egyptian Politics and Society*, 32–54. See also U. Haarmann, "The Sons of Mamluks as Fief-holders in Late Medieval Egypt," in T. Khalidi (ed.), *Land Tenure and Social Transformation in the Middle East* (Beirut: American University of Beirut, 1984), 141–68; R. Irwin, "Iqta' and the End of the Crusader States," in P. M. Holt (ed.), *The Eastern Mediterranean Lands in the Period of the Crusades* (Warminster: Aris & Phillips, 1977), 62–77.

office-holders, the transfer of an *iqṭāʿ* from father to son was recognized by law. The author of a fifteenth-century legal manual provides several model documents for transfer of *iqṭāʿ* through the mechanism of "handing down."[56]

Dowries and *iqṭā*'s were seen as two complementary gender-specific mechanisms of transmitting property, as is exemplified in the following anecdote regarding the redistribution of *iqṭāʿ* following the outbreak of the plague. Faced with high mortality rates among the *iqṭāʿ*-holders, the vice-regent of Egypt handed over the *iqṭā*'s of deceased soldiers to one of their surviving sons. When a soldier's widow prostrated herself before the vice-regent and told him that her husband had left her with only two daughters, the vice-regent sold the deceased soldier's *iqṭāʿ* to another officer for 12,000 dirhams. He then gave the money to the widow, telling her to use it to provide dowries for her two daughters.[57]

## Land, cash and credit: elite women in the economy

Possessing a large dowry did not necessarily mean economic independence for elite women. The gender division of property among the Mamluk elites meant that daughters received their share of patrimony in the form of trousseaux, "personal items" or heirlooms that were not easily exchanged in the market. Elite daughters did not receive cash, nor were they entitled to positions in the military and religious hierarchy and to the landed revenue that came with these positions. The exclusion of elite women from landed revenue was a distinctive feature of Mamluk political institutions, and marks a clear departure from earlier practice. Female members of the Ayyubid family received hereditary appanages as late as the middle of the thirteenth century.[58] In the Ayyubid principalities of Syria women of the ruling households held villages and agricultural land in what appears to have been full private ownership. The daughter of the Ayyubid prince al-Malik al-Amjad Ḥasan, for example, owned several villages in the Jordan Valley and, upon her death, passed them on to her son.[59] A question put to the Syrian jurist Ibn al-Ṣalāḥ (d. 643/1245) deals with a woman who owned a village on a riverbank, and let her husband assume the daily administration of the property.[60]

[56] Al-Jarawānī, "Mawāhib," fol. 23a. Another legal manual provides a model document that lays down the rights of the minor orphans of an Amir of Ten. The revenues of their late father's *iqṭāʿ* are to be used towards their own military equipment and personnel, and to finance a follower (*tabaʿ*) who will take up their place in royal military expeditions (Shams al-Dīn Muḥammad al-Minhājī al-Asyūṭī, *Jawāhir al-ʿUqūd wa-Muʿīn al-Quḍāh wa'l-Muwaqqiʿīn wa'l-Shuhūd*, 2 vols. [Cairo: Maṭbaʿat al-Sunnah al-Muḥammadiyyah, 1955], vol. II, 226–27). In the chronicles there are only occasional references to *nuzūl* over *iqṭāʿ* (al-Ṣafadī, *Aʿyān*, vol. I, 699; Chamberlain, *Knowledge*, 94, n. 16).

[57] Al-Ṣafadī, *Aʿyān*, vol. II, 86.

[58] R. S. Humphreys, *From Saladin to the Mongols* (Albany: State University of New York Press, 1977), 371–75, 415; H. Rabie, *The Financial System of Egypt, AH 564–741/1169–1341* (London: Oxford University Press, 1972), 42–43.

[59] Shihāb al-Dīn Aḥmad al-Nuwayrī, *Nihāyat al-Arab fī Funūn al-Adab* (Cairo: Dār al-Kutub al-Miṣriyya; al-Hay'ah al-Miṣriyya al-ʿĀmmah li'l-Kitāb, 1923–), vol. XXX, 193.

[60] Ibn al-Ṣalāḥ al-Shahrazūrī, *Fatāwā wa-Masā'il Ibn al-Ṣalāḥ*, ed. ʿAbd al-Muʿṭī Qalʿajī (Beirut: Dār al-Maʿrifa, 1986), 502 (no. 490).

A tangible product of Ayyubid women's access to landed property was their unusual prominence among patrons of public institutions. In Ayyubid Damascus (1174–1260), the womenfolk of the ruling elite established twenty-six religious institutions, including fifteen madrasas and six Sufi hospices. All in all, twenty-one individual women, mostly wives or daughters of Ayyubid rulers, established about 15 percent of the total number of charitable institutions. The financial backing came from endowed rural revenues.[61] In other cities female patrons were not as visible, but still managed to leave an impact on the urban landscape. In Cairo female members of the Ayyubid household established two madrasas, as well as other religious buildings, such as Shajar al-Durr's mausoleum.[62] Ḍayfa Khātūn, who effectively ruled Aleppo in the name of an Ayyubid prince, established one of the largest madrasas in the city.[63]

During the second half of the thirteenth century the Mamluk sultans confiscated or bought much of the privately owned land and then distributed it as *iqṭā'*. Women, it seems, were especially vulnerable. The life of Khātūn, daughter of the Ayyubid ruler of Damascus al-Malik al-Ashraf Mūsā, illustrates the way Ayyubid women were stripped of their landed assets.[64] In 685/1286, when Khātūn was in her seventies, officials in the Syrian administration went to court and claimed that she had been in a state of mental incompetence (*sifh*) when she sold her lands in several villages near Damascus thirty years earlier. Because of her supposed mental incapacity, she had been under the interdiction of her uncle and was not qualified to dispose of her property. The proofs brought by the state's representatives were accepted, and the sale was retroactively invalidated.

Legal mechanisms, and especially that of interdiction, were frequently deployed to limit the control of elite women over their property. Interdiction (*ḥajr*) is a legal mechanism that allows a responsible adult to exercise control over property owned by individuals whom the law considers unfit, such as minors and the mentally incapacitated.[65] In late thirteenth-century Damascus a Shāfi'ī *qāḍī* granted the request of a minor grandson, himself under interdiction, to impose interdiction on his sixty-year-old grandmother on the grounds of her mental incapacity.[66] In a case from Upper Egypt, an orphan girl remained under interdiction even after her

61 R. S. Humphreys, "Women as Patrons of Religious Architecture in Ayyubid Damascus," *Muqarnas* 11 (1994), 35–54.

62 Berkey, "Women and Islamic Education," 144; Howyda al-Harithy, "Female Patronage of Mamluk Architecture in Cairo," *Harvard Middle Eastern and Islamic Review* 1 (1994), 157; D. Behrens-Abouseif, *Islamic Architecture in Cairo: An Introduction* (Leiden: Brill, 1989), 91–93.

63 Humphreys, "Women as Patrons," 35; Y. Tabbaa, *Constructions of Power and Piety in Medieval Aleppo* (University Park: Pennsylvania State University Press, 1997), 44–49, 193.

64 J. Sublet, "La folie de la princesse Bint al-Ašraf (un scandale financier sous les mamelouks bahris)," *Bulletin d'études orientales* 27 (1974), 45–50; Faḍlallāh b. Abī al-Fakhr Ibn al-Suqā'ī, *Tālī Kitāb Wafayāt al-A'yān*, ed. J. Sublet (Damascus: Institut Français de Damas, 1974), 72, 159; al-Nuwayrī, *Nihāyat al-Arab*, vol. XXXI, 147. On her father, see Ibn Kathīr, *al-Bidāya* (Beirut), vol. XIII, 257; Humphreys, *From Saladin to the Mongols*, 208–38.

65 M. Shatzmiller, "Women and Property Rights in al-Andalus and the Maghrib: Social Patterns and Legal Discourse," *ILS* 2 (1995), 229–30.

66 Al-Fazārī, "Fatāwā," fol. 23a; cited in 'Isā b. 'Uthmān al-Ghazzī (d. 799/1397), "Adab al-Qaḍā'," Chester Beatty MS 3763, fol. 170a.

marriage, and the court's representative sold her property without her permission.[67] The fourteenth-century jurist and *qāḍī* al-Subkī warned his colleagues that proving women's mental incapacity had become too facile. He specifically criticized judges who maintained that a proof of mental incapacity prevails over any counter-evidence the woman may produce. These *qāḍī*s did not require any substantial testimony or circumstantial evidence, but only the signatures of two men who were ready to support the claim.[68]

As more and more land was alienated in favor of men, and as the economic activity of elite women was subject to increasing controls, the number of public institutions founded by women fell dramatically. Against the twenty-six religious and charitable institutions women established during less than a century of Ayyubid rule in Damascus, only four were founded in the following century. In Cairo the womenfolk of the royal court had more of a chance to contribute to the city's landscape, especially in the days of al-Nāṣir Muḥammad. Urdutekin bt. Nogāy, the Mongol wife of the sultan, funded the establishment of a tomb for her son by endowing tenement houses, a covered market, two bathhouses, and agricultural land.[69] Sitt Ḥadaq, a slave-girl and wet-nurse who became the senior governess in al-Nāṣir's court, established a mosque that has survived to our day.[70] Overall, however, women's representation among the patrons of public buildings in Cairo remained low.

The relative exclusion of elite women from control over land must have pushed them towards the credit market, although the extent of this involvement remains vague. On a rudimentary level, a woman could rent out the jewelry and textiles of her trousseau for weddings or other social occasions.[71] But women were also involved in the cash economy. A couple of cases put to Ibn Taymiyya deal with women buying textiles or jewelry, and then re-selling them for a higher price (in one instance, a third more), to be paid at a later date. These were most probably fictitious sales, intended to circumvent the prohibition on interest.[72] In a case brought before the court of Damascus, a certain ʿUmar al-Kurdī from Jerusalem took a loan of 200 silver dirhams from a Jewish woman called Ḥusniyya, pawning his vineyard as security. When the debt was not paid, the woman appealed to the local deputy *qāḍī*, who proceeded to register the vineyard in her name.[73]

67 Jaʿfar b. Thaʿlab al-Udfūwī, *al-Ṭāliʿ al-Saʿīd al-Jāmiʿ li-Asmāʾ al-Fuḍalāʾ waʾl-Ruwāt bi-Aʿlā al-Ṣaʿīd* (Cairo: al-Dār al-Miṣriyya liʾl-Taʾlīf waʾl-Tarjamah, 1966), 227; al-Ṣafadī, *Aʿyān*, vol. II, 231.

68 Al-Subkī, *Fatāwā*, vol. I, 340–44.

69 Al-Harithy, "Female Patronage," 157–59.

70 C. Williams, "The Mosque of Sitt Ḥadaq," *Muqarnas* 11 (1994), 55–64. The *khānqāh* of Ṭughāy, a concubine of al-Nāṣir and the mother of his eldest son, was most probably established before the founder's death in 749/1348. On these structures, see A. ʿAbd al-Rāziq, "Trois foundations féminines dans l'Egypte mamlouke," *Revue d'études islamiques* 41 (1973), 97–126.

71 Ibn Taymiyya, *Majmūʿ Fatāwā Shaykh al-Islām Aḥmad Ibn Taymiyya*, ed. ʿAbd al-Raḥmān b. Muḥammad al-ʿĀṣimī al-Najdī, 35 vols. (Riyadh: Maṭbaʿat Riyāḍ, 1381–86 [1961–66]), vol. XXX, 194.

72 Ibn Taymiyya, *Fatāwā al-Nisāʾ*, 179–80.

73 Al-Subkī, *Fatāwā*, vol. II, 542–43. The case is dated 741/1340–41.

The deathbed declaration of Nafīsa bt. ʿAlī, wife of a baker in Jerusalem, shows that she was engaged in extensive credit operations, apparently geared towards the family business. Two villagers owed her about 30 dirhams each, one man owed her 350 dirhams, and a bean-maker in the city owed her as much as 500 dirhams. Her husband owed her 1,000 dirhams as the late payment of her marriage gift. Finally, the couple co-owned a vineyard in the vicinity of Jerusalem, and at the time of her death she still owed her husband 60 dirhams as the price of her share.[74] But it is much more common to find husbands who owed money to their wives. Bīrū, a shaykh of a Sufi *zāwiya* in Jerusalem and one of the richest persons to appear in the Ḥaram documents, owed his wife 1,600 dirhams.[75] Shams al-Dīn al-Baʿalbakī, a merchant, owed his wife 10,000 dirhams, and his entire estate had to be sold in order to cover this sum.[76] A Jewish man from Jerusalem owed his wife a total of 500 dirhams, half of which were the remainder of her marriage gift and the rest a loan.[77] One Cairene husband, who went on a business trip to the Red Sea, not only borrowed money from his wife but also had to promise on pain of divorce that he would pay back by the end of the month.[78] This aspect of marriage – the creditor wife and the indebted husband – becomes a standard feature of fifteenth-century marriages.

A striking illustration of women's credit activities comes from the legal *responsa* of the Cairene jurist Walī al-Dīn Ibn al-ʿIrāqī (d. 826/1423). The question put to the jurist deals with the legality of exclusively female credit associations. According to the question, the "well-known practice" was that several women pooled their financial resources by appointing one of them, known as "the Collecting Woman" (*al-mar'ah al-jamʿiyyah*), to collect a fixed sum from each of them. The woman would collect 1,000 dirhams every week from ten participating women. She then gave the entire sum to each woman in her turn, and continued doing so until the end of the term agreed to in advance. The legality of this communal fund was questioned because the collecting woman received a fee for her efforts – in the example cited, 5 percent of the money she collected – and this profit was suspect as interest.[79] The description clearly fits the female rotating savings and credit associations found up to this day in many urban societies in the developing world, including contemporary Cairo. As with the modern institution, the appearance of savings associations may have been related to the entry of a large number of women – not necessarily from the upper classes – into the cash economy.[80]

[74] Ḥaram document no. 607, published in Lutfi, *al-Quds*, 54–60.

[75] Ḥaram document no. 210, published in Lutfi, "*Iqrārs*," 278 ff. and in al-ʿAsalī, *Wathāʾiq*, vol. II, no. 43.

[76] Ḥaram document no. 591, published in Donald P. Little, "Documents Related to the Estates of a Merchant and his Wife in Late Fourteenth Century Jerusalem," *MSR* 3 (1999), 93–177.

[77] Ḥaram document no. 554, published in Donald P. Little, "Ḥaram Documents Related to the Jews of Late Fourteenth-Century Jerusalem," *Journal of Semitic Studies* 30 (1985), 233 ff.

[78] Ibn Taymiyya, *Majmūʿ Fatāwā*, vol. XXXIII, 115. For husbands borrowing from their wives in the Geniza, see Goitein, *A Mediterranean Society*, vol. III, 181.

[79] Chester Beatty MS 4665, fols. 53b–54a. The work was copied in Cairo in 879/1475.

[80] On rotating savings associations in contemporary societies in general, see S. Ardener and S. Burman (eds.), *Money-go-rounds: The Importance of Rotating Savings and Credit Associations for Women* (Oxford: BERG, 1995). On savings associations in contemporary Cairo, see Evelyn Early, *Baladi*

## Impact of the Black Death

The plague that hit the Near East in the middle of the fourteenth century posed an immediate challenge to the prevailing gender division of property. Those daughters of military and civilian elite households who survived benefited by inheriting unusually large fortunes. A treatise written in Damascus immediately following the first outbreak reveals a deep anxiety about the sudden surge in wealthy young heiresses.[81] The following decades saw a revival in female patronage of religious buildings, part of a general spate of building activity.[82] In Jerusalem, after a long hiatus, women established at least three madrasas.[83] In Cairo, female members of the military elite founded as many religious institutions in two decades as they had in the preceding century. These include Madrasat Umm al-Sulṭān, the most remarkable achievement of female patronage in Mamluk Cairo, established by the concubine mother of al-Ashraf Shaʿbān in 770/1368.[84]

Yet this side-effect of the plague was temporary. The high visibility of the wives and daughters of the military elite as patrons of religious buildings was short-lived, like the contemporary political prominence of *awlād al-nās*.[85] In the long run, however, the impact of the plague on the gender division of property was twofold. First, the lavish dowries of elite women circulated more easily. In the fifteenth century we often hear about spendthrift women who converted their trousseaux into cash only to squander them completely. Sitt al-Khulafāʾ, the daughter of the caliph al-Mustanjid Yūsuf, wasted away the major part of her dowry. Ibn Qāwān, her third husband (she was divorced twice), inherited her debts when she died in 892/1487 at the age of 32.[86] Fāṭima, daughter of Sultan al-Ẓāhir Ṭaṭar, received a trousseau estimated at 100,000 dinars upon her marriage to al-Asharf Barsbāy.

*Women of Cairo. Playing with an Egg and a Stone* (Boulder: Lynne Rienner, 1993), 5 ff. See also W. Jordan, *Women and Credit in Pre-industrial and Developing Societies* (Philadelphia: University of Pennsylvania Press, 1992).

81 Al-Ṭarsūsī, *Kitāb Tuḥfat al-Turk*, 20.

82 M. Dols, *The Black Death in the Middle East* (Princeton: Princeton University Press, 1977), 270; D. Behrens-Abouseif, "Patterns of Urban Patronage in Cairo: A Comparison between the Mamluk and the Ottoman Periods," in Phillip and Haarmann (eds.), *The Mamluks in Egyptian Politics and Society*, 229.

83 See Mujīr al-Dīn al-ʿUlaymī, *al-Uns al-Jalīl fī Taʾrīkh al-Quds waʾl-Khalīl*, 2 vols. (Najaf: al-Maṭbaʿa al-Ḥaydariyya, 1969), vol. II, 36, 43. The endowment deed for the al-Bārūdiyya madrasa, established by Sufrā Khātūn bt. Sharaf al-Dīn al-Bārūdī in 768/1367, has survived (Ḥaram document no. 76; discussed in Donald P. Little, "The Ḥaram Documents as Sources for the Arts and Architecture of the Mamluk Period," *Muqarnas* 2 [1984], 69).

84 ʿAbd al-Rāziq, *La femme*, 22–23; al-Harithy, "Female Patronage," 161–67; Behrens-Abouseif, *Islamic Architecture*, 129–31. For biographical details, see al-Maqrīzī, *Sulūk*, vol. III, 210; Abū Bakr b. Aḥmad Ibn Qāḍī Shuhba, *Taʾrīkh Ibn Qāḍī Shuhba*, ed. ʿAdnān Darwīsh, 3 vols. (Damascus: Institut Français de Damas, 1977–94), vol. III, 429, 439.

85 On the prominence of *awlād al-nās* in this period, see R. Irwin, *The Middle East in the Middle Ages: The Early Mamluk Sultanate, 1250–1382* (London: Croom Helm, 1986), 143; Jamāl al-Dīn Yūsuf Ibn Taghrī Birdī, *al-Manhal al-Ṣāfī waʾl-Mustawfā Baʿd al-Wāfī*, ed. Muḥammad Muḥammad Amīn (Cairo: al-Hayʾah al-Miṣriyya al-ʿĀmmah lil-Kitāb, 1984–), vol. V, 126; al-Maqrīzī, *Sulūk*, vol. III, 63.

86 Al-Sakhāwī, *Ḍawʾ*, vol. XII, 55 (no. 324).

She left the Citadel after the death of her husband and moved to a private residence in the city. In order to finance an elegant lifestyle, which was condemned by some chroniclers, Fāṭima pawned her expensive clothes with Cairene female brokers. Eventually, she was unable to pay back the loans and was heavily in debt when she died in 874/1469.[87]

Another important change in the gender division of the economy was the re-entry of elite women into the land market. By and large, women were still excluded from holding official positions and collecting the tax revenues that came with them (although even this happened towards the end of the fifteenth century, when a widow of a Sufi shaykh was elected to head his *zāwiya*).[88] Yet, the share of agricultural surplus that was channeled to these positions was gradually decreasing. More and more land was alienated to support endowments that were for the most part private or familial, although charitable in appearance.[89] This was especially true in Egypt. By the end of the fifteenth century it was estimated that two-fifths of all Egyptian arable land was endowed in some way or another.[90] The rapid growth of family endowment at the expense of *iqṭā'* allowed elite women greater access to landed revenue; they could – and did – become beneficiaries, administrators and founders.

Overall, women profited from the establishment of endowments more often than not. While Islamic law allows the founder of an endowment complete freedom in choosing its beneficiaries, many founders still stipulated that the revenues of the endowment would be divided according to Islamic inheritance law (*bi'l-farīḍa al-shar'iyya*). Most of the endowment deeds preserved in the legal literature explicitly state that males should receive twice the share of females.[91] In these cases, we may assume that the endowment was established with the sole purpose of protecting the property from confiscation. But some family endowments were intentionally designed to circumvent the Islamic inheritance law in order to improve the lot of daughters. It was quite common for a founder to stipulate equal

[87] Petry, "Class Solidarity," 131–32; al-Khaṭīb al-Jawharī Ibn al-Ṣayrafī, *Inbā' al-Haṣr bi-Abnā' al-'Aṣr*, ed. Ḥasan Ḥabashī (Cairo: Dār al-Fikr al-'Arabī, 1970), 131; al-Sakhāwī, *Ḍaw'*, vol. XII, 92 (no. 572).

[88] Berkey, "Women and Islamic Education," 145. On the unusual appointment of a widow as shaykha, see Abū al-Barakāt Ibn Iyās, *Badā'i' al-Zuhūr fī Waqā'i' al-Duhūr*, ed. M. Muṣṭafā, 5 vols. (Wiesbaden: F. Steiner, 1975–92), vol. III, 233.

[89] The literature on fifteenth-century endowments is quite extensive. See in particular M. M. Amīn, *al-Awqāf wa'l-Ḥayāh al-Ijtimā'iyya fī Miṣr, 648–923 H./1250–1517 M.* (Cairo: Dār al-Nahḍa al-'Arabiyya, 1980); C. Petry, *Protectors or Praetorians? The Last Mamlūk Sultans and Egypt's Waning as a Great Power* (Albany: State University of New York Press, 1994), 190–219; J.-C. Garcin and M. A. Taher, "Enquête sur le financement d'un *waqf* égyptien du XV$^{e}$ siècle: Les comptes de Jawhār Lālā," *JESHO* 38 (1995), 262–304.

[90] H. Halm, *Ägypten nach den mamlukischen Lehensregistern*, 2 vols. (Wiesbaden: Reichert, 1979–80), vol. I, 50–52; N. Michel, "Les *rizaq iḥbāsiyya*, terres agricoles en mainmorte dans l'Egypte mamelouke et ottomane. Etude sur les *Dafātir al-Aḥbās* ottomans," *AI* 30 (1996), 105–98.

[91] For examples of endowment deeds in which males receive twice the share of daughters, see al-Subkī, *Fatāwā*, vol. I, 475, 484, 494, 500, 501, 511, 517, vol. II, 9, 10, 29, 40, 50, 50, 72, 167, 168, 177, 183, 187; al-Anṣārī, *I'lām*, 164, 165, 167, 168, 171, 175, 182, 185, 187, 189, 191.

shares for sons and daughters, or males and females.[92] There are several examples of family endowments in which the primary beneficiaries are daughters or their children.[93] Some founders specifically excluded male descendants,[94] while others excluded females.[95] Yet, in a sample of preserved endowment deeds from late fifteenth-century Damascus, the portions of what women obtained as beneficiaries are explicitly higher than what they would have received by the Qur'ānic laws of inheritance. The reverse does occur, but is considerably rarer.[96]

By the latter half of the fifteenth century, elite women were often nominated as administrators of their families' endowments. A standard endowment deed specified that following the founder's death the supervision should pass to the "most discerning" (*al-arshad*) among the founder's descendants. As shown by Carl Petry, this vague definition was often understood to include women.[97] It is possible to identify thirty-eight individual women who served as administrators of family endowments in late fifteenth- and early sixteenth-century Cairo, representing one-fifth of the total number of known administrators.[98] The daughter of the *dawādār* Azbak was appointed as supervisor of the endowment established by her mother's second husband, ʿAbd al-Ghanī b. al-Jīʿān. She attracted the attention of the chroniclers in 841/1437–8, when she sold the main asset of the endowment, a

92 Al-Subkī, *Fatāwā*, vol. I, 473, 478, 481, 485, 506, 509, 514, vol. II, 143; al-Anṣārī, *Iʿlām*, 162, 170, 174, 187. Equal shares for females are also stipulated in a fifteenth-century endowment established by a wealthy physician from Cairo. See D. Behrens-Abouseif, *Fatḥ Allāh and Abū Zakariyā': Physicians under the Mamluks* (Cairo: Institut français d'archéologie orientale, 1987).

93 Al-Subkī, *Fatāwā*, vol. I, 474, 485, 494; al-Anṣārī, *Iʿlām*, 159, 162, 165, 189. Endowments for the benefit of daughters are also mentioned in the Ḥaram documents (nos. 606, 257; Little, *Catalogue*, 93, 265). See also M. M. Amīn, *Fihrist Wathā'iq al-Qāhirah ḥattā Nihāyat ʿAṣr al-Mamālīk. Catalogue des doucments d'archives du Caire de 239/853 à 922/1516* (Cairo: Institut français d'archéologie orientale, 1981), 441 ff.

94 For the exclusion of males from a thirteenth-century endowment, see H. Rabie, "Ḥujjat Tamlīk wa-Waqf," *Majallat al-Jamʿiyya al-Miṣriyya lil-Dirāsāt al-Ta'rīkhiyya*, 12 (1964); Amīn, *Awqāf*, 94.

95 Al-Subkī, *Fatāwā*, vol. I, 493, 497, 510, vol. II, 40, 66; al-Anṣārī, *Iʿlām*, 165, 181. In the Ḥaram documents, we find an enquiry concerning an endowment for the benefit of the male progeny of a family from Nablus (Ḥaram document no. 25, Little, *Catalogue*, 40).

96 M. Winter, "Mamluks and their Households in Late Mamluk Damascus: A *Waqf* Study," in A. Levanoni and M. Winter (eds.), *The Mamluks in Egyptian and Syrian Politics and History* (Leiden: Brill, 2004), 297–316. For similar conclusions regarding endowment deeds in contemporary North Africa, see D. Powers, "The Mālikī Family Endowment: Legal Norms and Social Practices," *IJMES* 25 (1993), 379–406.

97 Petry, "Class Solidarity," 133 ff. I do not agree, however, with Petry's argument that women were seen as a stabilizing element in a world of incessant factionalism, and therefore the administrators of choice among the military elite. Women still represented only a minority of all endowment supervisors. Furthermore, the appointment of women as administrators was by no means limited to the military elite. The relative growth in the number of women who acted as supervisors of endowments was rather a combined result of the demographics of the plague and of a loosening of the restrictions on the economic activity of elite women.

98 The data was collected from Amīn, *Fihrist*. The name of an endowment's administrator appears routinely in the documents, mainly in connection with the sale of endowed property through *istibdāl*. Petry estimated that women constituted almost 30 percent of the endowment administrators in this period ("Class Solidarity," 133).

big house in Cairo worth tens of thousands of dinars, for a ludicrous price.[99] In a case from 877/1472, Shaqrā', daughter of the former sultan al-Nāṣir Faraj, brought a lawsuit against an amir who refused to pay the rent on agricultural lands he had leased from her.[100] The same Shaqrā' also contested the control of the family's endowment with her sister's daughter Āsiyya.[101] In 884/1479–80 an elderly aunt who managed the endowment of the *qāḍī* Walī al-Dīn al-Sifṭī was deemed "the most discerning" in the family line in spite of a legal challenge by her young nephew.[102] These examples clearly show that women were now trusted to manage family property. The legal mechanism of interdiction, popular in the thirteenth and fourteenth centuries, is hardly mentioned in later sources.

Most important, fifteenth-century elite women were not only beneficiaries and administrators of endowments, but also a sizable minority among the founders. The best-known example is that of the lifelong wife of Sultan Qā'itbāy, Fāṭima bt. 'Alī Ibn Khāṣṣbak (d. 909/1504). Fāṭima started acquiring real estate in 878/1473, when she bought ten units of urban property and six agricultural tracts located in the Delta provinces of al-Gharbiyya, al-Sharqiyya and al-Qalyūbiyya. According to the purchase deed, all six units had originally been held in the Army Bureau for distribution as *iqṭā'*. In the next thirty years Fāṭima constantly bought urban and rural real estate, and continued to invest at the same rate even after the death of her husband – a clear indication that her hold over this property was real. The agricultural units formed between one-third and one-half of her overall investments, estimated to be several tens of thousands of dinars.[103]

Female founders of endowments appear to constitute about 15–20 percent of the total number of known founders in fifteenth-century Cairo.[104] As opposed to the grand institutions built following the first outbreak of the plague, fifteenth-century elite women endowed relatively small family tombs and neighborhood mosques, of which few survived.[105] Elite women, mostly from military households, established eleven out of the twenty-three charitable endowments providing bread for the poor in fifteenth-century Cairo. The purpose of these endowments was to

99 Al-Sakhāwī, *Ḍaw'*, vol. IV, 236; Shihāb al-Dīn Aḥmad Ibn Ḥajar al-'Asqalānī, *Inbā' al-Ghumr bi-Abnā' al-'Umr*, ed. Ḥasan Ḥabashī, 3 vols. (Cairo: Lajnat Iḥyā'al-Turāth al-'Arabī, 1971–76), vol. III, 411.

100 Petry, "Class Solidarity," 130; Ibn al-Ṣayrafī, *Inbā' al-Haṣr*, 471.

101 Ibn Iyās, *Badā'i'*, vol. III, 79.

102 Al-Sakhāwī, *Ḍaw'*, vol. XII, 8; Muḥammad b. 'Abd al-Raḥmān al-Sakhāwī, *Wajīz al-Kalām fī al-Dhayl 'alā Duwal al-Islām*, ed. Bashshār 'Awwād Ma' rūf, 'Isām Fāris al-Ḥarastānī and Aḥmad al-Khutaymī, 3 vols. (Beirut: Mu'assasat al-Risāla, 1995), vol. III, 897, 1068. See further examples of late fifteenth-century female administrators of family endowments in Petry, "Class Solidarity," 132–33.

103 C. Petry, "The Estate of al-Khuwand Fāṭima al-Khāṣṣbakiyya: Royal Spouse, Autonomous Investor," in Levanoni and Winter (eds.), *The Mamluks in Egyptian and Syrian Politics and History*, 277–94; Petry, *Protectors or Praetorians*, 200–01; Petry, "Class Solidarity," 134–36.

104 For a statistical analysis of the late Mamluk endowment deeds preserved in Dār al-Wathā'iq in Cairo, see S. Denoix, "Pour une exploitation d'ensemble d'un corpus: Les waqf mamelouks du Caire," in R. Deguilhem (ed.), *Le waqf dans l'espace islamique: outil de pouvoir socio-politique* (Damascus: Institut français d'études arabes de Damas, 1995), 29–44.

105 Al-Harithy, "Female Patronage," 159.

support a family tomb and the pious works associated with it, while simultaneously protecting the family's property.[106] In 871/1477 the amir Jaqmaq al-Maḥmūdī established one such endowment together with his wife, a daughter of a civilian dignitary. The endowment supported the tomb of the wife's father, where food was distributed, and a large share of its revenue was reserved for the couple's descendants.[107] While married couples established only a small proportion of fifteenth-century endowments,[108] their mere existence demonstrates the changes that occurred in the gender division of property in the aftermath of the plague. The lines dividing specifically male and specifically female property became so blurred as to allow some husbands and wives to merge their assets into one marital fund.

Did dowries make women financially independent? Could women rely on their trousseaux if they wanted to get out of an unwanted marriage? The answer is yes, but only for the wealthy. Dowries were a form of gender-specific pre-mortem inheritance and represented a daughter's share in her parents' patrimony. The value of a dowry of a princess, or even the daughter of an amir, was often fantastically high, and certainly much higher than the marriage gifts offered by the groom. But, while dowries were important in the marriages of all social classes, the less affluent could not have provided their daughters with long-term security, and the value of the dowries they donated was much more modest. Even for elite women dowries came with restrictions attached. Dowries were given in the form of trousseaux, reinforcing a gendered division of the economy. As long as elite women had limited access to landed revenue – and this was the case until the second half of the fifteenth century – they were not fully incorporated into the economy, and were unable to make the most out of their share of their families' inheritance. However, the opening up of the market in land and the general monetization of the fifteenth century allowed for greater economic integration of elite women, and, as a by-product, enhanced their position vis-à-vis their husbands.

106 A. Sabra, *Poverty and Charity in Medieval Islam. Mamluk Egypt, 1250–1517* (Cambridge: Cambridge University Press, 2000), 90–93.

107 *Ibid.*, 93.

108 Qānī Bay (d. 863/1459), the governor of Damascus, needed the contribution of his wife in order to fund improvements to the minaret of the Umayyad Mosque (Ibn al-Ḥimṣī, *Ḥawādith*, vol. I, 144). The amir Hoşgeldi (Khushkaldī) and his wife, Zahrā' bt. Yaḥyā al-Muhājirī, established a joint trust in 864/1460, which they administered together for at least thirty-five years (Amin, *Fihrist*, nos. 389, 403, 428, 525, 526, 527, 529, 557, 560, 561). For other joint endowments, see Amin, *Fihrist*, nos. 163, 404, 405, 194, 247, 254.

CHAPTER 2

# Working women, single women and the rise of the female *ribāṭ*

In the year 655/1257–58, after ten years of marriage, the Damascene scholar Shihāb al-Dīn Abū Shāma composed a poem in praise of his wife, Sitt al-ʿArab bt. Sharaf al-Dīn al-ʿAbdarī. After mentioning her noble lineage, Abū Shāma proceeds to commend her impeccable character. Sitt al-ʿArab is modest and obedient to her husband, attends to her family and shows mercy to orphans. She is wise, while striving to understand what she does not know, and eloquent, her words are like pearls. She guards the secrets of the house, and the property of her husband:

> Better still, to her all this virtue/
> is no burden, but comes natural/
> Do not reproach me for my love for her/
> for few of the women of her age are her equal/
> At our wedding she was a girl of fourteen/
> with all these traits already installed/
> She never strayed from that path/
> and each passing year her virtue increased manifold/
> What more to say: in ten years with me/
> she has never given me any reason to complain.[1]

An extraordinary feature of the poem is the realistic appreciation of Sitt al-ʿArab's contribution to the household economy. Abū Shāma writes:

> She always attends to household chores
> despite her youth she shies away from nothing
> *ṭirāz* embroidery, needlework with golden threads
> cutting cloth, sewing and spinning
> She moves from this to that and from that to this
> not to mention the cleaning, the cooking and the washing.[2]

[1] ʿAbd al-Raḥmān b. Ismāʿīl Shihāb al-Dīn Abū Shāma, *Tarājim Rijāl al-Qarnayn al-Sādis wa'l-Sābiʿ al-Maʿrūf bi'l-Dhayl ʿalā al-Rawḍatayn*, ed. M. Zāhid al-Kawtharī (Cairo: Dār al-Kutub al-Malikiyya, 1947), 196–98. On the birth of his son, see *ibid.*, 189. It is rare to find husbands expressing their love for their wives so openly. On this poem see also Joseph Lowry, "Time, Form and Self: The Autobiography of Abū Shāma," *Edebiyât: Special Issue – Arabic Autobiography* 712 (1997), 313–25.

[2] Abū Shāma, *al-Dhayl*, 196.

Thus, Sitt al-ʿArab did not just bring honor to her husband. Abū Shāma appreciated the way she fulfilled her domestic duties. In particular, the poem gives the impression that Sitt al-ʿArab spent most of her day working on various stages in the production of textiles – from the spinning of yarn to the final touches of embroidery. At least some of these tasks, and especially the spinning of yarn, were almost certainly done for wages. The cleaning and the cooking were a second priority, and the little baby Aḥmad, born a year earlier, is not even mentioned.

Whatever dowries they brought to their marriages, the vast majority of wives had to work hard, even the wife of a scholar like Abū Shāma. Moreover, much of what they did had a market value, even if the male authors of the texts at our disposal seldom give credit to women's contribution to the urban economy. A large proportion – perhaps the majority – of urban women, regardless of their marital status, worked for wages. Some worked outside their homes – hairdressers and midwives, as well as the omnipresent female peddler, had to go around the city in order to offer their services. But even when women worked at home, and this was true for the vast majority of working women, their work was an integral and indispensable part of the urban textile industry. The garments worn by everyone in Mamluk cities, from the elite to the paupers, were embroidered, sewn, and certainly spun, by women.

Women's remunerative work, both within and outside marriage, is crucial for understanding the balance of power between husbands and wives, and the phenomenon of frequent divorce. Even if women received lower wages than men, they still gained a substantial degree of economic independence. Wages from work in the textile industry allowed many women, not necessarily elite women, to remain single for long periods of time. Mamluk cities always had a large population of widowed and divorced women, who did not remarry but lived on wages they received for their work as spinners and seamstresses. The existence of these single women posed a problem to the patriarchal self-image of Mamluk society, and occasionally there were futile attempts to ban women from the streets of the cities. Mamluk society accommodated these single women by the establishment of exclusively female religious houses, built with the purpose of providing them with their own moral and physical space within the male public sphere. It is the large and unprecedented number of female religious houses established in the Mamluk period that demonstrates how many women managed without husbands.

## Women and the textile industry

In Mamluk society, as in the Jewish community of the Geniza and in other medieval Muslim societies, women were represented in a limited range of gender-specific professions.[3] Women performed services directly related to female life, such as

[3] Goitein, *A Mediterranean Society*, vol. I, 127–30; M. Shatzmiller, *Labour in the Medieval Islamic World* (Leiden: Brill, 1994), 347–68.

midwives,[4] hairdressers,[5] matchmakers,[6] washers of the dead,[7] and female attendants in baths and hospitals.[8] Midwives and hairdressers were paid generously, and were considered quite profitable professions.[9] In his diary, Ibn Ṭawq records the gifts his wife regularly sent to her midwife, and the hefty sums she paid to her hairdresser before going to a wedding. The women attending her during visits to the bathhouse received smaller fees.[10] As in the Geniza period, women appear mostly as peddlers rather than as shopkeepers.[11] The female cloth-peddlers were a familiar sight, and had a crucial role in the distribution of the textile industry's products. They also had privileged access to the private domains of elite households.[12] In non-skilled professions, wet-nurses and prostitutes had to compete with the unsalaried services of slave-girls.[13] Salaried domestic servants were completely absent. Women competed with men only in a few skilled crafts. There are references to both male and female instructors of girls.[14] Female and male barbers performed a variety of services, such as bloodletting, cleansing and whitening teeth, or removing excessive hair, mainly for women.[15]

[4] Ibn al-Ḥājj, *Madkhal*, vol. III, 290; anonymous Shāfiʿī treatise on marriage, Chester Beatty MS 4665, fols. 28a–29b. See also ʿAbd al-Rāziq, *La femme*, 62, 83.

[5] ʿAbd al-Rāziq, *La femme*, 82, and the sources cited there.

[6] Muḥammad Ibn Daniyāl, *Kitāb Ṭayf al-Khayāl*, ed. Paul Kahle, with a critical apparatus by D. Hopwood (Cambridge: Trustees of the E. J. W. Gibb Memorial, 1992), 22 ff. See also Ibn Baydakīn al-Turkumānī, *Kitāb al-Lumaʿ fī al-Ḥawādith waʾl-Bidaʿ*, ed. Ṣubḥī Labīb (Wiesbaden: F. Steiner Verlag, 1986), 163.

[7] ʿAbd al-Rāziq, *La femme*, 81; H. Lutfi, "Manners," 106; Ibn al-Ḥājj, *Madkhal*, vol. II, 172, vol. III, 246; Ibn al-Ukhuwwa, *Maʿālim al-Qurba fī Aḥkām al-Ḥisba*, ed. R. Levy (London: Luzac & Co., 1938), 101–02.

[8] Female orderlies (*farrāshāt*) were employed in the hospital of Qalāwūn in the beginning of the fourteenth century (Sabra, *Poverty*, 76). On bath-attendants, see ʿAbd al-Rāziq, *La femme*, 44.

[9] On the career of al-Nāṣir Muḥammad's midwife, see al-Jazarī, *Taʾrīkh*, vol. III, 701. In one case, we are told that a hairdresser employed a slave-girl as her assistant (al-Jazarī, *Taʾrīkh*, vol. III, 939; al-Maqrīzī, *Sulūk*, vol. I, 521).

[10] See examples in Ibn Ṭawq, *Taʿlīq*, vol. I, 35 (3/12/885), 132 (16/1/887), 150 (27/2/887), 154 (12/3/887), 196 (5/10/887).

[11] An exception is the widow of a Cairene bookseller, who continued to sell his books nine years after his death. The husband, Shāfiʿ b. ʿAlī Nāṣir al-Dīn Ibn ʿAsākir, died in 730/1330 (al-Ṣafadī, *Aʿyān*, vol. II, 503).

[12] For female peddlers (*dallālāt*) who acted as government spies, see al-Yūsufī, *Nuzhat al-Nāẓir*, 261–64. On the type of transactions made by female brokers in fifteenth-century Granada, see M. Shatzmiller, "Women and Wage Labour in the Medieval Islamic West," *JESHO* 40 (1997), 196.

[13] For a comprehensive study of wet-nurses in medieval Islam, see A. Giladi, *Infants, Parents and Wet Nurses: Medieval Islamic Views on Breastfeeding and their Social Implications* (Leiden: Brill, 1999). See also ʿAbd al-Rāziq, *La femme*, 83–85; Shatzmiller, "Women and Wage Labour," 183–88. For model contracts for the hiring of wet-nurses in Mamluk legal sources, see al-Jarawānī, "Mawāhib," fols. 37b, 99b; al-Asyūṭī, *Jawāhir al-ʿUqūd*, vol. II, 206. For references to wet-nurses in Mamluk chronicles, see al-Jazarī, *Taʾrīkh*, vol. II, 522; al-Maqrīzī, *Sulūk*, vol. IV, 1116. On prostitutes, see ʿAbd al-Rāziq, *La femme*, 45 ff., and the rich sources cited there.

[14] ʿAbd al-Raḥmān b. Naṣr Al-Shayzarī, *Nihāyat al-Rutba fī Ṭalab al-Ḥisba*, ed. al-Sayyid al-Bāz al-ʿArīnī (Cairo: Maṭbaʿat Lajnat al-Taʾlīf waʾl-Tarjama waʾl-Nashr, 1946), 104; Ibn al-Ukhuwwa, *Maʿālim al-Qurba*, 261; Muḥammad b. Aḥmad Ibn Bassām, *Kitāb Nihāyat al-Rutba fī Ṭalab al-Ḥisba*, ed. Ḥusām al-Dīn al-Samarrāʾī (Baghdad: Maṭbaʿat al-Maʿārif, 1968), 161–63. See also Shatzmiller, *Labour*, 355.

[15] Ibn al-Ḥājj recommends the use of female barbers in order to limit unnecessary physical contact between men and women, but then warns that these women try to show off their merchandise by

The vast majority of women, however, worked in the production of textiles, traditionally "the main field of female remunerative occupation."[16] Spinning and embroidery were the female professions par excellence, as demonstrated in an anecdote told by the historian Ibn Kathīr. During a visit to Baalbek in 754/1353–54, Ibn Kathīr met a hermaphrodite who was brought up as a girl until the age of fifteen. Then a tiny penis appeared, and the local governor gave an order to celebrate the transformation of the girl into a man by bestowing a military uniform upon him. The young soldier boasted before Ibn Kathīr that he was "skilled in all the professions of women, including spinning, decorating with *ṭīrāz* bands and embroidery with gold and silver threads (*zarkāsh*)."[17] Girls were taught spinning and embroidery at a young age. Al-Jazarī mourns with sadness and pride two of his young nieces, who were not only beautiful and pious, but also excelled in the arts of embroidery and sewing.[18] While spinning was done by women, weaving was generally done by men. There were, however, a few exceptions. Zayn al-Nisā' bt. 'Imād al-Dīn Ibn al-Mulḥim (d. 735/1335) was known for her cooking, sewing, embroidery and weaving.[19] 'Ā'isha bt. Muḥammad Ibn Muslim (d. 736/1336), an impoverished daughter of a Damascene scholarly family, made her living out of working the loom.[20]

The women who worked in embroidery and sewing, and in particular spinning, could perform these tasks at home.[21] Ibn al-Ṣalāḥ ruled that a husband could not prevent his wife from working at home in embroidery, spinning or sewing.[22] Most women spun at home and organized domestic chores around their work. Ibn al-Ḥājj describes the domestic work cycle of women, and admonishes those who refrain from spinning and carding on Fridays, making it their day off.[23] But working women had to go out of the house at some point, if only to buy raw material and sell the finished product. Women congregated in front of the cotton and flax traders' shops, waiting for the carding process to be finished,[24] and later sold the threads

going about their business unveiled (*Madkhal*, vol. IV, 105–07). See also 'Abd al-Rāziq, *La femme*, 75, and the sources cited there.

16 Goitein, *A Mediterranean Society*, vol. I, 128. See also Shatzmiller, *Labour*, 352.

17 Ibn Kathīr, *Bidāya* (Beirut), vol. XIV, 198. On the social reaction to hermaphrodites see Tamer al-Leithy, "Of Bodies Chang'd to Various Forms . . .: Hermaphrodites and Transsexuals in Mamluk Society" (unpublished paper, Princeton University, 2001).

18 The two sisters followed each other to the grave in 737/1336–37 (al-Jazarī, *Ta'rīkh*, vol. III, 976, 980).

19 *Ibid.*, 827–28.

20 Al-Ṣafadī, *A'yān*, vol. II, 640; Shams al-Dīn al-Dhahabī, *Siyar A'lām al-Nubalā'*, ed. Shu'ayb al-Arnā'ūṭ and Ḥusayn al-Asad, 25 vols. (Beirut: Mu'assasat al-Risāla, 1981–88), vol. XVII, 520.

21 Shatzmiller, *Labour*, 351.

22 Ibn al-Ṣalāḥ, *Fatāwā*, 452 (no. 415). Cited by al-Ghazzī, "Adab al-Qaḍā'," fol. 154a.

23 Ibn al-Ḥājj, *Madkhal*, vol. I, 278–79; Lutfi, "Manners," 105. There is a striking similarity between Ibn al-Ḥājj's comments and those of a seventeenth-century Franciscan moralist, who admonished women in Lyon for not spinning on Saturdays out of superstition. See N. Davis, "Women and the Crafts in Sixteenth-Century Lyon," in B. Hanawalt (ed.), *Women and Work in Pre-industrial Europe* (Bloomington: Indiana University Press, 1986), 180.

24 Al-Shayzarī, *Nihāyat al-Rutba*, 69, 70; Ibn al-Ukhuwwa, *Ma'ālim al-Qurba*, 225; Ibn al-Bassām, *Kitāb Nihāyat al-Rutba*, 74. Ibn al-Ukhuwwa notes that spindle makers and flax traders have dealings mainly with women (*Ma'ālim al-Qurba*, 279).

directly to the yarn trader, who weighed the finished product.[25] Alternatively, women brought their yarn to mosques, where they negotiated the prices with a male broker acting as their agent. Ibn al-Ḥājj was infuriated, not least because these women often brought with them toddlers who urinated in the mosque.[26] The need of working women to go out was recognized by contemporary jurists. Widows and divorcées in their waiting periods, when their contact with strangers should be kept to a minimum, retained the right to leave their homes during the day in order to purchase raw material or sell the finished threads. At night these women were also allowed to go to neighbors' houses to spin together and chat.[27]

The routine work of female spinners comes alive in the stories about the miracles of saints. In one case from Jabal Nablus, we find a woman who used to donate half of her annual production, sixty cubits of spun yarn, to the local shaykhs. The amount was so extraordinarily high that one shaykh refused the gift, suspecting the woman of association with the devil.[28] One of the miracles associated with al-Sayyida Nafīsa concerns a widow and her four daughters who made their living from spinning. Each Friday the old woman would take the week's yarn to the market and sell it for 20 dirhams. With half the money she earned she would purchase the raw flax needed for spinning the next week's quota of yarn. With the other half she would buy necessities for herself and her daughters. One Friday, however, while she was on her way to the market, a bird suddenly swooped down and seized the woman's bundle of finished yarn. The story ends well – the bird dropped the yarn just in time to allow the merchants on board a foundering ship to plug the hole in their vessel. Through the intercession of al-Sayyida Nafīsa, the old woman was repaid many times over for the yarn she had lost. Although al-Sayyida lived many centuries earlier, the story was tailored to a late medieval audience that must have recognized the situation as familiar – the poor spinner who came to market every Friday and so sustained herself and her children.[29]

The biography of Ḍayfa bt. ʿUmar (d. 728/1328) provides a touching illustration of the difficulties facing a female wage-earner, and also provides precious information about wages and standards of living. Ḍayfa's husband, Muḥammad Ibn al-Irbilī, suffered from an eye disease that prevented him from working. As the sole provider for the family, Ḍayfa used to sew for remuneration,[30] and received half a dirham for a day's work. Things got difficult during a famine, almost certainly

25 Ibn Bassām, *Kitāb Nihāyat al-Rutba*, 73.

26 Ibn al-Ḥājj, *Madkhal*, vol. II, 226; Lutfi, "Manners," 106.

27 Al-Rāfiʿī, *al-ʿAzīz Sharḥ al-Wajīz*, ed. ʿAlī Muḥammad Muʿawwaḍ and ʿĀdil Aḥmad ʿAbd al-Mawjūd, 14 vols. (Beirut: Dār al-Kutub al-ʿIlmiyya, 1997), vol. IX, 510; al-Subkī, *Fatāwā*, vol. II, 314–20. According to the established doctrine, such permission was granted only to single women not entitled to marital support.

28 Daniella Talmon-Heller, "The Cited Tales of the Wondrous Doings of the *Shaykh*s of the Holy Land, by Ḍiyāʾ al-Dīn Abū ʿAbd Allāh Muḥammad b. ʿAbd al-Wāḥid al-Maqdisī (569/1173–643/1245)," *Crusades* 1 (2002), 123 (Arabic), 141 (English).

29 Taylor, *In the Vicinity of the Righteous*, 131. The reference to flax – rather than cotton – sets the story in an Egyptian context.

30 Text: *tukhīṭu bi'l-kawāfī* (al-Jazarī, *Ta'rīkh*, vol. II, 375).

the one that began in 694/1295.[31] On Ramaḍān food prices went up, and the 1 dirham she received every other day from the master artisan could only buy them ten ounces of bread, some beans or a bit of cauliflower. When evening came the couple would cut a big slice of the bread for their daughter, and divide the rest between them. On the following night, with nothing to eat, all they could do was drink water and look at each other in despair. Eventually, things got better when the husband was appointed a tax-collector. He continued, however, to entrust his wife with all his financial affairs. Al-Jazarī adds that, following Muḥammad's death, Ḍayfa managed on her own to marry off their three daughters and bring up their minor son.[32]

Judging by this anecdote, the wages paid for the sewing performed by Ḍayfa were low, but not insubstantial. Thanks to Adam Sabra's study it is possible to calculate that in that period, with a moderate level of prices, a monthly salary of 15 dirhams could buy about 200 pounds of bread – enough for two adults and one child to subsist on.[33] Ḍayfa's family was severely affected by the famine, but so were, most probably, many male-headed households. While one should keep in mind that embroiderers and seamstresses were probably better paid than the majority of simple spinners, Ḍayfa's case does prove that some women did receive a living wage, and that a woman's work in the textile industry could even support a small family.

An ample demonstration of the importance of women to the urban economy came in 841/1438 when Sultan Barsbāy, who blamed the debauchery of women for the current outbreak of the plague, issued an edict banning all women from frequenting the streets and markets of Cairo, with catastrophic results. Al-Maqrīzī notes the plight of widows and other single women, women practicing a profession, and female beggars. The damage extended also to the markets for clothes and perfumes, now emptied of their usual customers.[34] Partial relief came only after three days, when slave-girls were allowed to go out in order to purchase basic household supplies, so long as they did not veil and could easily be distinguished from free women. Old women were also allowed to go out for their necessities. The general ban remained in force for at least another week.[35] The chroniclers are unanimous in dismissing the whole affair as a blunder.[36] There was no consistent

[31] If the price of bread cited here is correct, the shortages must have been severe and indicate a famine. The crisis of 694/1295 represents the only major famine of that period. See Sabra, *Poverty*, 141–44; M. Chapoutot-Remadi, "Une grand crise à la fin du XIIIe siècle en Egypte," *JESHO* 26 (1983), 217–45.

[32] Al-Jazarī, *Ta'rīkh*, vol. II, 375. For a contemporary reference to a seamstress in the legal literature, see Ibn Taymiyya, *Majmū' Fatāwā*, vol. XXIX, 397; Ibn Taymiyya, *Fatāwā al-Nisā'*, 169.

[33] Sabra, *Poverty*, 119–21.

[34] A century earlier, Ibn al-Ḥājj wrote a vivid description of women shopping in these markets (*Madkhal*, vol. II, 17, vol. IV, 32; Lutfi, "Manners," 103).

[35] Al-Maqrīzī, *Sulūk*, vol. IV, 103 ff.; al-Khaṭīb al-Jawharī Ibn al-Ṣayrafī, *Nuzhat al-Nufūs wa'l-Abdān fī Tawārīkh al-Zamān*, ed. Ḥasan Ḥabashī, 4 vols. (Cairo: al-Hay'ah al-Miṣriyya al-'Āmmah li'l-Kitāb, 1970–94), vol. II, 404–09; Ibn Taghrī Birdī, *Nujūm*, vol. XV, 93–96; Ibn Iyās, *Badā'i'*, vol. II, 182–83. For a short summary, see Sabra, *Poverty*, 60–61.

[36] Another ban on the appearance of women in public was pronounced three years later, in 844/1440. But slave-girls and old women were exempted, and the ban lasted only a day (al-Maqrīzī, *Sulūk*, vol. IV, 1209).

state policy against working women, and towards the end of the fifteenth century state authorities even made attempts to protect the livelihood of female spinners against adverse market conditions. In 873/1468 the *dawādār* Yashbak min Mahdī abolished taxes imposed on yarn sold by women.[37] During the famine of 892/1487, when the value of copper coins was debased, merchants were given orders to pay women in silver for their spinning.[38]

Among the Jewish community of the Geniza women's remunerative work became more widespread during the Mamluk period. Most Jewish marriage contracts from the Mamluk period included a clause allowing wives to retain their earnings.[39] This stipulation, which was very rare in earlier centuries, was needed since under rabbinic law (and contrary to Islamic law) a wife's earnings belong to her husband, as compensation for his marital support. In some cases, the bride retained her rights both to her earnings and to the clothing owed by the husband. Usually, however, prospective wives absolved their grooms from the obligation of providing them with clothing. In this kind of settlement the bride chose to keep her wages even at the price of giving up part of her husband's monetary support. As Goitein concluded, Jewish marriage contracts from the Mamluk period reflect a society in which women's salaried labor was considered the norm. Goitein suggested that this change was symptomatic of the economic decline of the Jewish community of Cairo, as only the poor would allow their wives to work for wages. But when one considers the extent of women's work among the Muslim majority, it is evident that the phenomenon could not have been limited to the Jews or to Cairo.

The explanation for the normative attitude towards female labor, among both Muslims and Jews, should be sought in the expansion and technological innovation of the contemporary textile industry. The volume of textile production significantly increased in the thirteenth and fourteenth centuries.[40] Evidence of this expansion comes, first of all, from the great variety of materials and designs in early Mamluk textile fragments.[41] Official dress in the Mamluk court was gradually beautified and elaborated, a trend that reached its peak under Sultan al-Nāṣir Muḥammad in the first half of the fourteenth century.[42] The industry attained a higher degree of specialization, also indicating an expansion in the volume of production and in the number of persons employed.[43] This was also a period of technological innovation. The introduction of the draw-loom in the middle of the thirteenth century facilitated

tech. advmts. in textile ind.

[37] Ibn al-Ṣayrafī, *Inbā' al-Haṣr*, 39.

[38] Al-Sakhāwī, *Wajīz al-Kalām*, vol. III, 1000; cited in Sabra, *Poverty*, 163.

[39] Goitein, *A Mediterranean Society*, vol. III, 132–35. For published documents, see Ashtor-Strauss, *Tōldōt*, vol. III, nos. 39 (dated 1310), 41 (fourteenth century), 43 (1316), 53 (1379), 54 (1379).

[40] For general summary, see Bethany J. Walker, "Rethinking Mamluk Textiles," *MSR* 4 (2000), 167–95. I would like to thank the author for elucidating several points in a personal communication. For a very different view of the textile industry in the Mamluk period, see R. B. Serjeant, *Islamic Textiles: Material for a History up to the Mongol Conquest* (Beirut: Librairie du Liban, 1972).

[41] For a summary of these changes, see Walker, "Rethinking," 176–78; S. Māhir, *al-Nasīj al-Islāmī* (Cairo: al-Jihāz al-Markazī li'l-Kutub al-Jāmi'iyya wa'l-Madrasiyya wa'l-Wasā'il al-Ta'līmiyya, 1977), 88.

[42] L. A. Mayer, *Mamluk Costume: A Survey* (Geneva: A. Kundig, 1952), 21 ff.; Walker, "Rethinking," 168.

[43] Shatzmiller, *Labour*, 240–49.

the weaving of repeat patterns, large figures and inscriptions.[44] In addition to the draw-loom, spinning-wheels, apparently previously unknown in Egypt and Syria, are mentioned in the Ḥaram documents from the late fourteenth century.[45] The introduction of the spinning-wheel may have increased the productivity of spinners threefold, as well as the uniformity of the threads. Together with the draw-loom, the spinning-wheel allowed for rapid and cheap production.[46] Since the vast majority of working women participated in the production of textiles, the expansion of the industry and the introduction of the spinning-wheel may have meant growing employment opportunities for Muslim and Jewish women alike.

## Single women: the *ribāṭ*

Our understanding of Mamluk divorce rates hinges on the way Mamluk society treated non-married women. To a large extent, this is an economic question. Decisions about divorce must have been directly related to the question of whether the dowries of the elite, or the wages of the vast majority of working women, could provide economic security for a woman who was no longer married. But this was also a question of public morality. Was it acceptable for women to remain unmarried for long periods of time? Could they live on their own without fear for their reputation or safety? Did they have a physical and moral space that would accommodate their existence in a patriarchal society?

At first sight, the near-universal marriage pattern in Mamluk society appears to suggest that unmarried women had no place in the public sphere. Authors of biographical dictionaries do mention women who never married, but they seem to be the exception rather than the rule.[47] Moreover, the majority of girls were married off in their early or mid-teens, probably not long after reaching puberty.

44 Walker, "Rethinking," 174 ff.: L. Mackie, "Towards an Understanding of Mamluk Silks: National and International Considerations," *Muqarnas* 2 (1984), 127–46. For a reference to the use of the draw-loom in the Dār al-Ṭirāz in Alexandria in 770/1369, see Muḥammad Ibn al-Qāsim al-Nuwayrī, *Kitāb al-Ilmām bi'l-I'lām fīmā Jarat bihi al-Aḥkām wa'l-Umūr al-Muqḍiyya fī Waq'at al-Iskandriyya*, ed. A. S. Atiyya, 7 vols. (Hyderabad: Dā'irat al-Ma'ārif, 1968–76), vol. VI, 4; cited in M. Marzouk, *History of the Textile Industry in Alexandria, 331 BC–1517 AD* (Alexandria: Alexandria University Press, 1955), 65–67.

45 Lutfi, *al-Quds*, 297. A woman working with a spinning-wheel appears in a thirteenth-century illustration of the *Maqāmāt* (Ahmed Y. al-Hassan and Donald R. Hill, *Islamic Technology: An Illustrated History* [Cambridge: Cambridge University Press, 1986], 186). There are no references to spinning-wheels in the Geniza (Goitein, *A Mediterranean Society*, vol. I, 99). Ibn al-Ukhuwwa, writing at the beginning of the fourteenth century, discusses the proper manufacture of a spindle (*mirdan*), but does not refer to spinning-wheels (*Ma'ālim al-Qurba*, 279).

46 On spinning-wheels in the Italian cotton industry, see Maureen F. Mazzaoui, *The Italian Cotton Industry in the Later Middle Ages, 1100–1600* (Cambridge: Cambridge University Press, 1981), 78. Eliyahu Ashtor-Strauss famously argues that the Mamluks stifled any technological innovation, and that the treadle loom and the spinning-wheel were never introduced to the medieval Near Eastern textile industry ("Levantine Sugar Industry in the Later Middle Ages – an Example of Technological Decline," *Israel Oriental Studies* 7 [1977], 262–66). On this point, his argument seems to be off the mark.

47 Zaynab bt. Aḥmad b. 'Abd al-Karīm (646/1248–49–740/1339–40), a traditionist from Jerusalem, never married during her long life. Her celibacy is attributed to an eye-disease from which she had

Sitt al-ʿArab married Abū Shāma when she was fourteen. Rābiʿah, the daughter of the scholar Ibn Ḥajar al-ʿAsqalānī, first married at the age of fifteen, and his granddaughter married at the age of sixteen.[48] Some married earlier. Al-Sakhāwī married an eleven-year old girl.[49] Al-Maqrīzī's mother first married when she was twelve.[50] Orphan girls were usually married off while still minors, between ten and twelve.[51] But it should be noted that some women were married at an older age. The historian al-Birzālī's daughter first married when she was nineteen.[52] The virgin bride of Ibn Ḥajar was eighteen.[53]

Yet, even if we assume that almost all girls were married off and at an early age, there were still a lot of single women in Mamluk cities. After their first marriage, women still faced a real possibility of having to live on their own. Marriages were of relatively short duration, a result of high mortality rates and of high rates of divorce. Many remained unmarried for long periods far beyond the legally prescribed waiting period of three months, and sometimes for the rest of their lives. These women were often removed from their natal homes, and had to make a living on their own, usually as spinners, seamstresses and embroiderers. Many found shelter in an unprecedented number of exclusively female religious houses, usually known as *ribāṭ*s.

The *ribāṭ* came to be identified with female piety from the Fatimid period. The involvement of women in mystical movements was not new, and dates to the early Islamic period.[54] But the establishment of exclusively female Sufi institutions started only in the sixth/twelfth century. According to al-Maqrīzī, the wives and slave-girls of the later Fatimid caliphs established a number of female hospices in the Qarāfa cemetery, in which old widows and pious women lived in seclusion.[55] Similar institutions appeared in Mecca and Baghdad.[56] Along with the *zāwiya* and

suffered since childhood (Ibn Ḥajar, *Durar*, vol. II, 117). See also the biographies of Fāṭimah bt. Salmān (d. 708/1308–09) and Ḥabība bt. Zayn al-Dīn al-Maqdisiyya (d. 733/1332–33) (al-Dhahabī, *Siyar Aʿlām al-Nubalāʾ*, vol. XVII, 376; Ibn Ḥajar, *Durar*, vol. II, 5). One daughter of the Ayyubid prince al-Malik al-Ṣāliḥ Ismaʿīl never married (Ibn Kathīr, *al-Bidāya* [Beirut], vol. XIV, 87).

48 The daughter married in 826/1423 (Ibn Ḥajar, *Inbāʾ al-Ghumr*, vol. III, 374; al-Sakhāwī, *Ḍawʾ*, vol. XII, 199). The granddaughter married in 852/1448–49 (al-Sakhāwī, *Ḍawʾ*, vol. XII, 122 [no. 747]; Muḥammad b. ʿAbd al-Raḥmān al-Sakhāwī, *Kitāb al-Tibr al-Masbūk fī Dhayl al-Sulūk* [Būlāq: al-Maṭbūʿāt al-Amīriyya, 1896], 211). Similarly, a daughter of a Cairene Ḥanbalī scholar first married when she was fifteen (al-Sakhāwī, *Ḍawʾ*, vol. VI, 321, vol. XII, 104 [no. 657]).

49 The marriage took place in 848/1444 (al-Sakhāwī, *Ḍawʾ*, vol. XII, 144 [no. 895]; al-Sakhāwī, *al-Tibr al-Masbūk*, 93).

50 Taqī al-Dīn al-Maqrīzī, *Durar al-ʿUqūd al-Farīdah fī Tarājim al-Aʿyān al-Mufīdah*, ed. ʿAdnān Darwīsh and Muḥammad al-Miṣrī, 2 vols. (Damascus: Wizārat al-Thaqāfah, 1995), vol. II, 225. For a girl who was already a widow at the age of thirteen, see al-Jazarī, *Taʾrīkh*, vol. II, 134.

51 In all the cases of child marriages put to Ibn Taymiyya, the brides are described as orphan girls who "need someone to provide for them" (Ibn Taymiyya, *Majmūʿ Fatāwā*, vol. XXXII, 43–51).

52 Al-Jazarī, *Taʾrīkh*, vol. II, 477; al-Ṣafadī, *Aʿyān*, vol. IV, 30.

53 Al-Sakhāwī, *Ḍawʾ*, vol. XII, 11 (no. 55).

54 In a study of female asceticism in the first three Islamic centuries, Rkia E. Cornell found no evidence for female hermitages or religious houses (*Early Sufi Women*. Dhikr al-Niswa al-Mutaʿabbidāt aṣ-Ṣūfiyyāt *by Abū ʿAbd ar-Raḥmān as-Sulamī* [Louisville, KY: Fons Vitae, 1999]).

55 Al-Maqrīzī, *Khiṭaṭ*, vol. III, 652.

56 A. Schimmel, *My Soul is a Woman: The Feminine in Islam*, trans. Susan H. Ray (New York: Continuum, 1997), 48–49.

the *khānqāh*, the *ribāṭ* was associated with the Sufi mystical movement, but the functions of these institutions became somewhat differentiated during the Mamluk period. While the *zāwiya* was usually linked to a specific Sufi order and the *khānqāh* to prayers for the dead, the *ribāṭ* emerged as a hospice for the needy, with social welfare as its main goal.[57] In principle, *ribāṭ*s could also be exclusively male, and there were some *ribāṭ*s for men in the Mamluk period. It seems, however, that women came to be considered the natural recipients of the *ribāṭ*'s charitable role.

The establishment of *ribāṭ*s in all Mamluk urban centers reached a peak in the latter half of the thirteenth century and the first half of the fourteenth. The Ribāṭ al-Baghdādiyya, established in Cairo in 684/1285, was the most famous *ribāṭ* devoted exclusively to women. The daughter of the Sultan Baybars, Tidhkārbāy Khātūn, endowed the institution for the benefit of a female mystic called Zaynab al-Baghdādiyya, after whom it was named. Zaynab had already acquired a large following among the women of Damascus when Tidhkārbāy invited her to come to Cairo. The *ribāṭ* was located next to Baybars' *khānqāh*, and was probably intended as a sister institution.[58] In 694/1295, the amir ʿAlāʾ al-Dīn al-Barābāh established a *ribāṭ* for the use of Sitt Kalīla, the widow of another senior amir. In 715/1315, the amir Sunqur al-Saʿdī attached a women's *ribāṭ* to the madrasa he endowed in the city. Al-Maqrīzī and Ibn Ḥajar agree that the primary function of these *ribāṭ*s was to provide shelter for widows, divorcées and abandoned women.[59] At least six additional *ribāṭ*s for widows and old women operated in the Qarāfa cemetery during the fourteenth century.[60]

Syrian cities had an even larger number of women's religious houses. Six were established in Aleppo during the thirteenth century, although there they were called *khānqāh*s rather than *ribāṭ*s. An inscription on one of the *khānqāh*s, erected by an Ayyubid princess in the first half of the century, said that it was built "for the poor women (*faqīrāt*) who wish to reside in it, so that they would perform the five daily prayers and sleep there."[61] In Damascus the term *ribāṭ* had come to mean a specifically female place of worship. A Damascene author, Ibn Zufar al-Irbīlī (d. 726/1326), remarks that a *ribāṭ* is a *khānqāh* devoted exclusively to women (*al-rubuṭ hiya al-khawāniq allatī takhtaṣṣu bi'l-nisāʾ*). He then enumerates twenty such institutions, fifteen within the city itself and an additional five in its suburbs.[62]

57 T. Emil Homerin, "Saving Muslim Souls: The Khānqāh and the Sufi Duty in Mamluk Lands," *MSR* 3 (1999), 67. For a somewhat different view, see D. Little, "The Nature of *Khānqāh*s, *Ribāṭ*s and *Zāwiya*s under the Mamlūks," in W. Hallaq and D. Little (eds.), *Islamic Studies Presented to Charles J. Adams* (Leiden: Brill, 1991), 91–107; Sabra, *Poverty*, 25.

58 On Ribāṭ al-Baghdādiyya, see al-Ṣafadī, *Aʿyān*, vol. II, 181; Ibn Ḥajar, *Inbāʾ al-Ghumr*, vol. I, 480; al-Maqrīzī, *Khiṭaṭ*, vol. III, 602–03; Sabra, *Poverty*, 84.

59 On the Ribāṭ al-Sitt Kalīla, see al-Maqrīzī, *Khiṭaṭ*, vol. III, 603. On the *ribāṭ* built by Sunqur, *ibid.*, 523. See also Fernandes, *Evolution*, 11; Berkey, "Women and Islamic Education," 150.

60 Al-Maqrīzī, *Khiṭaṭ*, vol. III, 652, 660, 672.

61 Anne-Marie Eddé, *La principauté ayyoubide d'Alep (579/1183–658/1260)* (Stuttgart: Franz Steiner Verlag, 1999), 428.

62 Ibn Zufar al-Irbilī, *Madāris Dimashq wa-Rubuṭihā wa-Jawāmiʿuhā wa-Ḥammāmatihā*, ed. Muḥammad Aḥmad Duhmān (Damascus: Maṭbaʿat al-Taraqqī, 1947), 11; cited in L. Pouzet, *Damas au VII^e/XIII^e siècle. Vie et structures religieuses d'une métropole islamique* (Beirut: Dar el-Machreq Sarl, 1988), 211.

Some of the the money for these institutions came from the pockets of the womenfolk of the Damascene elite. In 730/1330, the wife of the governor of Damascus endowed the largest female *ribāṭ* in the city, next to her own tomb.[63]

Quite a few elite women lived in these *ribāṭ*s, whether established by themselves or by others. The daughter of a Ḥanafī *qāḍī* established one around the middle of the thirteenth century, and assumed its leadership.[64] The position then passed in her family line. Al-Jazarī reports the death of one of her successors, a woman called Zaynab bt. Shams al-Dīn Ibn ʿĀṭā', in 733/1333.[65] Fāṭima bt. Aḥmad Ibn Qāḍī al-ʿAskar (d. 685/1286), originally from Aleppo, was the shaykha of a *ribāṭ* in the suburb of al-Mizza near Damascus.[66] Āsiyya bt. Zayn al-Dīn Aḥmad b. ʿAbd al-Dā'im (d. 686/1287), known as Umm ʿAbdallāh the Qur'ān-reciter, was the teacher of the female occupants of a convent (*dayr*).[67] Zayn al-ʿArab al-Juwayrānī, a scholar's daughter, divorced in 658/1259–60 and never remarried. She lived in the Ribāṭ Darb al-Naqqāshah until her death in 704/1304. Sitt al-ʿUlamā' (d. 712/1312) was the shaykha of the Ribāṭ Darb al-Mahrānī. An Ayyubid princess led one of the Damascus *ribāṭ*s until her death in 697/1298.[68]

A fifteenth-century legal manual provides a detailed model document for the endowment of a women's *khānqāh*. At this time the movement was past its heyday; what this document says may be extended to earlier institutions only with caution. Here we find a mixture of spiritual meditation, strict discipline and charitable purposes. The endowment should provide living quarters and assembly rooms for about ten women, who are expected to be old, pious and poor. Except for a monthly visit to the public baths, the women should remain confined in the *khānqāh*, where a small team of household personnel takes care of their basic needs. Their duties consist of attending the *dhikr* ceremony and prayers. Spiritually, they are placed under the guidance of a resident shaykha, who preaches to them every Friday. The author of the legal manual adds a short discussion of model endowment deeds for men and women's *ribāṭ*s. The *ribāṭ*s are intended to house the old and the destitute, including poor widows who have no financial resources of their own.[69]

Al-Maqrīzī dwells on the authoritarian element in the Ribāṭ al-Baghdādiyya. According to his description, widows and divorcées stayed there during their waiting period so as to protect them from forbidden sexual contacts. The shaykha enforced the performance of the five daily prayers and other devotional acts.[70]

63 Ibn Kathīr, *Bidāya* (Beirut), vol. XIV, 121; ʿAbd al-Qādir b. Muḥammad al-Nuʿaymī, *al-Dāris fī Ta'rīkh al-Madāris*, ed. Jaʿfar al-Ḥusaynī, 2 vols. (Damascus: Maṭbaʿat al-Taraqqī, 1948–51), vol. II, 274–75. Zaynab bt. ʿUmar (d. 699/1300), the wife of a military official in Baalbek, is also said to have built a women's *ribāṭ* (al-Ṣafadī, *Aʿyān*, vol. II, 388).

64 Her name was Ṣafiyya al-Qalʿiyya. According to al-Nuʿaymī, she died in 633/1235–36, but this date is questioned by Humphreys (al-Nuʿaymī, *Dāris*, vol. II, 193; Humphreys, "Women as Patrons," 40).

65 Al-Jazarī, *Ta'rīkh*, vol. III, 656.

66 Shams al-Dīn al-Dhahabī, *Ta'rīkh al-Islām wa-Wafayāt al-Mashāhīr wa'l-Aʿlam*, ed. ʿUmar ʿAbd al-Salām Tadmurī (Beirut: Dār al-Kitāb al-ʿArabī, 1987–), vol. LXIX, 230.

67 *Ibid.*, 297.

68 See their respective biographies in al-Ṣafadī, *Aʿyān*, vol. II, 387, 402, vol. V, 501.

69 Al-Asyūṭī, *Jawāhir al-ʿUqūd* , vol. I, 364–66. Discussed in Little, "The Nature," 99–102.

70 Al-Maqrīzī, *Khiṭaṭ*, vol. III, 602. Cited in Sabra, *Poverty*, 84–85.

It would seem that at least some women were put in the al-Baghdādiyya against their will. In an anecdote told by al-Maqrīzī, a woman came before Ḥusām al-Dīn al-Ghūrī, chief Ḥanafī *qāḍī* in the first half of the fourteenth century, to claim a debt from her husband. When the *qāḍī* gave orders to put the husband in jail, the latter demanded that his wife would be put in al-Baghdādiyya, in order to safeguard her chastity during his term in prison. The *qāḍī*, by the way, refused, suspiciously suggesting that the woman would be better protected in his own private residence.[71]

But reducing the female *ribāṭ*s to their authoritarian aspects does an injustice to the spiritual aspirations of medieval Muslim women. Some of the founders were female, and quite a few elite women *chose* to spend their widowhood years there. Rather, the *ribāṭ*s should be considered as an aspect, albeit a unique one, of the spread of the mystical orders during the thirteenth century. Women must have been moved by the same ideals of asceticism and inner reflection as men, but were not integrated into the exclusively male institutions. An indication of the primarily religious function of the *ribāṭ*s was their status as sister institutions to male Sufi establishments. The Ribāṭ al-Baghdādiyya was adjacent to Baybars' *khānqāh*. Al-Irbīlī regarded the female *ribāṭ*s of Damascus as the counterparts of the male *khānqāh*s. Moreover, not all the women who took the mystical path resided in *ribāṭ*s. Ibn al-Ḥājj, writing in the first half of the fourteenth century, notes the growth of exclusively female Sufi groups in Cairo, but does not mention any association with an institution or establishment.[72] As we have seen, Zaynab al-Baghdādiyya had a large following even before she was appointed as shaykha of a *ribāṭ*. In her case, and most probably in others, the establishment of a *ribāṭ* was intended to support existing groups of pious women. Thus, the *ribāṭ*s represented only the physical manifestation of a wider religious and spiritual phenomenon.

Besides their spiritual functions, the female *ribāṭ*s catered for the needs of poor single women who were excluded from other Sufi foundations. The dual nature of the Sufi institutions that provided men both with spiritual space and with lodging options held true for the female *ribāṭ*s. The use of the term poverty is confusing for, as demonstrated by Adam Sabra, the medieval sources do not make a clear distinction between poverty as a social phenomenon and poverty as a religious ideal.[73] A man finding himself in a strange town, or in a sudden state of destitution, could go to one of the Sufi hospices and hope to receive a bed and a meal. But these institutions were meant to accommodate men only. When a lonely woman squatted in a room of a *zāwiya*, she was thrown out. Ibn Taymiyya, who ruled in her case, explained that her sex made her ineligible.[74] It is for homeless women like this squatter that female *ribāṭ*s were established, with parallel charitable functions. In an anecdote about a fourteenth-century Damascene scholar, it is told that he used to live near the Ribāṭ al-'Ajā'iz (of the Old Women), which functioned as a washing

[71] In the published edition, the institution is called *riwāq* rather than *ribāṭ* (al-Maqrīzī, *Sulūk*, vol. II, 611).
[72] Ibn al-Ḥājj, *Madkhal*, vol. II, 141; Lutfi, "Manners," 116.
[73] Sabra, *Poverty*, 31.
[74] Ibn Taymiyya, *Fatāwā al-Nisā'*, 189.

place for poor women and their children. Whenever a woman needed soda-ash for bodily wash, or soap for laundry, she received some from the scholar's family.[75]

The proliferation of the female *ribāṭ*s, however, must also have been fueled by an increase in the numbers of single women in urban society, itself a probable by-product of an expanding textile industry. There was one common denominator to practically all the women who stayed in *ribāṭ*s, and that was freedom from matrimonial obligations. A woman who wanted to join a *ribāṭ* was not necessarily poor; but she almost certainly had to be single. This was true even for the women mystics who were not affiliated with a *ribāṭ*. Ibn al-Ḥājj describes pious women who choose to remain unmarried.[76] Ibn Baydakīn, a thirteenth-century author, similarly rebukes women who refrain from marriage out of misguided piety.[77] While virginity had a certain saintly value in popular culture,[78] prior marriages did not pose an obstacle in the spiritual path taken by Sufi women. All contemporary sources agree that the residents of *ribāṭ*s were widows or divorcées – that is, women who were *no longer* married, and who needed a physical and moral space of their own.

The fifteenth century witnessed a decrease in the number of female religious houses. The rapid inflation that accompanied the collapse of the monetary system had a detrimental influence on religious endowments in general, since salaries were fixed by preexisting documents. Most of the Sufi *khānqāh*s were unable to disburse sufficient food or cash to their beneficiaries, and many of the residents left.[79] The Ribāṭ al-Baghdādiyya was hit hard by the crisis of 806/1403–04. Al-Maqrīzī says that male residents, perhaps those of the adjacent *khānqāh*, prevented divorced and widowed women from spending their waiting period there.[80] The institution is not mentioned again in later sources, and appears to have closed its doors. The women's *ribāṭ*s in the Qarāfa cemetery suffered a similar fate. Like large parts of the cemetery, they were deserted in the aftermath of the economic crisis.[81] Occasionally, royal edicts prohibited women even from visiting the cemetery.[82]

Female hospices did not disappear from the Cairene landscape, but fifteenth-century institutions seem fewer and smaller compared with their predecessors. Zaynab bt. Ibn Khāṣṣbak, wife of Sultan Īnāl, established a *ribāṭ* for widows in

[75] Jamāl al-Dīn Yūsuf Ibn al-Mibrad, *al-Jawhar al-Munaḍḍad fī Ṭabaqāt Muta'akhkhirī Aṣḥāb Aḥmad*, ed. ʿAbd al-Raḥmān al-ʿUthaymīn (Cairo: Maktabat al-Khānjī, 1987), 174.

[76] Ibn al-Ḥājj, *Madkhal*, vol. II, 141.

[77] Ibn al-Baydakīn, *Kitāb al-Lumaʿ*, 144.

[78] A tombstone in the Qarāfa cemetery commemorated the piety of Khadīja (d. 1295), the daughter of Shaykh Hārūn b. ʿAbdallāh, who had performed the pilgrimage fifteen times and died a virgin (Taylor, *In the Vicinity of the Righteous*, 95).

[79] Sabra, *Poverty*, 153.

[80] Text: *manaʿa mujāwirūhu min sajn al-nisā' al-muʿtādāt bihi* (al-Maqrīzī, *Khiṭaṭ*, vol. III, 602–03). See also Sabra, *Poverty*, 85.

[81] Al-Maqrīzī, writing at the beginning of the fifteenth century, already refers to these institutions in the past tense (*Khiṭaṭ*, vol. III, 652, 660, 672). Parts of the cemetery were deserted at the beginning of the fifteenth century (Taylor, *In the Vicinity of the Righteous*, 34 ff.).

[82] Sultan Barqūq's vice-regent was apparently the first to prohibit women from visiting the Qarāfa in 793/1391 (Ibn Qāḍī Shuhba, *Tā'rīkh*, vol. I, 383; al-Maqrīzī, *Sulūk*, vol. II, 749). On later edicts, see al-Maqrīzī, *Sulūk*, vol. IV, 594, 619, 870.

northern Cairo.[83] Fāṭima bt. Jamāl al-Dīn Yūsuf Ibn Sunqur (d. 855/1451), wife of the scholar Tāj al-Dīn al-Bulqīnī, built a *zāwiya* for widows and other poor women.[84] Ḥasnā' bt. 'Alī b. Muḥammad al-Shādhilī (d. 888/1483), a daughter of a Sufi shaykh, extended the activities of the order by building a female *ribāṭ*.[85] The chief Ḥanafi *qāḍī* 'Izz al-Dīn al-Kinānī al-'Asqalānī (d. 876/1471) allowed a group of widows and other single women into his former house, which he turned into a hospice.[86] By the end of the fifteenth century, Damascus still had at least five female *ribāṭs*.[87] Al-Sakhāwī even tells of women, including his own mother, who used to open their private houses to widows and divorcées.[88] The reliance on this form of neighborhood charity suggests a decline in the importance of hospices. So does the late fifteenth-century account of Felix Fabri, who describes poor women lying, and even giving birth, in the streets of Cairo.[89]

The rise and decline of the female *ribāṭ*s bear intriguing similarities to the fate of the female religious houses, especially those of the Beguines, which dotted western European cities in the thirteenth and fourteenth centuries.[90] Like the Beguinages, the foundation of *ribāṭs* presupposes a large number of single women in the cities, and, as a necessary corollary, a normative attitude to female labor. Some elite women, like the Ayyubid princess who headed a *ribāṭ* in Damascus, could choose to remain single by relying on the dowry they received at their first marriage. But, judging by the sheer number of *ribāṭ*s founded during the thirteenth century, most of their residents must have come from the lower classes. In either case, these single women did not want, or were not able, to return to their natal families or to find new husbands. Instead, they found in the *ribāṭ* a sheltered female space, and eked out their living as spinners, seamstresses and embroiderers in an expanding textile industry.

## Pilgrims, beggars and spinners in Jerusalem

Ultimately, the question of divorce is a demographic one. High rates of divorce swell the ranks of women who are not married at any given time, numbers which

83 'Abd al-Rāziq, *La femme*, 25; al-Sakhāwī, *Ḍaw'*, vol. XII, 45 (no. 261).

84 Al-Sakhāwī, *Ḍaw'*, vol. XII, 113 (no. 683). 85 *Ibid.*, 20 (no. 106).

86 *Ibid.*, vol. I, 207; cited in Sabra, *Poverty*, 51.

87 Al-Nu'aymī, *Dāris*, vol. II, 193–95. His contemporary Ibn al-Mibrad mentions only one single women's *ribāṭ* in the city, established in the first half of the fourteenth century (*Thimār al-Maqāṣid fī Dhikr al-Masājid*, ed. Muḥammad As'ad Ṭalas [Beirut: Institut Français de Damas 1943], 124). Obadiah, who visited Jerusalem in 1488, noted the existence of several community houses for Jewish widows (E. Adler [ed.], *Jewish Travelers* [London: Routledge, 1930], 235; Obadiah Bertinoro, *Me-Italyah li-Yerūshalayim. Igrōtav shel R. Ovadyah mi-Bartenūra me-Erets Yisrael*, ed. A. David and M. Hartom [Ramat Gan: Bar Ilan University, 1997], 65, 69).

88 On open houses for widows and poor women, see al-Sakhāwī, *Ḍaw'*, vol. XII, 131, 148; Lutfi, "al-Sakhāwī's *Kitāb al-Nisā'*," 119.

89 Sabra, *Poverty*, 108.

90 On the Beguines, see S. Murk-Jansen, *Brides in the Desert: The Spirituality of the Beguines* (Maryknoll, NY: Orbis Books, 1998); C. Neel, "The Origins of the Beguines," in Judith M. Bennett, Elisabeth A. Clark, Jean F. O'Barr, B. Anne Vilen and Sarah Westpahl-Wihl (eds.), *Sisters and Workers in the Middle Ages* (Chicago: University of Chicago Press, 1989), 240–60.

were already high under the existing mortality rates. This demographic trend can only be sustained when women can find work and space of their own. The gendered demography, the gendered economy and the gendered morality were interrelated, as is well illustrated in the Ḥaram documents from late fourteenth-century Jerusalem.

Let us take demography first. In terms of gendered demography, late fourteenth-century Jerusalem was bustling with single women. Going through the preserved estate inventories in the Ḥaram documents, Huda Lutfi found a very skewed sex ratio. The number of estate inventories for men is only 182, as opposed to 271 for women; for every 100 males there are 150 females.[91] Surprising as these figures may be, they are probably representative of the sex ratio of the adult population in Jerusalem during the last decades of the fourteenth century. As far as we know, the court of Jerusalem ordered an estate inventory after the death of every person. We find documents concerning free and adult members of all three religious communities, and of all echelons of local society, from the very wealthy to the beggars.[92] The evidence of the documents may be supported by the account of the Jewish scholar Obadiah Bertinoro, who visited Jerusalem a century later. Obadiah noted that many old Jewish widows came to Jerusalem from all over the world, so that the community had a ratio of seven women to one man.[93] A surplus of women may have been a constant feature of medieval Jerusalem.

Female migration into the city appears as the obvious reason for the skewed sex ratios. A large number of the women in the sample of the Ḥaram documents studied by Lutfi, 123 (45 percent), were unmarried at the time of their death, as compared with 64 men (32 percent). Eighty-four of the unmarried women, almost a third of all women, did not have any relatives residing in Jerusalem. The size of this group of unattached female migrants roughly corresponds to the difference in numbers between the estate inventories for men and for women. Obviously, late fourteenth-century Jerusalem attracted single women. Part of the attraction of the city was its holiness. As suggested by Lutfi, many of these women probably came to Jerusalem out of piety: after the death of their husbands, widows moved to the city in order to die there.[94] Indeed, the notaries identified four women as *mujāwiras*, religious sojourners. Two other women worked as water-carriers within the Ḥaram al-Sharīf, most probably serving pilgrims.[95]

But even if we assume that they were motivated by a spiritual calling, we still need to answer two more mundane questions regarding the large numbers of single

91 Lutfi, *al-Quds*, 226.

92 Ibid., 19–30. The sample includes a high proportion of foreigners and single persons and only a few non-Muslims. But this was probably the demographic composition of the pilgrimage city devastated by the plague. From Jewish *responsa* we know that there were no more than two hundred Jews living in Jerusalem at the time (Y. Hecker, "The Immigration of Spanish Jews to Palestine, 1391–1492" [Hebrew], *Cathedra* 36 [1985], 3–35).

93 Adler (ed.), *Jewish Travelers*, 235; Obadiah Bertinoro, *Me-Italyah li-Yerūshalayim*, 65, 69.

94 Lutfi, *al-Quds*, 227.

95 Female water-carriers were apparently associated with holy sites. A former wife of an Ayyubid prince, who fell into destitution, started working as a water-carrier in Mecca (Humphreys, "Women as Patrons," 44). Apart from these two women, the Ḥaram estate inventories also identify eight men as water-carriers.

women in the city: how did they make ends meet? and where did they live? The first question, in fact, is more difficult to answer. While scribes identified nearly all men by their profession, they did so only for six women (about 2 percent). The small ratio of women carrying occupational titles, however, is more an indication of cultural attitudes than an indication of the actual economic contribution by women.[96] Lutfi tackled the problem of identifying women's occupations by examining ownership of tools, raw materials or commercial quantities of finished products at the time of death. Even this categorization may well underestimate female participation in the workforce. Some women (as well as men) must have passed on some of their possessions to relatives and friends on their deathbeds. We are also dependent to a large degree on the diligence of the court's clerks in counting the petty possessions of the deceased women.

Nonetheless, Lutfi's survey shows that a large proportion of all women, maybe even the majority, were engaged in some kind of remunerative work. Spinning tools, or remnants of crude or spun cotton and flax, were found in the estate inventories of eighty-two women, about 30 percent of all women. The majority of these women – like the majority of all women in Lutfi's sample – were unmarried at the time of their death. Some of these women owned spindles (*mirdan* or *mighzala*), but the most frequently mentioned spinning tool was the spinning-wheel (*dūlāb ghazl* or *rikka*). This is a rare indication to the use of spinning-wheels in the Mamluk period, but it is not only of interest to historians of textiles. The purchase of a spinning-wheel was probably a substantial investment for a poor woman. According to a record of the sale of one poor woman's chattels, a spinning-wheel, together with small quantities of wheat, cotton and yarn, fetched 20 dirhams. All her other assets put together, that is, her utensils and clothes, were sold for a similar amount.[97]

While spinning was by far the most common occupation of women, an additional eleven women engaged in other stages of textile production. Tools for combing flax were found in the estate inventories of two women. Two other women may have engaged in ginning, another stage in processing raw cotton.[98] In general, men controlled the later stages of production, especially weaving. But one woman owned three weaving shuttles at the time of her death, suggesting that she either worked in a weaving workshop or at least owned a loom.[99] The presence of silk threads in the estate inventories of six women suggests that they worked as embroiderers. In contrast, only one man is identified as an embroiderer.[100] No

96 The small ratio of women identified by profession is comparable with the evidence from the comprehensive Florentine Catasto of 1427. The Catasto, a census of both the rural and urban population, lists about 7,000 female-headed households; but only 270 of these women carry a professional title of any sort. Most were domestic servants, religious women, or beggars (D. Herlihy, *Opera Muliebria. Women and Work in Medieval Europe* [New York: McGraw-Hill, 1990], 158–62).

97 Ḥaram document no. 767G, published in Lutfi, *al-Quds*, 64–67.

98 One owned a small *dast lil-ḥalj*, either a tool for combing or a distaff for combed cotton or flax. The other had a box containing *ghazl maḥlūj*, carded cotton (Ḥaram document nos. 484, 521; Lutfi, *al-Quds*, 288).

99 Lutfi, *al-Quds*, 298.

100 *Ibid.*, 300.

woman can be identified as a seamstress. This is surprising, since, as noted earlier, literary sources refer to sewing as a female profession. By contrast, the documents mention only four male tailors.

At least nine women were peddlers or small-scale merchants. The scribes identified three women as brokers (*dallāla*). Four other women owned commercial quantities of finished textile products. One owned twenty-one pieces of footwear and eighteen pieces of headwear at her death, another owned eighteen kerchiefs produced in Jerusalem, and a third had 433 dirhams that she had received from the sale of textile products. At least two more women were involved in trading in raw cotton. One lived in the house of a cotton merchant, and owned 80 *raṭl* of ginned yarn that was in his safekeeping. It is unlikely that she worked this large quantity by herself. More probably, she had some role in distributing the cotton to female spinners around the city.[101] A peddler was also a pawnbroker. From the estate inventory of Jawhara, an Egyptian woman, we learn that she pawned one of her earrings with a female peddler, in return for a loan of 35 dirhams. The other earring, by the way, was pawned with a male merchant.[102]

The Ḥaram documents suggest that the great majority of women – in fact, very nearly all working women – were employed in the textile industry. Scribes identify only three women as providing services – two female water-carriers and one bath-attendant. In another document, a kind of death certificate, a female washer of the dead testifies that no signs of injury were found on the body she inspected.[103] The small number of women employed in services is in line with what we should expect. The proportion of midwives or hairdressers was small, despite their high visibility in the literary sources.

The textile industry was the mainstay of Jerusalem's economy at the end of the fourteenth century, even though the city was better known as a pilgrimage site rather than as a center for the manufacture of textiles. There are forty textile artisans in the sample, most of them weavers, and they account for 22 percent of all men and more than half of the total number of craftsmen. Most of the male merchants, 10 percent of all men, made their living out of trade in textiles or in raw cotton. In comparison, the total number of persons whose work was directly associated with the flow of pilgrims, including men who made their living by selling amulets and antique objects or by offering translation services, does not add up to more than a small minority.[104]

When we consider women as part of the urban economy, the number of persons employed in the textile industry is trebled. Women formed the majority of the industry's workforce, supplying most of the unskilled labor at the early stages of production. Ginning was probably done in the countryside, but the deseeded raw

[101] Ḥaram document no. 422; Lutfi, *al-Quds*, 288. The same is probably true of a wealthy woman who at the time of her death owned 2 *raṭl*s of raw cotton (Ḥaram document no. 607, published in Lutfi, *al-Quds*, 54–60).

[102] Ḥaram document no. 163, published in al-ʿAsalī, *Wathāʾiq*, vol. I, 267.

[103] Ḥaram document no. 288, published in al-ʿAsalī, *Wathāʾiq*, vol. II, 135.

[104] Lutfi, *al-Quds*, 293, 304.

cotton was then brought to the urban centers and spun by women.[105] In the Ḥaram documents we find more than three female spinners for every male weaver, and this is most probably an underestimate. The evidence of the estate inventories does not allow identification of all female spinners or embroiderers. In the contemporary European textile industry, which was at a comparable technological level, one weaver required up to fifteen spinners to supply him with threads.[106] It seems that many women, probably even the majority, could find some form of employment in the textile industry of late fourteenth-century Jerusalem. According to the estate inventories, 105 women out of 271, or 39 percent, were engaged in some kind of remunerative work, excluding income generated by rents and interest on loans.

While single women found work in the textile industry of Jerusalem, they found shelter in the city's *ribāṭ*s. The Ḥaram documents tell us about nine unmarried women who lived and died in six different *ribāṭ*s in the city.[107] These *ribāṭ*s mainly accommodated single women, although they also admitted a married woman and even a male resident. Three more single women lived in *khān*s[108] and two in *zāwiya*s (although most of the inhabitants of *zāwiya*s were, as expected, single men). None of the women's *ribāṭ*s of Jerusalem is mentioned in the literary sources. For example, without the Ḥaram documents we would not have known about the generosity of a certain Fāṭima bt. Muḥammad, who endowed a part of her house in favor of poor old Maghribi women on 25 Rabīʿ al-Awwal 747 (17 July 1346). The building, not coincidentally, was adjacent to a Maghribi *zāwiya* for men.[109] One can assume that the chroniclers only mention the largest female hospices of Cairo and Damascus, while omitting many smaller institutions endowed by less powerful persons. The Ḥaram documents also tell us that some female residents of these institutions worked in textile production. Six of the women residing in the *ribāṭ*s, *zāwiya*s and *khān*s of Jerusalem can be identified as spinners by the tools or raw materials found in their estate inventories.

As in Cairo and Damascus, the proliferation of *ribāṭ*s in Jerusalem was primarily a manifestation of the participation of women in the mystical and ascetic movements of the time, but these institutions were tailored to the needs of a growing number of single women, who depended on an expanding textile production for their livelihood. It should be noted that the female religious houses presented a housing solution for only a small minority of single women. The majority did not

105 According to the German traveler von Harff, visiting Palestine a century later, the beating and preparing of the raw cotton was done in the villages (cited in Carl J. Lamm, *Cotton in Mediaeval Textiles of the Near East* [Paris: P. Geuthner, 1937], 233).

106 Claudia Opitz, "Life in the Late Middle Ages," in Georges Duby and Michelle Perrot (eds.), *A History of Women in the West* (Cambridge, MA: Harvard University Press, 1992), vol. II: *Silences of the Middle Ages*, 304. Another study puts the number of carders and spinners required to supply thread to one weaver at twenty (M. Wiesner, "Spinsters and Seamstresses: Women in Cloth and Clothing Production," in Margaret W. Ferguson, Maureen Quilligan and Nancy J. Vickers [eds.], *Rewriting the Renaissance: The Discourses of Sexual Difference in Early Modern Europe* [Chicago: University of Chicago Press, 1986], 194).

107 Lutfi, *al-Quds*, 252–55. The estate inventories provide only partial data regarding residence.

108 The term *khān* may be shorthand for *khānqāh* (I owe this suggestion to Baki Tezcan).

109 Ḥaram document no. 833, published in al-ʿAsalī, *Wathāʾiq*, vol. I, 235.

live in *ribāṭ*s or in any other public institution. At least seven single women rented rooms in houses belonging to other families, and many others owned their living quarters. This was an urban society that had a large proportion of female-headed households and regarded women's remunerative work as normal. The large number of unattached women in late fourteenth-century Jerusalem looked for spiritual salvation through pilgrimage and mysticism, but it was the textile industry that sustained their bodies.

It is even possible that some poor women moved to Jerusalem from the countryside in search of work. We do not know whether the wages female spinners received for their work could make them economically independent. Judging from their estate inventories, many were desperately poor. Men surely had better chances of making a living on their own. Some of these immigrant women were probably part-time spinners, part-time beggars and part-time pilgrims. But, since so many women did come to the city, it stands to reason that they were fleeing from something worse. Jerusalem offered holy sites and promises for the Hereafter, but also a chance to work as a spinner. And perhaps, at least in this respect, Jerusalem was not that unique a place.

Working women were the subject of at least three intriguing literary works composed during the second half of the fifteenth century. Ibn Ṭūlūn devoted a treatise to traditions about spinners, entitled *Qiṭf al-Zahrāt fīmā qīla fī al-Ghazzālāt* (Bunch of Flowers on the Sayings concerning Female Spinners).[110] The Cairene litterateur Shihāb al-Dīn al-Ḥijāzī al-Ḥazrajī (d. 875/1471) composed a collection of epigrams directed to various types of women, including spinners, seamstresses and other women of professions.[111] The Damascene Ibn al-Mibrad (d. 909/1503) collected an anthology of traditions and anecdotes about women, most of them in praise of women who work the spindle.[112] He also tells us that his own concubine Bulbul spun for wages, some of which she spent on charity.[113]

The first tradition in Ibn al-Mibrad's work, "accustom your womenfolk to the spindle, for it makes them more beautiful and more serene," is attributed to the Prophet, and found in early Islamic sources.[114] Its inclusion in a late fifteenth-century anthology is a testimony to aspects of continuity in the pattern of urban women's labor in medieval Islam. The range of female professions remained remarkably stable. Throughout medieval Islam, the textile industry was divided largely along gender lines – women spun, men wove. Similarly, in spite of patriarchal ideals, medieval Near Eastern cities always had a significant proportion of single women. In community charity lists from the Geniza, dating from the beginning of the eleventh century, a third of the hundred-odd beneficiaries are

[110] A copy of this treatise is listed in the catalogue of the Taymūriyya library, but I was unable to consult it. See Ibn Ṭūlūn, *al-Fulk al-Mashḥūn fī Aḥwāl Muḥammad Ibn Ṭūlūn*, ed. Muḥammad Khayr Ramaḍān Yūsuf (Beirut: Dār Ibn Ḥazm, 1996), 142.

[111] Shihāb al-Dīn al-Ḥijāzī al-Ḥazrajī (d. 875/1471), *al-Kunnas al-Jawārī fī al-Ḥisān min al-Jawārī*, ed. Riḥāb ʿAkkāwī (Beirut: Dār al-Ḥarf al-ʿArabī, 1998).

[112] Jamāl al-Dīn Yūsuf Ibn al-Mibrad, *Akhbār al-Nisāʾ al-Musammā al-Rusā lil-Ṣāliḥāt min al-Nisāʾ*, ed. Māhir Muḥammad ʿAbd al-Qādir (Homs: Dār al-Maʿārif, 1993).

[113] *Ibid.*, 16–17 (editor's introduction). [114] *Ibid.*, 45.

female-headed households.[115] More than four centuries later, a fifteenth-century list of inhabitants in a Cairene tenement house shows women leading a substantial minority of the fifty families in the building.[116]

The prospects of those women who had to live on their own, or chose to do so, were usually not high; but at some periods they were at least somewhat better. I have suggested here that an expansion in the textile industry during the thirteenth century may have increased the demand for female spinners and embroiderers. Most women worked at home, and they carried on working whether they were married or unmarried. But as increasing opportunities allowed more women to become economically independent, more women remained single for long periods of time. This economic independence was one of the factors behind the proliferation of female *ribāṭ*s and the emergence of new forms of female piety. It also explains how a large number of women made their living out of wedlock, their mere presence challenging the patriarchal ideal of female economic dependency.

[115] Goitein, *A Mediterranean Society*, vol. III, 62–65. [116] Sabra, *Poverty*, 104.

CHAPTER 3

# The monetization of marriage

Meshullam of Volterra, a perceptive Italian Jewish merchant who visited the Mamluk domains in 1481, thought that Near Eastern marriages brought women none of the security found in the marriages of Europeans. He also thought this was the reason for the high rates of divorce in Mamluk society. During his stay in Jerusalem Meshullam wrote the following:

> The customs of the Muslims are diverse from all people . . . The men give marriage gifts to the women. From the day of marriage the man is only bound to give his wife food, but her clothes and all other things she requires she has to make herself . . . The wife is bound to pay for the food and clothes of all her sons and daughters. Therefore, the women are all harlots.[1] When they do not wish to stay with their husbands they go to the Niepo [i.e., *nā'ib* or governor] of the city, and say that their husband does not give them food. They are believed, and the husband must divorce his wife. For the Muslims give divorce like the Jews. All men and women and children, Jews as well as Muslims, have these customs . . . And these customs are usual in the whole kingdom of the Sultan, and not in Jerusalem only . . . They are all alike.[2]

According to Meshullam, husbands were absolved from giving support in any way other than food. Wives paid for their clothing through their independent earnings, and even bore the financial responsibility for their children. With understandable horror, he concluded that Near Eastern husbands (both Jews and Muslims), unlike Italian men, left their wives to their own devices. Meshullam was also unfavorably impressed with the ability of wives to secure a divorce on the grounds of lack of support. His disgust with divorce only shows how much this Jewish merchant was a product of late medieval Florentine society. His description of wives asking the court for a divorce on the grounds of non-maintenance is repeated some fifteen years later by the German traveler von Harff. According to von Harff's

[1] Text: *zōnōt mfūrsamōt*.

[2] Adler (ed.), *Jewish Travelers*, 194–95; Meshūllam of Volterra, *Massa' Meshūllam mi-Volterra be-Erets Yisra'el (1481)*, ed. Avraham Ya'arī (Jerusalem: Mosad Byalik, 1948), 75–76. Meshullam wrote a similar passage during his visit to Alexandria: "When a man marries a wife he gives her a marriage gift and from henceforward he is only obliged to feed her, eating and drinking alone, but not clothing, for she must dress herself from her own money. And also, when she has children, she is bound to feed them" (Adler [ed.], *Jewish Travelers*, 159; Meshūllam of Volterra, *Massa'*, 46).

account, if a woman complained that her husband did not give her due support, the judge would order the husband to be flogged, and allow her to divorce him while taking all the property she brought into the marriage.[3]

Did marriage bring with it financial security for women? In Islamic law, the prevailing assumption is that this is the case. The jurists conceived of the husband as the provider, who, upon concluding a valid marriage, takes upon himself two sets of financial obligations: the marriage gift, or the *ṣadāq*, and marital support, or *nafaqa*. Although the chapters on marriage gifts and marital support in the law books tend to be quite extensive, there are essentially few requirements. According to the majority of the schools, there are no minimum or maximum limits to the marriage gift, nor is it necessary to pay the entire marriage gift before the termination of the marriage contract through death or divorce. The extent of marital support is fixed according to the needs of the wife (and sometimes also according to the financial capabilities of the husband). The simplicity of the law conceals a wide variety of real-life arrangements; in fact, the nature of Mamluk marriage depended to a large extent on the actual application and enforcement of these laws. In particular, much depended on how much a husband was expected to give his wife, the timing of the payment or the support, and the form it took, whether in cash or in kind.

According to a patriarchal ideal of conjugal harmony, espoused by many Mamluk jurists, a household should constitute one indivisible economic unit, and marriage should not be contaminated by the monetary transactions taking place outside the household. Husbands should feed and clothe their wives, but not give them money. Ibn Qayyim al-Jawziyya (d. 751/1350), a fourteenth-century Ḥanbalī scholar from Damascus, equated the support of wives with the support of slaves. Slavery, rather than being a contemptible institution, was the exemplary patriarchal model, with the bond between a master and his slave the organizing principle of the military elite. According to Ibn al-Qayyim, the strength of this bond was partly due to the absence of any monetary exchange. Slaves cannot earn wages; they may receive money, but their property ultimately belongs to their master. The absence of wages shields the supposed mutual loyalty and love between a master and his slave from the disharmonious market economy.[4] The same should hold true, ideally, for the relations between husband and wife: "The wife is her husband's prisoner, a prisoner being akin to a slave. The Prophet directed men to support their wives by feeding them with their own food and clothing them with their own clothes; he said the same about maintaining a slave."[5]

However, Ibn al-Qayyim was reacting to social realities that were increasingly removed from this patriarchal ideal. During the fourteenth century, and even more

[3] Arnold von Harff, *The Pilgrimage of the Knight Arnold von Harff*, trans. M. Letts (London: Hakluyt, 1946), 112. See similar remarks by F. Suriano, *Treatise on the Holy Land*, trans. T. Bellorini and E. Hoade (Jerusalem: Franciscan Press, 1949), 204.

[4] On this distinction, see I. Lapidus, "The Grain Economy of Mamluk Egypt," *JESHO* 12 (1969), 2; B. Shoshan, "Grain Riots and the 'Moral Economy': Cairo, 1350–1517," *Journal of Interdisciplinary History* 10 (1980), 459. Sabra prefers the term tributary economy, pointing out that urban largesse was funded by the extraction of surpluses from the peasantry (*Poverty*, 134–36).

[5] Ibn Qayyim al-Jawziyya, *Ighāthat al-Lahfān min Maṣā'id al-Shayṭān*, ed. Muḥammad Ḥāmid al-Fiqī, 2 vols. (Cairo: Maṭba'at Muṣṭafā al-Bābī al-Ḥalabī, 1939), vol. II, 60.

so in the fifteenth, husbands and wives attached a cash value to various aspects of their relationships. This "monetization" of marriage was largely driven by wives who sought to receive payments of marriage gifts and support during their marriage, rather than wait for its dissolution. While in earlier centuries wives had received an advance portion of their marriage gifts before consummation with the rest being paid only after dissolution, in the Mamluk period many wives gained the right to demand the payment of the remaining portion of their marriage gift whenever they so wished. Some also demanded that the support owed by their husbands be paid in cash rather than in kind, in the form of daily or yearly allowances. As more of husbands' obligations acquired pecuniary value, their wives obtained additional grounds for a judicial divorce. The autonomous and hierarchical household was challenged by the intrusion of cash contracts typical of the marketplace, and this monetization of marriage was a major factor determining the rates and patterns of divorce in Mamluk society.

## The marriage gift (*ṣadāq*)

The main function of the marriage contract, apart from testifying to the validity of a marriage, was to record the marriage gift pledged by the groom at the time of the marriage. The groom's marriage gifts were specified in cash.[6] They were divided into advance and deferred portions, with the advance payment almost always smaller than the deferred portion.[7] Before the Mamluk period, the late payment was usually postponed for a set number of years. For example, a husband would pledge to pay the remainder of the marriage gift after five, eight or ten years.[8] But by the thirteenth century it had become common to divide the late portion into yearly installments.[9] Alternatively, in some Mamluk marriage contracts the deferred portion was designated as a due debt, which was payable upon demand. These three methods of payment – advance gift, yearly installments and due debt – appear together in various combinations.[10] Each marriage contract was different, and the parties to the contract were at liberty to choose the methods of payment.

6 In the legal literature there is one example of a marriage gift consisting of a share in a house (Ibn al-Ṣalāḥ, *Fatāwā*, 437 [no. 386]). The author of a legal manual mentions the possibility of a marriage gift consisting of a slave, a ring, a sword, real estate or textiles (al-Asyūṭī, *Jawāhir al-'Uqūd*, vol. II, 52).

7 This was true for Jewish marriage contracts as well. See Goitein, *A Mediterranean Society*, vol. III, 122. For the division of the *ṣadāq* in royal marriages, see A. 'Abd al-Rāziq, "'Aqdā Nikāḥ," 76.

8 Y. Rapoport, "Matrimonial Gifts in Early Islamic Egypt," *ILS* 7/1 (2000), 1–37.

9 The earliest mention of a division into installments comes from an Egyptian marriage contract dated 598/1202. The number of annual installments varied considerably, and could spread over fifteen years. For division into monthly installments in a model document see al-Asyūṭī, *Jawāhir al-'Uqūd*, vol. II, 93.

10 The authors of legal manuals allow the contracting parties to choose whether the *ṣadāq* should be paid at the time of marriage (*maqbūḍ, mu'ajjal*), paid in installments (*munajjam, muqassaṭ*) or designated as payable upon demand (*ḥāll*). See al-Jarawānī, "Mawāhib," fol. 67b; al-Asyūṭī, *Jawāhir al-'Uqūd*, vol. II, 62.

Despite the careful record of the marriage gifts in the marriage contracts, the written obligations did not usually correspond to real payments made by husbands. This was partly because marriage contracts were means of conveying social status. Among the very wealthy, it was common to write down the marriage contract on silk,[11] or to insert a preamble to the contract, written in refined language, extolling the virtues of the bride and groom.[12] Another way of enhancing one's social status through a marriage contract was to exaggerate the value of the marriage gifts. It followed that the amounts written down and declared publicly were often higher than the sums pledged in private and informal agreements. The practice of doubling the actual value of the marriage gifts is well attested in the Geniza,[13] and the same practice was common among the Muslim majority. A question put to the Damascene jurist Ibn al-Ṣalāḥ dealt with a marriage contract in which the marriage gift was double the sum previously agreed in private.[14] Ibn Taymiyya criticized families who inflated the marriage gift for self-glorification, without any intention of demanding or delivering the bloated amount.[15]

Because marriage gifts were signs of status, they were designated in gold dinars, even by people who had never had the chance to hold a gold piece in their hand. The main currency in circulation was the silver dirham, but in most marriage contracts the marriage gift was specified in gold. In the documents of al-Ḥaram al-Sharīf, marriage contracts are practically the only transactions made in dinars; in almost all other documents the amounts are given in dirhams.[16] Again, the same was true for contemporary Jewish marriage contracts from the Geniza.[17] Tāj al-Dīn al-Fazārī (d. 690/1291), a Damascene jurist, explained that people wrote the amounts of the marriage gift in dinars merely as an embellishment. The actual payment was made in silver coins after calculating the exchange rate.[18] This practice gave plenty of

11 See Yūsuf Rāġib, "Un contrat de mariage sur soie d'Egypte fatimide," *AI* 16 (1980), 31–37. Contemporary jurists, such as the Shāfi'ī al-Nawawī (d. 676/1277), prohibited this practice (Yaḥyā b. Sharaf al-Nawawī, *Fatāwā al-Imām al-Nawawī al-Musammā bi'l-Masā'il al-Manthūra*, ed. 'Alā' al-Dīn Ibn al-'Aṭṭār [Beirut: Dār al-Kutub al-'Ilmiyya, 1982], no. 224). For a more permissive position, see Tāj al-Dīn al-Subkī, *Mu'īd al-Ni'am*, 61.

12 See G. Guellil, *Damaszener Akten des 8./14. Jahrhunderts nach at-Tarsusis* Kitāb al-I'lām. *Eine Studie zum arabischen Justizwesen* (Bamberg: Aku, 1985), 223–31; al-Ṣafadī, *A'yān*, vol. V, 260; al-Qalqashandī, *Ṣubḥ al-A'shā*, vol. XIV, 300–21; al-Asyūṭī, *Jawāhir al-'Uqūd*, vol. II, 53–82. Among the preserved marriage contracts, elaborate proems are found only in the marriage contracts of the military elite. See Māhir, "'Uqūd al-Zawāj" and Ḥaram document no. 47.

13 Marriage and engagement contracts from the Geniza occasionally state that the marriage gifts have been written down at an inflated value (Goitein, *A Mediterranean Society*, vol. III, 126–27; Ashtor-Strauss, *Tōldōt*, vol. III, 44–45).

14 Ibn al-Ṣalāḥ ruled that the original private agreement was binding (*Fatāwā*, 655 [no. 930]). In another case, he was asked about a groom who pledged a marriage gift of 1,000 dirhams, even though all the parties concerned were aware of his inability to pay this sum (*ibid.*, 425–26 [no. 362]).

15 Ibn Taymiyya, *Majmū' Fatāwā*, vol. XXXII, 192–95, 199. See also Ibn Qayyim al-Jawziyya, *I'lām al-Muwaqqi'īn 'an Rabb al-'Ālamīn*, ed. Ṭāhā 'Abd al-Ra'ūf Sa'd, 4 vols. (Beirut: Dār al-Jīl, 1964), vol. III, 91–92.

16 Lutfi, *al-Quds*, 285–86.

17 In thirteenth-century Jewish marriage contracts from the Geniza, the exchange rate between gold and silver is written down as part of the contract (Ashtor-Strauss, *Tōldōt*, vol. III, 91–93; Goitein, *A Mediterranean Society*, vol. III, 119–20, 451).

18 Al-Fazārī, "Fatāwā," fols. 88a–90b.

headaches to *qāḍīs* who attempted to enforce the financial obligations undertaken in marriage contracts. In two cases of disputes over marriage contracts written down in provincial towns in Syria, Ibn al-Ṣalāḥ went to the length of making inquiries at the moneychangers' market.[19] In the fifteenth century the state even found it necessary to regulate the type of specie designated in contracts in order to avert excessive litigation.[20]

Moreover – and this is perhaps the most significant gap between the written record and actual praxis – it was very uncommon for husbands to pay the yearly installments of the marriage gifts on time. The only concrete example of punctual payment comes from an early thirteenth-century marriage contract, and even there the payment was made to the wife's father and not to the woman herself.[21] At the beginning of the fourteenth century, a question put to Ibn Taymiyya summed up the situation as follows: "For many years, a wife is incapable of demanding the marriage gift owed to her by her husband, in order not to cause a divorce. Eventually, she is either given real estate as compensation or receives the payments after a long time."[22]

Under normal circumstances, the yearly installments of the marriage gift were only paid after the death of one of the spouses (as was also the case among the Geniza Jewish community). A woman predeceasing her husband would sometimes forfeit her claim to the remainder of the marriage gift on her deathbed.[23] Otherwise, it was divided as part of her estate.[24] When the husband predeceased his wife, as was more often the case, the remaining portion of the marriage gift was paid out of his inheritance. The payment of marriage gifts out of deceased husbands' estates is well attested in the Ḥaram documents.[25] Because women generally outlived their husbands, men often took steps to secure the rights of their future widows.

19 He also notes that the custom in Damascus was to write down the *ṣadāq* in gold dinars, but to pay it in dirhams according to the exchange rate prevalent at the time of the contract (Ibn al-Ṣalāḥ, *Fatāwā*, 433–34 [nos. 379, 380]).

20 In 806/1403–04, during a shortage of gold and silver, the chief *qāḍī* of Cairo prohibited the city's notaries from designating the amounts of *ṣadāq* in dinars or dirhams. Thirty years later, following a shortage of copper, the decree was overturned, and only gold and silver were now permissible (al-Maqrīzī, *Sulūk*, vol. IV, 795). The decision to prohibit the use of copper coins was made by Ibn Ḥajar al-ʿAsqalānī in 832/1428–29. In his chronicle, he explains that amounts written down in copper had become meaningless due to the scarcity of copper coins (Ibn Ḥajar, *Inbāʾ al-Ghumr*, vol. III, 419).

21 A. Dietrich, "Eine arabische Eheurkunde aus der Aiyūbidenzeit," in J. Fück (ed.), *Documenta Islamica Inedita* (Berlin: Akademie Verlag Berlin, 1952), 121–54. It was not uncommon for daughters to claim portions of their *ṣadāq* from the estates of their late fathers (Ibn al-Ṣalāḥ, *Fatāwā*, 322 [no. 199], 432 [no. 375], 493 [no. 480]; al-Anṣārī, *Iʿlām*, 120, 314–15).

22 The subject of the question was whether the marriage gift, when it is eventually paid to the woman, is liable to retroactive taxation. Ibn Taymiyya ruled that no tax should be levied (*Majmūʿ Fatāwā*, vol. XXV, 47; Ibn Taymiyya, *Fatāwā al-Nisāʾ*, 60). The Shāfiʿīs, however, held that a deferred *ṣadāq* is taxable (al-Anṣārī, *Iʿlām*, 257). I have found no reference to the actual collection of such a tax.

23 Ḥaram document no. 607, published in Lutfi, *al-Quds*, 54–60.

24 When the mother died leaving minor children, they did not receive the *ṣadāq* until their father's death (al-Asyūṭī, *Jawāhir al-ʿUqūd*, vol. II, 227). For a case of adult children claiming their deceased mother's *ṣadāq* from the estate of their father, see Ibn al-Ṣalāḥ, *Fatāwā*, 536 (no. 543).

25 Lutfi, *al-Quds*, 285, 289.

Pre-mortem settlements saved widows the trouble of having to go through the court system, often a costly and complicated affair, not least because very few women could read their marriage contracts, and required the services of notaries, who demanded hefty fees.[26] One option was a testamentary disposition affirming the amount of the *ṣadāq*.[27] A second option was to pay when death was approaching. When al-Ẓāhir Barqūq's troops left for battle in 791/1389, some of the soldiers were so overcome by a sense of doom that they paid the marriage gifts of their wives.[28]

Some wealthy husbands preferred a pre-mortem settlement called *taʿwīḍ* (compensation), in which the wife received property, usually real estate, in lieu of her promised marriage gift which had been designated in cash. References for this kind of settlement abound in the legal literature.[29] These settlements could also take place after the husband's death, between the widow and his heirs.[30] An example of this kind of pre-mortem settlement comes from the marriage contract of a tribal amir from Aswan, dated 742/1341. At marriage the amir gave an advance payment of 50 gold dinars, and pledged 150 dinars as postponed payment, to be divided into fifteen yearly installments. These installments were never actually paid. In a settlement reached thirty years later, in 772/1370, the wife received half of her husband's lands in the village of Niklā in the region of Giza, not far from Cairo. She also acquired possession of a female slave and the slave's adult son. In return for this property, she forfeited her rights to the full amount of her postponed marriage gift, 150 gold dinars.[31]

In contrast to marriage gifts payable upon death or divorce, however, some marriage contracts designated a portion of the marriage gift as due debt (*ḥāll*) "payable upon demand." This term is found in documents and legal literature from the second half of the thirteenth century onwards.[32] By the middle of the fourteenth century it was standard practice in Damascus to designate part of the marriage gift as payable upon demand.[33] This new feature of marriage contracts attracted the

[26] Ibn al-Ḥājj, *Madkhal*, vol. II, 161–62.

[27] For examples, see al-Sakhāwī, *Ḍaw'*, vol. V, 223; al-Anṣārī, *Iʿlām*, 205, 211; Goitein, *A Mediterranean Society*, vol. III, 251, 255.

[28] Ibn Qāḍī Shuhba, *Ta'rīkh*, vol. I, 292.

[29] Ibn al-Ṣalāḥ, *Fatāwā*, 428 (no. 366). For other examples of property given to a wife as *taʿwīḍ* for her *ṣadāq*, see al-Fazārī, "Fatāwā," fol. 87b (livestock); Ibn al-Ṣalāḥ, *Fatāwā*, 321 (no. 197); cited in al-Ghazzī, "Adab al-Qaḍā'," fol. 109a (a horse); al-Subkī, *Fatāwā*, vol. II, 485–88 (a house), 504 (a slave); al-Anṣārī, *Iʿlām*, 225 (a house), 310 (a third of a house). For similar settlements in the Jewish community and in contemporary Granada, see Goitein, *A Mediterranean Society*, vol. III, 252; Shatzmiller, "Women and Property Rights," 244.

[30] Al-Jarawānī, "Mawāhib," fols. 18a–19b. A settlement for a widow is also mentioned in Ibn Taymiyya, *Majmūʿ Fatāwā*, vol. XXXII, 203.

[31] Māhir, "ʿUqūd al-Zawāj," 50–53.

[32] The earliest mention of the term comes from an Egyptian marriage contract dated 677/1278, where the *ṣadāq* is divided into due portion of 100 dirhams and ten yearly installments of 40 dirhams (ʿAbd al-Rāziq, "ʿAqdā Nikāḥ," 76–88).

[33] Guellil, *Damaszener Akten*, 169–70. In a marriage contract from Upper Egypt, dated 749/1348, the parties agreed that only half of the advance portion would be delivered at marriage, while the rest would become payable upon demand (A. Grohmann, "Einige arabische Ostraka und ein Ehevertrag aus der Oase Baḥriya," in *Studi in onore di Aristide Calderini e Roberto Paribeni*, 3 vols. [Milan: Ceshina, 1957], vol. II, 499–509).

attention of Najm al-Dīn al-Ṭarsūsī (d. 758/1357), the chief Ḥanafī *qāḍī* of the city, who devoted a treatise to the interpretation of the clause. It is customary, al-Ṭarsūsī explains, to pay the deferred portion only after death or divorce. However, the text of standard marriage contracts does specifically allow the wife to demand the marriage gift "whenever she wants." A *qāḍī* presented with such a contract must enforce the payment of the remaining marriage gift at the wife's request, and send the husband to jail if he refuses.[34]

The "payable upon demand" clause undermined the notion of marriage as a harmonious and non-monetized relationship of dependency, and therefore attracted considerable attention from upholders of patriarchal values. Ibn Qayyim al-Jawziyya, who also devotes a separate discussion to this clause, condemns *qāḍīs* who imprison husbands for failing to pay the marriage gift of their wives. This phenomenon, he explains, is a result of the change in the way the *ṣadāq* was being paid. In the past the wife could not demand the deferred or postponed portion before it matured. In his days, however, it is had become customary to write into marriage contracts that the deferred portion is a due debt, "payable upon demand." According to Ibn al-Qayyim, there was still an informal private agreement between the parties to defer the payment until the dissolution of the marriage, and the promise to pay upon demand was an embellishment, only meant to honor the bride and her family. At most, the wife might demand this payment in case of marital discord, such as when the husband takes a second wife.[35]

When some women, assisted by *qāḍīs*, did not wait until death or divorce but actually went to court and demanded this portion of their marriage gifts, the results were disastrous (for men):

> Only God knows how much evil and corruption have spread since women were given the power to demand the deferred portions of their marriage gift, and to cause the imprisonment of their husbands. If a husband scolds his wife for her housekeeping, or prevents her from stepping out or leaving his house, or does not let her go wherever she wishes, the wife then demands her marriage gift. The husband is sent to prison, while she goes wherever she wants. The husband is writhing and wriggling in jail, while she spends the night wherever she pleases.[36]

The image of fourteenth-century Damascus as a city where men languish in jail while their wives sleep where they please is somewhat exaggerated, but is not completely imaginary. Some wives did bring their husbands to court and even caused their imprisonment. In a case put to Ibn Taymiyya, a husband was imprisoned for two months at the request of his wife, while the court searched in vain for any

[34] Najm al-Dīn al-Ṭarsūsī, *al-Fatāwā al-Ṭarsūsiyya aw Anfaʿ al-Wasāʾil ilā Taḥrīr al-Masāʾil*, ed. Muṣṭafā Muḥammad Khafājī (Cairo: Maṭbaʿat al-Sharq, 1926), 29–34. The established doctrine allowed a bride to refuse consummation as long as the due portion was not paid (Ibn Taymiyya, *Majmūʿ Fatāwā*, vol. XXXII, 203–04 [two similar cases]; al-Subkī, *Fatāwā*, vol. II, 277; al-Jarawānī, "Mawāhib," fol. 67a; Chester Beatty MS 4665, fol. 27b).

[35] Ibn Qayyim al-Jawziyya, *al-Ṭuruq al-Ḥukmiyya fī al-Siyāsa al-Sharʿiyya* (Cairo: Maṭbaʿat al-Ādāb, 1317/1898–99), 63–65.

[36] *Ibid.*, 64. On Ibn Taymiyya's views on the subject, see *Majmūʿ Fatāwā*, vol. XXXII, 76.

property in his name. Eventually, the husband had to be released.[37] Ḥusām al-Dīn al-Ghūrī, chief Ḥanafī *qāḍī* of Egypt, earned a reputation for siding with wives against their husbands. One anecdote concerns a woman who appealed to Ḥusām al-Dīn for marital support and the installments of her marriage gift, 1 dinar each year. After instructing the woman to remove her veil, Ḥusām al-Dīn admonished her father: "You wretch! How could you marry off such a beautiful girl like this for just one dinar a year? By God, even one night with her is worth one hundred dirhams."[38]

By designating a portion of the marriage gift as a due debt, women were in a better position to impose favorable conditions in their marriage contracts. In one marriage contract put to Ibn Taymiyya, the groom undertook to support the wife's child from a previous marriage, and in return the bride promised not to claim a due payment of 5 dinars.[39] A cautious bride stipulated that she would have rights over her outstanding marriage gifts if her husband took back his previous wife as a second wife.[40] In another case, a bride's father required her husband to pay the due portion of the marriage gift before taking off on a journey. When the man did eventually desert his wife, her father was in a position to appeal for judicial divorce on the grounds that the due portion was not paid.[41] In a case put to Qāri' al-Hidāya (d. 829/1426), a wife refused to relocate to her husband's town until he paid his due debt.[42] In another fifteenth-century case, a wife's father demanded from the husband a conditional bill of divorce that would come into effect were the husband to be absent for two months, threatening to demand the full marriage gift if he did not comply.[43] A husband who wished to preserve his authority had to make his wife swear not to demand the due portion of her marriage gift as long as they were married.[44]

When a couple agreed to insert the "payable upon demand" clause, they were steering away from a patriarchal model of marriage. The clause allowed wives to claim money from their husbands while still married, and then follow up the claim in court if the husband proved recalcitrant. Women were also entitled to yearly installments, although in practice these were seldom paid in their due time. These changes in the method of paying the marriage gift reinforced the contractual nature of marriage. The marriage gift was no longer paid only twice, once at the beginning of the marriage and once after its dissolution. It was now transformed into a series of payments that were supposed to be delivered throughout the marriage; it therefore

[37] Ibn Taymiyya, *Majmū' Fatāwā*, vol. XXXV, 197.

[38] Al-Maqrīzī, *Sulūk*, vol. II, 611; cited in J. Escovitz, *The Office of Qadî al-Qudât in Cairo under the Bahrî Mamlûks* (Berlin: Klaus Schwarz, 1984), 158. For a slightly different version, see Ibn Ḥajar, *Durar*, vol. II, 42.

[39] Ibn Taymiyya, *Majmū' Fatāwā*, vol. XXXIV, 100.

[40] Ibn Taymiyya, *Fatāwā al-Nisā'*, 295–96.

[41] Ibn Taymiyya, *Majmū' Fatāwā*, vol. XXXIV, 92.

[42] Qāri' al-Hidāya, "al-Fatāwā al-Sirājiyya," fol. 40a.

[43] Al-Anṣārī, *I'lām*, 267. Stipulating a due debt, sometimes in addition to the yearly installments, was a standard feature of fifteenth-century Egyptian marriage contracts. See Al-Anṣārī, *I'lām*, 229; al-Suyūṭī, *al-Ḥāwī lil-Fatāwā fī al-Fiqh wa-'Ulūm al-Tafsīr wa'l-Ḥadīth wa'l-Uṣūl wa'l-Naḥw wa'l-I'rāb wa-Sā'ir al-Funūn*, 2 vols. (Cairo: Idārat al-Ṭibā'a al-Munīriyya, 1352/1933), vol. I, 248.

[44] Al-Suyūṭī, *Ḥāwī*, vol. I, 249.

amplified the already existing similarity between a marriage relationship and a business partnership.

## Marital support and cash allowances

Even more than the changes in the way marriage gifts were paid, it was the changes taking place in the form of marital support that brought about increasing monetization of the daily relations between husbands and wives. Nothing changed, of course, in the essence of husbands' legal obligation to feed, clothe and lodge their wives. This was the husband's primary duty during marriage, or even immediately following the engagement.[45] What did change during the late medieval period was the way this obligation was carried out. Before the Mamluk period, or at least up to the end of the thirteenth century, husbands supported their wives by buying food in the market and, quite literally, putting bread on the table. From the beginning of the fourteenth century, however, we find some husbands delivering maintenance by paying cash allowances to their wives. By the fifteenth century, a variety of cash payments, especially in lieu of undelivered clothing, had become a common form of marital support.

The traditional position in Islamic law was that a husband is only required to provide support in kind. In early thirteenth-century Damascus, we are told by the Syrian jurist Ibn al-Ṣalāḥ, a husband was expected to deliver three-and-a-half ounces of flour every day, to which the price of grinding and baking should be added. If the husband so wished, the couple could agree on a daily number of bread loaves, and on *idam*, i.e., something to go with the bread, such as cheese or oil. The husband was also required to provide his wife with a new set of clothes twice a year, including a chemise, a pair of trousers, a headgear and a pair of shoes, as well as one cloak for the winter months.[46] This list might tell us something about the standard of living among the poor in thirteenth-century Damascus.[47] For our purpose here, however, the list is significant because it reiterates the traditional legal position, and represents the actual practice at the time. When one husband could not afford to buy new clothes even once a year, he asked whether he could give his wife washed clothes that were, supposedly, as strong as new.[48] Another husband could not afford the winter cloak, and wanted to make do with pieces of inferior cloth commonly used for making tents.[49] As in the Jewish

[45] A man was even expected, in return for the promise of a future alliance, to support his fiancée immediately after the engagement, before the wedding. Ibn Taymiyya, *Majmūʿ Fatāwā*, vol. XXXII, 8; al-Anṣārī, *Iʿlām*, 218 (two cases).

[46] Ibn al-Ṣalāḥ also mentions cleaning utensils, such as a broom, and basic furniture (*Fatāwā*, 456 [no. 423]).

[47] For an overview, see Sabra, *Poverty*, 109–16. See also similar lists compiled by jurists from Ottoman Syria and Palestine (Tucker, *In the House of the Law*, 43). The lists tend to be formulaic, but there are slight differences indicating that they had some practical significance.

[48] Ibn al-Ṣalāḥ, *Fatāwā*, 453 (no. 415).

[49] *Ibid.*, 455 (no. 420). See also al-Nawawī, *Fatāwā*, nos. 264, 266.

community of the Geniza, husbands bought food and clothes and brought them home. They did not give their wives household money, but rather did the shopping themselves.[50] This practice was facilitated by the availability of prepared food in the markets, itself a result of the scarcity of wood, which meant that most people could not cook at home.[51]

But by the fourteenth century jurists started to voice alarm over husbands who gave their wives cash allowances. Ibn Taymiyya and his disciple Ibn al-Qayyim denounced wives who made retroactive demands for maintenance, and *qāḍī*s who allowed such claims to be heard. They cite the case of a woman who appeared before the *qāḍī* after fifty years of marriage, and claimed that her husband had never fed or clothed her. The *qāḍī* believed her, put the husband in prison and gave his property to the wife. Ibn Taymiyya argues that this must have been a fraudulent claim, for the prevalent social circumstances are that the husband is the provider. If a wife denies receiving support, she needs to explain how exactly she sustained herself. After all, he points out, "women are not angels – they need to eat."[52] Ibn al-Qayyim further laments that husbands are now under a constant threat of being sued for support. Since they cannot invite witnesses for every meal their wives take, they have no choice but to give their wives a monthly cash allowance, and let them buy what they want. Alternatively, if they do not wish the wife to go out, they have to use the money as the wife tells them to. In any case, the correct hierarchy of power in marriage is reversed, and it is the husband who is now his wife's prisoner and slave.[53]

During the fourteenth century there are quite a few examples of husbands who undertook cash payments to their wives. The Egyptian moralist Ibn al-Ḥājj criticizes husbands who leave money with their wives in order to allow them to buy flax or water from the peddlers who knock on their doors.[54] Ibn al-Ḥājj also reports that wives often demand a small payment from their husbands before going to bed with

50 Goitein, *A Mediterranean Society*, vol. III, 167.

51 See *ibid.*, vol. I, 114; S. ʿA. ʿĀshūr, *al-Mujtamaʿ al-Miṣrī fī ʿAṣr Salāṭīn al-Mamālīk* (Cairo: Dār al-Nahḍa al-ʿArabiyya, 1962), 116. European travelers often noted the sale of food on the markets of Cairo, Damascus and Jerusalem. See, for example, Nicolá da Foggibonsi, *A Voyage Beyond the Seas, 1346–1350*, trans. T. Bellorini and E. Hoade (Jerusalem: Franciscan Press, 1945), 77; Leonardo Frescobaldi, Giorgio Gucci and Simone Sigoli, *Visit to the Holy Places of Egypt, Sinai, Palestine, and Syria in 1384*, trans. T. Bellorini and E. Hoade (Jerusalem: Franciscan Press, 1948), 49, 167, 183; E. Piloti, *L'Egypte au commencement du quinzième siècle, d'après le traité d'Emmanuel Piloti de Crète, incipit 1420*, ed. P.-H. Dopp (Cairo: Imp. Université Fouad 1er, 1950), 108; P. Casola, *Canon Pietro Casola's Pilgrimage to Jerusalem in the Year 1494*, trans. M. Newett (Manchester: Manchester University Press, 1907), 251; von Harff, *Pilgrimage*, 109.

52 Ibn Taymiyya, *Majmūʿ Fatāwā*, vol. XXXII, 80–82; Ibn al-Qayyim, *Ighāthat al-Lahfān*, vol. II, 55–68; Ibn al-Qayyim, *al-Ṭuruq al-Ḥukmiyya*, 20; Ibn al-Qayyim, *Iʿlām al-Muwaqqiʿīn*, vol. III, 351–53. A minority position in the Shāfiʿī school required husbands to submit proof of marital support, although the dominant opinion in the school (*mashhūr*) was that the burden of proof falls on the wife (Ibn ʿAbd al-Salām, "al-Qawāʿid al-Kubrā," MS British Library, Or. 3102, fol. 18a; ʿImād al-Dīn al-Aqfahsī, "Tawqīf al-Ḥukkām ʿalā Ghawāmiḍ al-Aḥkām," Chester Beatty MS 3328, fol. 106b; al-Asyūṭī, *Jawāhir al-ʿUqūd*, vol. II, 214; al-Anṣārī, "ʿImād al-Riḍā," fol. 57b; al-Anṣārī, *Iʿlām*, 268–71).

53 Text: *al-ʿānī waʾl-asīr waʾl-mamlūk* (Ibn al-Qayyim, *Ighāthat al-Lahfān*, vol. II, 56, 59–60). See also Ibn Taymiyya, *Majmūʿ Fatāwā*, vol. XXXIV, 83, 88.

54 Lutfi, "Manners," 104; Ibn al-Ḥājj, *Madkhal*, vol. IV, 103.

them, a payment which he calls a bed-fee (*ḥaqq al-firāsh*).[55] In a Geniza document dated 1334, drawn up after a domestic quarrel, a Jewish husband undertakes to send his wife half a dirham a day until they resume cohabitation. He also promises to buy her clothes and to send an additional sum of 5½ dirhams.[56] Around the same time, a Damascene Muslim husband left his wife a daily allowance of 2 dirhams before going on a business trip.[57] A Cairene amir by the name of Qijlīs (d. 731/1331) gave his wife a daily allowance of 2,000 silver dirhams when she asked to go and take a holiday on the banks of the Nile, away from the heat of the city. The wife, by the way, augmented this daily allowance by selling some of her trousseau for 10,000 dirhams, and then came home early, saying that the money had all been spent.[58]

By the latter half of the fourteenth century cash allowances had become widespread. Legal manuals from this period specifically approve of them as a permissible form of marital support.[59] The Italian merchant Frescobaldi, visiting Egypt in 1384, was bemused by Muslim husbands who promised their wives a marriage gift but did not deliver it. Instead, he writes, spouses reached a settlement on a daily allowance for the wife's support. The amounts of this allowance varied according to social position, from 1 to 3 dirhams a day, and less than that among the poor.[60] A century later, von Harff referred to cash payment of marital support as "the law of the country." According to his account, a husband must give his wife 3 silver dirhams every day, as well as money for the bath. During the day, the wife would eat with her husband and from his provisions, but she would take supper by her own, and her husband had to pay for that too.[61] Von Harff adds that a husband must provide each of his wives with a black slave-girl, thus revealing the class bias of his report.[62]

The diary of Shihāb al-Dīn Ibn Ṭawq contains minute records of his expenditures, including occasional references to the money he gave to his wife. Although Ibn Ṭawq did not seem to give his wife regular cash allowances, she could rely on him to give her money for her outings. On one occasion he gave his wife one gold coin and 34 dirhams for her visit to the bathhouse.[63] Before another visit he gave her 29 dirhams.[64] He also records giving her 10 silver coins for a farewell present to her midwife who was going on the pilgrimage.[65] Twelve days later he gave her thirty coins to give to his maternal cousin in the suburb of al-Ṣāliḥiyya, whom she visited without him. He also paid six coins for hiring a donkey driver to take her there.[66]

55 Lutfi, "Manners," 107–08; Ibn al-Ḥājj, *Madkhal*, vol. II, 169.
56 Published by Ashtor-Strauss, *Tōldōt*, vol. III, 80–81.
57 ʿAbd al-Rāziq, *La femme*, 195. 58 Al-Ṣafadī, *Aʿyān*, vol. IV, 78–79.
59 See late fourteenth-century Shāfiʿī jurists such as Muḥammad b. ʿAbd al-Raḥmān al-ʿUthmānī, "Kifāyat al-Muftiyyīn wa'l-Ḥukkām fī al-Fatāwā wa'l-Aḥkām," Chester Beatty MS 4666, fols. 49b–50a; al-Aqfahsī, "Tawqīf," fol. 106b.
60 Frescobaldi, et al., *Visit*, 49 (cited in E. Ashtor-Strauss, *Histoire des prix et des salaires dans l'Orient médiéval* [Paris: SEVPEN, 1969], 367).
61 For wives who did not take their meals together with their husbands see also Ibn al-Ḥājj, *Madkhal*, vol. I, 216 (cited in ʿĀshūr, *al-Mujtamaʿ al-Miṣrī*, 116).
62 Von Harff, *Pilgrimage*, 112. 63 Ibn Ṭawq, *Taʿlīq*, 35.
64 *Ibid.*, 166. 65 *Ibid.*, 404. 66 *Ibid.*, 407.

Wives clearly preferred to receive cash allowances, sometimes against their husbands' will. Some wives even appealed to the courts to have their support paid in cash rather than in kind. In a case put before Qāri' al-Hidāya, a wife had asked the *qāḍī* to impose a daily cash allowance on her husband. The jurist answered that the *qāḍī* should do so only if the husband was known to be maltreating her.[67] In a case from the end of the fifteenth century, a wife who had been living with her husband, and supposedly sharing his food, appealed in court for a daily cash allowance (in copper coins). The husband countered by approaching a Shāfi'ī *qāḍī*, who ordered that the support should be paid in kind.[68]

In addition to daily allowances, annual or monthly cash payments in lieu of clothing (*kiswa*) had become standard practice in the fifteenth century, and were added to the growing list of husbands' financial obligations. Often mentioned in fifteenth-century legal literature, formal settlements with regard to payments in lieu of clothing were registered before a *qāḍī* and were effectively an integral part of the marriage contract.[69] The annual payments for clothing could reach substantial sums. In a case from the end of the fifteenth century, a husband paid for his wife's clothing by transferring to her name an item of real estate.[70] Ibn Ḥajar al-'Asqalānī acknowledged in his will that he still owed his wife 300 gold dinars for undelivered clothing, a sum which could have allowed her to buy a large house in the center of Cairo.[71] In late fifteenth-century Damascus, one elite bride demanded thirty-five gold coins as her annual clothing budget.[72] Another Damascene bride stipulated that her husband would pay 200 silver pieces as her annual clothing payment, as well as another dirham a day from consummation; the two sums were to be used as support for her two daughters from a previous marriage. After their swift divorce, she married a textile merchant from Jerusalem, who undertook to pay 30 silver dirhams as monthly clothing, also to be spent on her two daughters.[73] Rabbi David b. Zekharya, writing in the early sixteenth century, noted that Jewish wives in Egypt and Palestine demanded cash instead of clothing in order to make small savings. The women would then buy second-hand clothes, or otherwise clothes of lesser value, and then invest the remaining sum in interest-bearing loans.[74]

Some husbands also had to pay rent to their wives. When a husband chose to live in his wife's house, she could, and sometimes did, require him to pay rent,

67 Qāri' al-Hidāya, "al-Fatāwā al-Sirājiyya," fols. 28b–29a.

68 Al-Anṣārī, *I'lām*, 268. The mystic al-Sha'rānī (d. 1565) was proud to say that one of his four wives was satisfied with only 2 dirhams a day (M. Winter, *Society and Religion in Early Ottoman Egypt: Studies in the Writings of 'Abd al-Wahhab al-Sha'rani* [New Brunswick: Transaction Books, 1982], 52).

69 Qāri' al-Hidāya, "al-Fatāwā al-Sirājiyya," fol. 29a; al-Suyūṭī, *Ḥāwī*, vol. I, 296; al-Anṣārī, *I'lām*, 269. For a model document, see al-Asyūṭī , *Jawāhir al-'Uqūd*, vol. II, 221–22.

70 Al-Anṣārī, *I'lām*, 242.

71 Al-Sakhāwī, *al-Jawāhir wa'l-Durar*, vol. III, 1203.

72 Ibn Ṭawq, *Ta'līq*, 379. For other examples of annual clothing payments, see *ibid.*, 407, 430.

73 *Ibid.*, 169.

74 R. Lamdan, *A Separate People: Jewish Women in Palestine, Syria, and Egypt in the Sixteenth Century* (Leiden: Brill, 2000), 121; Ashtor-Strauss, *Tōldōt*, vol. II, 345–46. This practice differed from the customs among the immigrant Jews coming from Spain, as illustrated in three marriage contracts of Spanish and Sicilian immigrants, dated 1511, published in R. Gottheil and W. H. Worrell, *Fragments from the Cairo Genizah in the Freer Collection* (New York: Macmillan, 1927), 178 ff.

monetization of marriage



since she was under no obligation to provide him with lodging.[75] In a case from the thirteenth century, a woman allowed her husband to reside in her house for free, but later changed her mind and demanded the rent retroactively.[76] Qāri' al-Hidāya and al-Aqfahsī discuss similar situations in the fifteenth century.[77] In the later period we have quite a few concrete examples of men who moved in with their brides. Following his arrival in Cairo in 807/1404–05, the scholar 'Umar b. Mūsā Ibn al-Ḥimṣī married a daughter of the Banū al-Bulqīnī and resided with them.[78] 'Umar b. Ḥasan al-Nawawī (b. ca. 820/1417) did likewise after he left his village in Lower Egypt and came to the capital.[79] Ibrāhīm b. Muḥammad al-Shādhilī, an acquaintance of the historian al-Sakhāwī, was forced to live with his in-laws after having been disowned by his father.[80] Towards the end of the fifteenth century Jalāl al-Dīn al-Suyūṭī even found it necessary to devote a treatise to the legal implications of residing in the wife's house.[81]

Cash payments for clothing and rent were additional layers in the process of the monetization and formalization of marriage. A fifteenth-century husband would usually have owed his wife an annual installment of the marriage gift, an annual payment for her clothing, a daily allowance and perhaps the rent for living in her house. In addition, she may have been entitled to demand the outstanding portion of the marriage gift at any point during the marriage. Some glimpses of how it all added up can be found in the Ḥaram estate inventories. In one case, a husband's estate was sold in order to pay his widow 360 dirhams for the remainder of her *ṣadāq* and undelivered clothing.[82] Similarly, the widow of a peasant received 200 dirhams from her late husband's brother for an unpaid marriage gift and for clothing.[83]

The best illustration for the variety of debts burdening a fifteenth-century husband comes from an Egyptian document dated 861/1456, which records a matrimonial financial settlement. The husband, an artisan by the name of Mūsā b. Riḍā al-Bardanūhī, acknowledges that he owes his wife, Umm al-Ḥasan, a total of 3,900 copper dirhams (about 13 gold dinars). These include 600 copper dirhams for the

75 Goitein, *A Mediterranean Society*, vol. III, 150–53. For Geniza engagement and marriage contracts allowing the bride to choose the domicile, see Ashtor-Strauss, *Tōldōt*, vol. III, 74–78 (nos. 42, 43). In one marriage contract, dated 1324, the bride allowed the groom to live in her house without paying rent; in return, the husband agreed to support her two daughters from a previous marriage (Goitein, *A Mediterranean Society*, vol. III, 311).

76 Ibn al-Ṣalāḥ, *Fatāwā*, 451–52 (no. 413).

77 Qāri' al-Hidāya, "al-Fatāwā al-Sirājiyya," fol. 51b; al-Aqfahsī, "Tawqīf," fol. 61b.

78 Al-Sakhāwī, *Ḍaw'*, vol. VI, 140. 79 *Ibid.*, 80.

80 *Ibid.*, vol. I, 164. For more examples, see *ibid.*, vol. II, 259, vol. X, 304 (no. 1176). For a contemporary case from Aleppo, see Sibṭ Ibn al-'Ajamī, *Kunūz al-Dhahab fī Ta'rīkh Ḥalab*, ed. Shawqī Sha'ath and Fāliḥ al-Bakkūr, 2 vols. (Aleppo: Dār al-Qalam al-'Arabī, 1996–97), vol. II, 212.

81 Al-Suyūṭī's goal is to refute anonymous contemporary jurists who allowed a wife to continue living in her own house against the wishes of her husband. If, however, it was the husband who chose to live in his wife's house, the woman was then entitled to both marital support and rent (al-Suyūṭī, *al-Nuqūl al-Mushriqah fī Mas'alat al-Nafaqa*, published in his *Ḥāwī*, vol. I, 299–309). On husbands paying rent in contemporary Granada, see Shatzmiller, "Women and Property Rights," 241.

82 Ḥaram document no. 205 (published in Lutfi, "*Iqrārs*," 269–73; al-'Asalī, *Wathā'iq*, vol. II, 40).

83 Ḥaram document no. 655.

due portion of his marriage gift; 800 for the postponed portion of his marriage gift, i.e., the yearly installments; 1,500 in lieu of clothing undelivered for the past two years; and 1,000 for the sale price of textile items that belonged to her. Mūsā undertakes, in front of the *qāḍī* and witnesses, to pay the remainder of the *ṣadāq* in ten annual installments. He also undertakes a monthly payment of 60 copper dirhams towards the other outstanding debts.[84] There is no indication that this document was drawn up as part of a divorce settlement. The couple, it seems, were expecting to continue living together, with Mūsā gradually paying off his debts to his wife.

## The marriages of Zumurrud

Given the scarcity of our documentary evidence, it is rarely possible to follow the marital history of non-elite women. We are therefore fortunate to have three consecutive marriage contracts of one such woman, a manumitted slave-girl by the name of Zumurrud, who lived in Jerusalem at the end of the fourteenth century. The importance of Zumurrud's marital history goes beyond the rare glimpse she offers us into the marriages of the common people. Her marriage contracts, concluded and then dissolved through divorce during the space of no more than two years, record the financial obligations undertaken by Zumurrud's respective husbands. Zumurrud's marriages are a concrete demonstration of the link between the monetization of marriage and the frequency of divorce.

The first marriage contract of Zumurrud preserved in the Ḥaram documents is dated 12 Ṣafar 791 (February 10, 1389), and records her marriage to the milkman Ibrāhīm b. ʿAlī b. Ibrāhīm al-Dimashqī. In this contract, Ibrāhīm al-Dimashqī bestowed on his fiancée, Zumurrud bt. ʿAbdallāh b. ʿAbdallāh, the manumitted slave-girl of Sitt Sutayta, three full coins (*mithqāl*s) of minted pure gold as marriage gift. Zumurrud, who is described as an adult woman free from any legal impediments to marriage, acknowledged taking possession of one full coin. The two remaining coins were originally to become due debt upon the husband, but this stipulation was crossed out in the original document. In its stead, the two coins were to be divided into two yearly installments, a dinar every year. Zumurrud was married, with her permission and agreement, by the judge, signatory of the document.[85]

Judging by this marriage contract, Zumurrud was a member of the lowest strata of urban society. She had no legal guardian, and therefore had to be represented by the court.[86] Zumurrud's guardian for marriage should have been her former

84 W. Diem, "Vier arabische Rechtsurkunden aus Ägypten des 14. und 15. Jahrhunderts," *Der Islam* 72 (1995), 206–27.

85 Ḥaram document no. 646, summary in Little, *Catalogue*, 305. The signatures of the witnesses and the *ʿalāma* of the judge are found on the margins of the document.

86 In theory, Ḥanafī *qāḍī*s could authorize marriage contracts in which an adult bride represented herself, but they did not practice this right. The Shāfiʿī Taqī al-Dīn al-Subkī ruled that a marriage

mistress, Sitt Sutayta, but this woman does not appear to have been involved in any of Zumurrud's marriages. Possibly she was not allowed to represent her former slave in marriage because of her sex,[87] but it is more likely that she was either absent or deceased. In any case, as far as we can tell, Zumurrud was acting on her own. From the marriage contract we also learn that this was not Zumurrud's first marriage, for otherwise she would have been described as a virgin bride.

As for the financial settlement mentioned in the contract, Ibrāhīm pledged a total marriage gift of 3 gold dinars, of which one was paid immediately to Zumurrud. As noted above, the actual payment was almost certainly made in dirhams. This is the smallest marriage gift found in the preserved marriage contracts,[88] equal to the sum accorded to Cairene prostitutes who were rounded up and married off during a campaign against vice in 827/1424.[89] The remainder of Zumurrud's marriage gift, just 2 dinars, was to be paid off in two yearly installments. Initially, the notary wrote that the remainder was a due debt (*'alā ḥukm al-ḥulūl*), which would have allowed Zumurrud to claim the money whenever she wished. For an unknown reason, however, the sentence was crossed out, and this small sum was divided into two installments of 1 dinar. The note at the end of the contract confirms the correction made to the text.

Ibrāhīm divorced Zumurrud on 17 Jumādā I 792 (May 4, 1390), that is, after one year and three months. The record of this divorce is found on the verso of the marriage contract.[90] As this was a consensual divorce, Zumurrud forfeited her rights to Ibrāhīm's debts towards her, including the remainder of the marriage gift. By this time, she should have already received one dinar as the first of her yearly installments, but there is no record of such a payment on the marriage contract.

concluded without a legal guardian is invalid, even if it was authorized by a Ḥanafī *qāḍī* (Tāj al-Dīn al-Subkī, *Ṭabaqāt al-Shāfi'iyya al-Kubrā*, 6 vols. [Cairo: Maṭba'at al-Ḥusayniyya, 1906], vol. VI, 185). Adult women could also ask the courts to marry them off if their legal guardians refused to do so (al-Aqfahsī, "Tawqīf," fol. 39a; al-Asyūṭī, *Jawāhir al-'Uqūd*, vol. II, 7; al-Sarūjī, *Kitāb Adab al-Qaḍā'*, ed. Ṣ. Yāsīn [Beirut: Dār al-Bashā'ir al-Islāmiyya, 1997], 204; al-Ṭarsūsī, *Anfa' al-Wasā'il*, 20–21; Ibn Taymiyya, *Majmū' Fatāwā*, vol. XXXII, 52).

87 Only the Ḥanafī law school approves of women assuming the role of guardians at marriage. Al-Asyūṭī provides a model marriage contract, which can only be authorized by Ḥanafī judges, in which an adult woman represents the bride (*Jawāhir al-'Uqūd*, vol. II, 82). The Ḥanafī school doctrine also allows a manumitted slave to marry without the permission of his or her ex-master. In a case put to Ibn Taymiyya, a manumitted slave-girl of a princess (*min banāt al-mulūk*) married without the consent of her ex-mistress. Ibn Taymiyya ruled that the marriage was valid according to the Ḥanafī law school (*Majmū' Fatāwā*, vol. XXXII, 58).

88 In a marriage contract of two slaves from Aswan, dated 744/1343, the groom promised 150 dirhams, of which 50 dirhams, about 2 dinars, were promptly paid (A. 'Abd al-Rāziq, "Un document concernant le mariage des esclaves au temps des mamlūks," *JESHO* 13 [1970], 309–14).

89 Al-Maqrīzī, *Sulūk*, vol. IV, 666. The prostitutes were married off for an advance marriage gift of 200 copper dirhams, and an equal sum of postponed *ṣadāq*. At the current exchange rates, 200 copper dirhams were worth a little less than 1 dinar (B. Shoshan, "Exchange-Rate Policies in Fifteenth-Century Egypt," *JESHO* 29 [1986], 33). During a public morality campaign in 667/1268, al-Ẓāhir Baybars gave orders to marry off prostitutes for a *ṣadāq* of 400 silver dirhams ('Abd al-Rāziq, *La femme*, 133).

90 Ḥaram document no. 646, verso, A (Little, *Catalogue*, 306).

Zumurrud was in a rush to get married again. A month later, on 23 Jumādā II 792 (June 8, 1390), Zumurrud married a man called Ṣabīḥ b. ʿAbdallāh, whose name indicates that he too was a manumitted slave. This second marriage contract was written down on the same sheet of paper.[91] In order for the marriage to be valid, Zumurrud testified under oath that she had completed the required waiting period of three menstrual periods. This was perjury, as must have been obvious to the court. But the Ḥanafī deputy who married her had no qualms about this particular breach of the law.

Ṣabīḥ, Zumurrud's second husband, pledged a total of 5 dinars as a marriage gift, divided into two portions. One dinar was designated as due, and was paid to Zumurrud at the time of the marriage. The remaining 4 dinars were to be paid in yearly installments of 1 dinar. Zumurrud was slightly better off compared to her previous marriage. Again she received 1 dinar as an advance payment, but this time she was promised four yearly installments of 1 dinar instead of 2. More important was Ṣabīḥ's obligation to support Muḥammad b. Ibrāhīm, Zumurrud's child from her previous marriage, who could not have been more than a few months old. Supporting Zumurrud's child involved a significant financial commitment on Ṣabīḥ's part, almost certainly more than the entire marriage gift.[92] It should be noted that, from a legal point of view, Zumurrud lost her right of custody as a result of her remarriage, but her ex-husband did not enforce his rights.

Six months later, Zumurrud was divorced again. Ṣabīḥ issued a single revocable divorce on the 12 Dhū al-Ḥijja 792 (November 22, 1390), and undertook to provide Zumurrud with maintenance for the duration of her waiting period.[93] This was a unilateral divorce, and Zumurrud did not forfeit her right to the postponed marriage gift. On 3 Shawwāl 793 (September 4, 1391) Ṣabīḥ made a payment of 1 dinar towards the remainder of Zumurrud's marriage gift.[94] This payment probably constituted the first yearly installment that was pledged in the marriage contract. But the document does not bear record of further payments by Ṣabīḥ. It is unlikely that these payments were made, for they too should have been registered on the same marriage contract.

By the time Zumurrud received Ṣabīḥ's solitary payment, she was already married for a third time, this time to a weaver by the name of Muḥammad b. ʿAlī al-Salḥadī. Their marriage, dated 8 Ṣafar 793 (January 10, 1391), took place only two months after Zumurrud's divorce from Ṣabīḥ.[95] Although the date of the divorce is specifically mentioned in the marriage contract, Zumurrud testified again under oath that she had already completed three menstrual periods. Her former husband, Ṣabīḥ, was required to testify that he did not revoke the divorce, and that they

91 Ḥaram document no. 646, verso, B (Little, *Catalogue*, 306).
92 The court of Jerusalem normally accorded 20 to 30 dirhams, about 1 dinar, as monthly support payments to orphans. See, for example, Ḥaram documents nos. 458, 667, 192, 52B, 183, 115, 604, 106.
93 Ḥaram document no. 646, verso, D (Little, *Catalogue*, 306).
94 Ḥaram document no. 646, verso, C (Little, *Catalogue*, 306).
95 Ḥaram document no. 610 (Little, *Catalogue*, 305). A cross-reference for the court's use is found in the margins of Ḥaram document no. 646, verso.

were no longer married to each other. In this third marriage, Zumurrud's new husband pledged a total of 6 dinars, of which 1 was paid immediately. The remaining 5 dinars were divided into two portions. One dinar was designated as a due debt, and the other 4 were to be paid in four yearly installments. Compared to her previous marriages, the total sum of Zumurrud's marriage gift was higher, but at marriage she received, again, only 1 dinar.

There is not much more that we know about Zumurrud. The last preserved entry regarding Zumurrud was made on 15 Dhū al-Qaʿda 793 (October 15, 1391).[96] At this date, the Shāfiʿī chief *qāḍī* of Jerusalem certified Zumurrud's third marriage contract, concluded nine months earlier by his Ḥanafī deputy. The reason for this is unclear. Perhaps some additional claim, unknown to us from the Ḥaram documents, required the belated certification of this marriage contract.[97] The document does not contain any further details about the payment of the postponed marriage gift by al-Salḥadī or about the fate of Zumurrud's third marriage.

The marriage contracts of Zumurrud were both highly monetized and extremely short. Zumurrud was always in a rush to be married. Like many other divorcées, she gave a false statement regarding the completion of three menstrual periods in order to shorten the waiting period between the dissolution of one marriage and the conclusion of another.[98] It appears that the financial benefits of marriage – that is, the marriage gift and the marital support of a husband – were the primary reason for her successive marriages. Although the sums involved seem paltry, each of her marriages was preceded by some negotiation over the financial settlements, which were different every time. In her first marriage contract we can even detect traces of the negotiations that were going on while the marriage contract was being written down, as the notary crossed out a due payment of 2 dinars and divided the sum into two yearly installments.

Yet it is equally striking that Zumurrud saw very little of the amounts promised by her husbands. From her first husband she apparently got nothing but a child. From her second husband she got 1 dinar out of 4. While we often hear about husbands who owed money to their wives, we rarely hear about husbands who paid up their debts. How much could women rely on their husbands' promises? Or were all these diverse financial obligations merely means of making it easier for husbands to shirk their responsibilities? In spite of the negotiations over the terms of the marriage gift before the marriage, women were not always able to have the promised amounts actually delivered to them. Finally, the main characteristic

[96] Ḥaram document no. 610, verso (Little, *Catalogue*, 305).

[97] The certifications found in the Ḥaram documents were probably needed in order to ensure that the document would not later be invalidated by another *qāḍī* (Little, "Documents Related to the Estates of a Merchant and his Wife," 143, 165; Little, *Catalogue*, 224).

[98] Perjury regarding the waiting period was not uncommon. In one of several cases brought before Ibn Taymiyya, a divorcée had taken a drug that was supposed to cause early menstruation (*Majmūʿ Fatāwā*, vol. XXXII, 78, vol. XXXIV, 22–24). In a fifteenth-century case, a pregnant woman falsely claimed to have lost her fetus in order to re-marry (al-Anṣārī, *Iʿlām*, 259). In a case from the North African city of Ceuta, a woman contracted two consecutive marriages without observing the full term of her waiting periods (Powers, "Women and Divorce," 36–39).

of Zumurrud's marriages is their temporary nature. These were short-term affairs. They entitled her to modest marital support for a short while, until the marriage was dissolved and Zumurrud went on to look for another husband.

Zumurrud's marriages reflect the shift in the nature of marriage in the cities of the Near East in the later middle ages. The relations between a husband and his wife tended to become much more formalized, and were accompanied by a myriad of pecuniary transactions. Husbands owed their wives yearly installments and due payments of their marriage gifts, daily cash allowances, annual clothing payments, and sometimes rent or support for children from previous marriages. On the other hand, it is hard to say how many husbands actually paid their dues. It is very likely that much of the financial obligations undertaken by husbands remained on paper. Yet, whether paid up or not, the all-pervading cash obligations meant that Mamluk marriages had little in common with the patriarchal ideal advocated by the jurists and the moralists. Marriage did not create a unified economic unit, with the husband as the provider and the wife as a dependant. Rather, unlike slavery, marriage was very clearly a contract, a complex business partnership, quite often leading to court litigation and with good chance of ending in divorce.

CHAPTER 4

# Divorce, repudiation and settlement

The basic inequality of Islamic law, whereby a husband can pronounce a unilateral repudiation while a wife needs either the husband's consent for divorce or the intervention of the courts, has been one of the major sources of husbands' power in marriage. The absolute right of husbands to disband the marriage contract at will, like the absolute right of a master to manumit his slave, were symbols of patriarchal authority, eclipsing other male privileges, such as polygamy, concubinage and the right of physical chastisement. It was also the ultimate threat against an insolent wife. The prevailing cultural assumption in Mamluk society, at least until the end of the fifteenth century, was that divorce was a disaster for women. It deprived them of support and protection; and if they remarried, the application of Islamic law meant that they were in danger of losing custody of their children.

A wife who wanted a divorce had limited legal tools. One option was to insert clauses in the marriage contract that would allow her to choose a divorce in the event of her husband taking another wife or a concubine, beating her or failing to sustain her. If such clauses were not inserted, judicial divorces were granted only in cases of desertion. The *qāḍīs*, ostensibly the protectors of women, were generally reluctant to intrude more assertively in the domestic sphere, where the word of the husband was supposed to reign supreme. This judicial policy shifted during the fifteenth century, when military officials encroached on the jurisdiction of *qāḍīs* and began adjudicating cases of family law, acting much more aggressively to protect the rights of abused wives. The same military courts, on the other hand, also pursued a more active policy of upholding patriarchal ideals. Instead of repudiating, threatening or punishing an insubordinate or adulterous wife, husbands now lodged their complaints in the court of law.

The majority of divorces in Mamluk society were neither unilateral repudiations nor judicial dissolutions, but consensual separations (*khulʿ*) in which wives gave up their rights to some, or all, of their financial rights in return for a divorce. The legal wording of a consensual divorce deed makes it apparent that these settlements were always initiated by the wife, who would ask her husband for a divorce in return for monetary compensation. But the formalities of divorce deeds concealed a complex interplay of various legal and extralegal pressures. On the one hand, husbands did have substantial leverage power in divorce negotiations, and were often able to impose a favorable settlement. On the other hand, divorce was rarely a one-sided affair. Some women (or their families) manipulated patriarchal ideals in order to initiate divorce, or used their financial leverage power in order to force a husband to grant them a divorce. In most accounts of individual cases divorce appears as a balanced affair, in which women very often had their say.

## The threat of repudiation

How often did Mamluk husbands use the privilege of unilateral repudiation? Some did so with impunity. Sultans repudiated their wives as a matter of course; in 777/1375 al-Ashraf Shaʿbān had all of his three wives divorced simultaneously.[1] A repudiation sometimes followed a change in the political circumstances that had brought about the marriage alliance in the first place. Al-Ẓāhir Baybars divorced his Kurdish wife after his alliance with Kurdish garrisons in Gaza came to an end.[2] Al-Naṣir Muḥammad divorced the daughter of Özbeg Khan, ruler of the Golden Horde, also for political reasons.[3] Repudiations were found among non-royalty as well. In 698/1299, the fifteen-year-old Taqī al-Dīn al-Subkī was married off to his paternal cousin on condition that she would not distract him from his studies. When she began pressing him for small gifts, he was told to repudiate her.[4] But throwing away one's wife for no good reason was not considered proper behavior. When the Ayyubid governor of Hama repudiated his wife and maternal cousin in 691/1292, the divorce was greeted with popular rebuke; thus, when a unilateral repudiation was perceived as arbitrary, it was condemned.[5] Similarly, al-Jazarī accused a notary by the name of Shams al-Dīn al-Anṣārī (d. 728/1328) of maltreating his wife by repeatedly divorcing her.[6]

In spite of the simplicity of the legal act of repudiation, arbitrary and unequivocally unilateral repudiations were not as common as one might expect. Most husbands were deterred, first and foremost, by the financial costs of divorce. Upon unilateral repudiation husbands were expected to pay up all their remaining financial obligations, including the late and due portions of the marriage gift, any arrears in payments of support and clothing, and other debts they may have incurred during the marriage. Divorced wives could also appeal to Ḥanafī *qāḍī*s, who upheld divorcées' claims to support and lodging during the waiting period (although husbands were equally entitled to register the divorce with a *qāḍī* from a different

1 Al-Maqrīzī, *Sulūk*, vol. III, 256.
2 Al-Nuwayri, *Nihāyat al-Arab*, vol. XXX, 367; al-Maqrīzī, *Sulūk*, vol. I, 640.
3 See Holt, "An-Nāṣir Muḥammad," 315–16. For the breakdown of an early thirteenth-century Ayyubid marriage alliance see Quṭb al-Dīn al-Yūnīnī, *Dhayl Mir'āt al-Zamān*, 2 vols. (Hyderabad: Dār al-Maʿārif, 1954–55), vol. I, 130; al-Maqrīzī, *Sulūk*, vol. I, 255.
4 Al-Subkī, *Ṭabaqāt*, vol. VI, 149.
5 The princess died shortly after her divorce (al-Nuwayri, *Nihāyat al-Arab*, vol. XXXI, 244; Muḥammad b. Ibrāhīm al-Jazarī, *La chronique de Damas d'al-Jazari, années 689–698 H.*, ed. J. Sauvaget [Paris: Librairie ancienne H. Champion, 1949], 21).
6 Al-Jazarī, *Ta'rīkh*, vol. II, 306.

school).[7] On top of these payments, husbands were also required to pay compensation (*mutʿa*) to their former wives. This was an obligatory payment, out of use in the classical period but actively revived by Mamluk jurists.[8] The payment, canonically set at 30 silver dirhams, was not always enforced.[9] The divorcée had a right to this compensation as long as she did not forfeit it in her divorce settlement, and when the divorce was not her fault.[10]

Rather than being a major factor in divorce, repudiation was more often used as a threat against a disobedient wife. Husbands threatened their wives with repudiation in response to any breach of their authority, even petty ones. Islamic Sunni law accords special status to threats of repudiation, which are usually called divorce oaths. These oaths are considered conditional phrases, the act of divorce being contingent on the fulfillment of the condition. Many husbands later regretted the use of such an oath, especially when the cause of conflict with their wives was trivial, and then asked a *muftī* for a way of circumventing the oath. Much can be learnt about the workings of day-to-day domestic life from *fatwā*s dealing with the validity of these divorces. A husband would threaten his wife with divorce in order to deter her from visiting a neighbor, from hosting a female friend, or from divulging a family secret.[11] Strained relations with the mother-in-law were also a common reason for pronouncing divorce oaths.[12] A husband who suspected his wife of pilfering his money threatened her with divorce if the money was not returned.[13] After another husband threatened to divorce his wife if she accepted a visit from her son from a previous marriage, the woman decided to prefer her son to her husband.[14]

The threat of repudiation was frequently evoked when the husband's honor was at stake. It was unacceptable to lock up a wife at home, although some tried.[15] But

7 According to Ḥanafī doctrine, every divorcée can claim marital support and lodging during the waiting period, while the Shāfiʿīs limit this right to pregnant divorcées (al-Ṭarsūsī, *Anfaʿ al-Wasāʾil*, 42–49; al-Subkī, *Fatāwā*, vol. II, 314–20). Appointment decrees specifically call on Ḥanafī *qāḍī*s to grant marital support to women during their waiting period (see Ibn Faḍl Allāh al-ʿUmarī, *al-Taʿrīf bi'l-Muṣṭalaḥ al-Sharīf* [Cairo, 1312/1894], 119–20; al-Qalqalshandī, *Ṣubḥ al-Aʿshā*, vol. XI, 95, 200). Ibn Qayyim al-Jawziyya offers his male readers several ways of circumventing payment of support during the waiting period, and notes that the husband must act swiftly, before the woman goes to a Ḥanafī judge (*Iʿlām al-Muwaqqiʿīn*, vol. III, 318, 378, vol. IV, 44).

8 On *mutʿa* payments in classical Islamic law, see Rapoport, "Matrimonial Gifts," 16–21.

9 Al-Nawawī, *Fatāwā*, no. 232. See also Ibn Taymiyya, *Majmūʿ Fatāwā*, vol. XXXII, 26, 341; al-Subkī, *Ṭabaqāt*, vol. VI, 185.

10 Al-ʿUthmānī, "Kifāyat al-Muftiyyīn," fol. 39a; al-Anṣārī, *Iʿlām*, 227; Chester Beatty MS 4665, fol. 41a; al-Jarāwānī, "Mawāhib," fol. 83a. For an actual case of payment, see Ḥaram document no. 653 recto (published in al-ʿAsalī, *Wathāʾiq*, vol. II, 19 [no. 1]).

11 Ibn Taymiyya, *Fatāwā al-Nisāʾ*, 253, 255; Ibn Taymiyya, *Majmūʿ Fatāwā*, vol. XXXIII, 162, 226–27.

12 Al-Nawawī, *Fatāwā*, 140; Ibn Taymiyya, *Majmūʿ Fatāwā*, vol. XXXIII, 112, 164–68.

13 Ibn Taymiyya, *Fatāwā al-Nisāʾ*, 253; Ibn Taymiyya, *Majmūʿ Fatāwā*, vol. XXXIII, 163, 229; al-Subkī, *Fatāwā*, 311.

14 Ibn Taymiyya, *Majmūʿ Fatāwā*, vol. XXXII, 287. In another case, a man threatened to divorce his wife if she bore him a daughter (*ibid.*, vol. XXXIII, 164).

15 In a question put to Ibn al-Ṣalāḥ, a man locked the doors of the house on his wife, contrary to the customary practice (*muʿtād*). The jurist allowed the man to do so if he had a specific cause for alarm, but prohibited him from blocking the windows (*sadd al-kuwwāt*) (*Fatāwā*, 453 [no. 415]).

a man could pronounce a conditional repudiation that would take effect were his wife to leave the conjugal home without permission. Judging by the number of references in the legal literature, this seems to have been a very common scenario.[16] Such behavior by husbands was not just a matter of individual choice, a private issue between a man and his wife. Society expected men to supervise the womenfolk of their household, and neglect of this duty could affect their social standing. Contemporary moralistic literature urged husbands to demonstrate appropriate manly jealousy. When married women danced unveiled at wedding ceremonies, mingled with men at mystical gatherings or rode behind the donkey-driver, it was their husbands who were held responsible.[17] As Ibn Taymiyya points out, the most demeaning curse is "husband of a bitch" (*zawj al-qaḥba*).[18] A cuckold – that is, any man who was careless about his wife's sexual behavior – was not to be allowed to marry into respectable families.[19]

The legal form of the majority of divorces in Mamluk society was consensual separation (*khulʿ*), although the formalities of divorce deeds concealed an interplay of various legal and extralegal pressures. In consensual separations the wife gave up her financial rights, and in particular her claim to the late marriage gift, in return for a divorce.[20] These settlements were so common as to be considered the standard form of divorce. Notaries assumed that couples coming to record a divorce had already agreed on a consensual separation.[21] According to the legal phrasing, women were always the initiators of consensual divorces; they would ask for the divorce and give up their financial rights in return. But jurists sometimes expressed concern as to whether women who entered divorce settlements were acting voluntarily.[22] Husbands had an obvious interest in coercing their wives into accepting a settlement. One woman appeared in the court of Taqī al-Dīn al-Subkī in Damascus and claimed that she had been coerced into a divorce settlement. Al-Subkī ruled that the circumstantial evidence supported her version of the events.[23]

16 Al-Nawawī, *Fatāwā*, 443 (no. 395); Ibn Taymiyya, *Fatāwā al-Nisāʾ*, 253, 256; Ibn Taymiyya, *Majmūʿ Fatāwā*, vol. XXXIII, 163, 229, 231.

17 Ibn Baydakin, *Kitāb al-Lumaʿ*, 170–73, 442; Ibn al-Ḥājj, *Madkhal*, vol. I, 266–69; Lutfi, "Manners," 115.

18 Interestingly, Ibn Taymiyya says that a fornicator is usually held in greater respect than a cuckold (*Majmūʿ Fatāwā*, vol. XXXII, 118).

19 Ibn Taymiyya, *Majmūʿ Fatāwā*, vol. XXXII, 143. See also al-Anṣārī, *Iʿlām*, 220.

20 Ḥaram documents nos. 44, 302, 646. There are two more records of *khulʿ* divorces, but in both cases the couple remarried shortly afterwards (ʿAbd al-Rāziq, "ʿAqdā Nikāḥ"; Ḥaram document no. 47). These were fictitious consensual divorces, known as *khulʿ al-yamīn*, intended to allow the man to violate an oath on pain of triple repudiation (see below, chapter 5).

21 Ibn Ṣalāḥ, *Fatāwā*, 439 (no. 390); Ibn Taymiyya, *Majmūʿ Fatāwā*, vol. XXXII, 288. In both cases couples came to register a unilateral repudiation, but the notaries, apparently out of habit, told them to pronounce the *khulʿ* formula.

22 Ibn Taymiyya, *Majmūʿ Fatāwā*, vol. XXXII, 355, 358–61 (in both cases, the bride was coerced by her father). In another case, the wife claimed that she was under interdiction and not authorized to make financial contracts, evidently as an excuse to invalidate the *khulʿ* settlement (*ibid.*, vol. XXXII, 285).

23 Al-Subkī, *Fatāwā*, vol. II, 297. In a similar case from twelfth-century Lisbon, an abused wife was able to provide evidence that she had been forcibly coerced into a settlement (Powers, "Women and Divorce," 31–35).

In a case put to Ibn Taymiyya, a husband suspected his wife of adultery after she failed to appear at a wedding she was supposed to attend. When the woman fled to the house of her maternal aunt, her husband then turned to her male relatives and demanded a divorce settlement absolving him of his financial obligations.[24]

Husbands could extract favorable divorce settlements by playing the custody card. In Islamic law divorced mothers lose their right of custody over minor children as soon as they remarry. They could also lose custody if the father wanted to take the child to another locality,[25] to provide him or her with better education or living standards,[26] or if the father could demonstrate neglect on the part of the mother.[27] Divorcées could secure custody only by accepting divorce settlements in which they undertook to pay for the upkeep of the child. A common divorce settlement allowed the mother to have custody for a fixed period of time (regardless of subsequent changes in her marital status) and, in return, not only to give up her financial rights, but also to pay part of the child support during that period.[28] In a case put before Ibn Taymiyya, a divorce settlement set the daily child support due from the father at about one-sixth of a dirham, a fraction of what would have been granted by a *qāḍī*. In return, the father allowed the mother to have custody of the child for two years.[29]

Wives too had their ways of provoking their husbands to grant them a divorce. Ibn Taymiyya discussed at length the variety of means employed by wives who wanted their husbands to divorce them, arguing that women can "pursue actions that will lead to separation in a manner that is usually effective." A wife could demand the full payment of the late marriage gift or the payment of her marital support in cash, and so bring about her husband's arrest. But she could also refuse sex, or stop doing housework, such as cooking, cleaning or washing. Women who used foul language or left home without permission might also be trying to provoke their husbands to divorce them.[30] Yet the informal means at wives' disposal should

24 Ibn Taymiyya, *Majmūʿ Fatāwā*, vol. XXXII, 283–84. See also *ibid.*, 141.

25 Ibn al-Ṣalāḥ, *Fatāwā*, 462–63 (no. 429); Ibn al-Qayyim, *Iʿlām al-Muwaqqiʿīn*, vol. III, 295. See also detailed accounts of custody cases put before the thirteenth-century Syrian jurist al-Fazārī. Contrary to the majority of contemporary jurists, al-Fazārī argued that the interests of the child's education and safety override the father's right to relocate the child (al-Fazārī, "Fatāwā," fols. 98a, 99b–101b).

26 Ibn Taymiyya, *Fatāwā al-Nisāʾ*, 289 (a merchant takes his child on a business trip to the Red Sea); Ibn al-Ṣalāḥ, *Fatāwā*, 463 (no. 431) (a father takes his child from the village to the city because of the better quality of education in the city).

27 In order to demonstrate neglect, neighbors were asked to testify that they had heard the baby crying when left alone in the house (al-Jarawānī, "Mawāhib," fol. 108b; al-Asyūṭī, *Jawāhir al-ʿUqūd*, vol. II, 239–40).

28 Al-Fazārī, "Fatāwā," fol. 93b (wife agrees to support the child for two years); al-Ṭarsūsī, *Anfaʿ al-Wasāʾil*, 44, 47 (in return for custody rights, a wife forfeits her *ṣadāq*, support during the waiting period and child support for seven years). For model documents, see al-Asyūṭī, *Jawāhir al-ʿUqūd*, vol. II, 228, 240–41, 247–48; al-Jarawānī, "Mawāhib," fol. 139b.

29 Ibn Taymiyya, *Majmūʿ Fatāwā*, vol. XXXII, 353–54. See also Ibn Taymiyya, *Fatāwā al-Nisāʾ*, 288–89. For a sixteenth-century treatise on custody settlements, see Sherman Jackson, "Kramer Versus Kramer in a Tenth/Sixteenth Century Egyptian Court: Post-Formative Jurisprudence between Exigency and Law," *ILS* 8 (2001), 27–51.

30 Ibn Taymiyya, *Iqāmat al-Dalīl fī Ibṭāl al-Taḥlīl*, published in the third volume *Majmūʿat Fatāwā Shaykh al-Islīm Taqī al-Dīn Ibn Taymiyya*, 5 vols. (Cairo: Maṭbaʿat Kurdistān, 1326–29/1908–11), 246, 261–64.

not obscure the overall legal framework in which they were embedded, a legal framework which drew a link between divorce and patriarchy. Unlike men, wives who wanted a divorce had either to pay for it or go to court.

## Divorce and the Islamic courts

As the weaker party, it was women who needed the assistance of the courts, and it is not surprising that appeals to the *qāḍī*s were made by wives rather than by husbands. Wives came to the courts to demand payments due to them, the fulfillment of favorable clauses inserted in their marriage contracts and the upholding of their rights within marriage. Mamluk jurists made important amendments to the Sunni law of marriage and divorce, mostly in order to protect wives from abuse by their husbands. They allowed wives to remain in their hometowns against their husbands' wishes, secured wives a compensation payment in cases of unilateral repudiation, and censured what they considered excessive wife-beating. But, all in all, the protection *qāḍī*s offered was limited. They rarely granted a judicial divorce against the wish of the husband, and were either incapable or unwilling to impinge too much on the patriarchal powers of the head of the household. As a result, most divorce negotiations were informal, and the role of the courts was mainly confined to putting an official stamp on the settlements brought before them.

A wife who wanted to secure her rights in marriage could insert clauses in the marriage contract that allowed her to opt for a divorce under certain conditions, most commonly if her husband took another wife or a concubine. Stipulations in the wife's favor have been added to Muslim marriage contracts since the early Islamic period, and are found in several eighth- and ninth-century marriage contracts from Egyptian provincial towns, as well in Jewish marriage contracts from the Geniza.[31] By the Mamluk period one finds a variety of clauses. One bride's family required the husband to promise, under pain of divorce, not to drink wine. Another family made the husband promise to postpone the consummation of his marriage with their minor daughter, and to allow the girl to live with her natal family. Husbands often committed to lodge and maintain their wives' children from previous marriages.[32]

[31] The most famous cases are of Umm Mūsā, wife of the Abbasid caliph al-Manṣūr, and Umm Salama, wife of al-ʿAbbās (See L. Ahmed, *Women and Gender in Islam: Historical Roots of a Modern Debate* [New Haven: Yale University Press, 1992], 77; N. Abbott, *Two Queens of Baghdad: Mother and Wife of Harun al-Rashid* [Chicago: University of Chicago Press, 1946], 15). For clauses in early Islamic marriage contracts, see A. Grohmann, *Arabic Papyri in the Egyptian Library*, 6 vols. (Cairo: Egyptian Library Press, 1934–62), vol. I, nos. 38, 39, 41; A. Grohmann, "Arabische Papyri aus den Staatlische Museen zu Berlin," *Der Islam* 22 (1935), 1–68, no. 8. For the Geniza, see M. A. Friedman, *Ribūi Nashīm be-Yisrael: Mekōrōt Ḥadashīm mi-Genīzat Kahīr* (Jerusalem: Mosad Byalik, 1986), 34–41; Goitein, *A Mediterranean Society*, vol. III, 147–50.

[32] The most comprehensive discussion is by Ibn Taymiyya, *Majmūʿ Fatāwā*, vol. XXXII, 164–70. See also Ibn al-Ṣalāḥ, *Fatāwā*, 684 (no. 1032); Ibn al-Qayyim, *Iʿlām al-Muwaqqiʿīn*, vol. III, 384. Ibn Taymiyya referred his readers to the "old Maghrebi marriage contracts," where these stipulations were to be found (Ibn Taymiyya, *Majmūʿ Fatāwā*, vol. XXXIII, 164–65). It is interesting to note that in the Geniza the stipulation against polygamy was known as the "Qayrawanese," i.e., the North African, condition (Goitein, *A Mediterranean Society*, vol. III, 149).

The Damascene notary Ibn Ṭawq records in his diary a few marriage contracts that included such stipulations, and these appear to be always associated with polygamous marriages. When Badr al-Dīn Ibn al-Yāsūfī married the daughter of a certain Ibn Nabhān as a second wife in Dhū al-Ḥijja 886/February 1482, he promised to divorce his first wife and to reside in the house of his new wife. But since he was unable to divorce his first wife, the marriage was dissolved the next day. Eventually, the couple married again eleven days later, with the bride consenting to a polygamous arrangement. This time Ibn al-Yāsūfī promised, in the presence of the bride's father, not to marry a third wife and not to lodge the two wives in the same house.[33] When ʿĀ'isha bt. Ibn al-Ḥawrānī suspected her husband Shihāb al-Dīn al-Raqqāwī of taking a concubine while on a trip to Cairo, he swore on divorce that since their marriage he had not had sexual relations with any slave-girl, apart from the one already in their house. Two years later, before going on another trip, al-Raqqāwī pledged again that were he to marry another wife or take a concubine, his wife was free to divorce him, provided that she was ready to give up the remainder of her marriage gift.[34] These pledges were common enough to be included in a notary's manual. Al-Asyūṭī provides a model document for an oath on pain of divorce taken by the husband. In the model, the husband takes it upon himself not to marry a second wife, not to take a concubine, and not to desert his wife.[35]

Mamluk judicial practice granted wives the right to remain in their hometowns, even against the wish of their husbands. A bride could insert a stipulation in the marriage contract that would allow her to remain in her hometown, and such a clause was common in the Geniza and in the early Islamic period.[36] Appointment decrees for Ḥanbalī *qāḍī*s singled out this clause as one of the beneficial aspects of Ḥanbalī law.[37] But these clauses became superfluous and out of use by the Mamluk period, as Ḥanafī and Shāfiʿī *qāḍī*s extended this right to all wives. According to the Ḥanafī jurist al-Ṭarsūsī, the dominant opinion and the practice of Ḥanafī judges was to give wives the right to remain in their hometowns, even though the founders of the school held a different position.[38] He also produces a model document, to

33 Ibn Ṭawq, *Taʿlīq*, 114, 121. 34 *Ibid.*, 198, 402.

35 Al-Asyūṭī, *Jawāhir al-ʿUqūd*, vol. II, 148. For husbands swearing not to take another wife, see also al-Anṣārī, *Iʿlām*, 244; Ibn Taymiyya, *Majmūʿ Fatāwā*, vol. XXXIII, 236. For the delegation of the power of divorce to the wife (*tawkīl* or *tamlīk*), see Ibn Taymiyya, *Majmūʿ Fatāwā*, vol. XXXIII, 119, 164, 168; Ibn al-Qayyim, *Iʿlām al-Muwaqqiʿīn*, vol. III, 343, 384.

36 For the Geniza, see Goitein, *A Mediterranean Society*, vol. III, 150–53, 177–79. For the early Islamic period, see Rapoport, "Matrimonial Gifts," 13.

37 Al-Qalqashandī, *Ṣubḥ al-Aʿshā*, vol. XII, 57; al-Ṣafadī, *Aʿyān*, vol. III, 1285–86. Ḥanbalī *qāḍī*s were expected to protect wives from this abuse (al-ʿUmarī, *Taʿrīf*, 122–23; al-Qalqashandī, *Ṣubḥ al-Aʿshā*, vol. XI, 95, 203). Ibn Qayyim al-Jawziyya regarded the condition allowing a wife to remain in her hometown as just and fair, since "no woman is willing to give away her vagina to a husband without it" (*Iʿlām al-Muwaqqiʿīn*, vol. III, 343).

38 The change in doctrine is attributed to Abū al-Qāsim al-Ṣaffār al-Balkhī (d. 319/931), who argued that a woman needs the protection of her own family because of the corruption of society (*fasād al-zamān*). Al-Ṭarsūsī complained that in his day wives even refused to move to a nearby neighborhood or village (*Anfaʿ al-Wasāʾil*, 40–42). For similar presentations of Ḥanafī doctrine in the fourteenth and fifteenth centuries, see al-ʿUthmānī, *Raḥmat al-Umma fī Ikhtilāf al-Aʾimmah*, ed. ʿAlī al-Sharbajī and Qāsim al-Nūrī (Beirut: Muʾassasat al-Risāla, 1994), 403; Qāriʾ al-Hidāya, "al-Fatāwā al-Sirājiyya," fols. 29b, 40b.

be issued by a Ḥanafī judge, which prohibits a husband from relocating his wife against her will.[39] Shāfiʿī doctrine achieved the same result in an indirect way. A woman who refused to travel with her husband could acknowledge a fictitious debt to a family relative, who in turn would then ask a Shāfiʿī judge to prevent the debtor – that is, the woman – from leaving the city.[40]

Clauses against wife-beating are relatively rare, perhaps as a result of attempts by the courts to curb the phenomenon. There is only one mention of a wife who demanded that her husband promise under oath of divorce not to beat her.[41] Some jurists advised husbands to beat their wives as a punishment for disobedience – especially for refusing to have sexual relations, but also for running away from home or swearing.[42] But the references to actual beatings are few. It may be that such cases reached public attention only when men used excessive force against child brides.[43] However, it also seems that *qāḍīs* actively attempted to limit the prevalence of domestic violence. Taqī al-Dīn al-Subkī limited wife-beating to cases of persistent disobedience. He ruled that it was not permitted to beat a wife who had merely refused to have sex or had left the house without permission, unless this had become a pattern.[44] In a model document included in a fourteenth-century legal manual, a dying woman testifies that her illness is the result of intentional beating and strangling by her husband and that were she to die from this illness her husband should be charged with her murder.[45]

Judicial divorce (*faskh*), the most drastic sanction a wife could hope for from the courts, was generally reserved for grass widows. Wives could appeal to a Ḥanbalī or Mālikī *qāḍī* for a judicial divorce on the grounds of abandonment. The wife was required to testify that her husband had been absent for at least six months, that he had left her no support, and that he had no property from which support payments could be derived.[46] Appointment decrees instructed Ḥanbalī *qāḍīs* to

39 Guellil, *Damaszener Akten*, 182 (no. 78). See also al-Jarawānī, "Mawāhib," fol. 139b.

40 For several thirteenth-century cases involving this legal subterfuge, see Ibn al-Ṣalāḥ, *Fatāwā*, 452 (no. 415), 455 (no. 419); al-Nawawī, *Fatāwā*, no. 267; al-Fazārī, "Fatāwā," fols. 21a, 90a. The Shāfiʿī jurists cited in these sources had conflicting opinions about the validity of the subterfuge.

41 Ibn al-Ṣalāḥ, *Fatāwā*, 658 (no. 945).

42 For Ḥanafīs, see al-Sarūjī, *Kitāb Adab al-Qaḍāʾ*, 223. For Shāfiʿīs, see Ibn ʿAbd al-Salām, "al-Qawāʿid al-Kubrā," fol. 116; Ibn al-Ṣalāḥ, *Fatāwā*, 432 (no. 376). Ibn Taymiyya also allowed beating after an act of gross immoral conduct, in order to force the wife into a *khulʿ* settlement (*Majmūʿ Fatāwā*, vol. XXXII, 274, 278–80, 283–84).

43 For physical abuse and rape of a ten-year-old bride, see Ibn Taymiyya, *Majmūʿ Fatāwā*, vol. XXXII, 167. On the limited extent of wife-beating in the Geniza see Goitein, *A Mediterranean Society*, vol. III, 184–89.

44 Al-Subkī, *Ṭabaqāt*, vol. VI, 193–95. A similar position is taken by al-ʿUthmānī, "Kifāyat al-Muftiyyīn," fol. 40a and al-Asyūṭī, *Jawāhir al-ʿUqūd*, vol. II, 50; but see also Chester Beatty MS 4665, fol. 33a.

45 Text: "*inna sabab maraḍihā min ḍarb zawjihā fulān. . . .wa-annahu ʿamada ilayhā wa-ḍarabahā wa-ḥanaqahā ḥattā balagha minhā al-juhd*" (Guellil, *Damaszener Akten*, no. 97).

46 The court had discretion with regard to the minimal period of absence required before granting a judicial divorce, and the wife was also required to testify that she had been obedient to her husband (see the model documents in al-Asyūṭī, *Jawāhir al-ʿUqūd*, vol. II, 123–25; al-Jarawānī, "Mawāhib," fol. 78b). The legal reason for a judicial divorce was the lack of marital support, not the wife's right

grant judicial divorces to abandoned women.[47] In the fifteenth century even Shāfiʿī *qāḍī*s, who had previously been bound by stringent rules of evidence, started to grant judicial divorces.[48] The courts also granted a judicial divorce when a husband refrained from consummating a marriage, thus withholding marital support from his prospective bride.[49] When an absentee husband left behind property, the court allowed the wife to use it for her support. In 797/1395, the wife of a certain Mūsā al-Qudsī appealed to the Shāfiʿī *qāḍī* in Jerusalem and testified that her husband had been in Yemen for the last thirteen years. During this period he did not send her anything for herself or for their two children, a boy and a girl. The court ruled that the woman was entitled to 13,000 silver dirhams (about 500 dinars) as due support for the entire period, and gave permission to sell the husband's property.[50]

Most cases of absentee husbands were settled without recourse to such judicial intervention, since husbands often deposited conditional bills of divorce with their wives before going on a journey. Conditional bills of divorce appear very often in the Geniza,[51] and were widely used among the Muslim majority. In such a bill, the husband made the divorce of his wife contingent on his absence for a certain period of time. If the husband did not return, the wife had the right to confirm the divorce in court.[52] Traveling husbands allowed their wives to choose whether to divorce or not, sometimes adding a condition that the divorce should only take effect if the wife would forfeit the remainder of her marriage gift.[53] It should be emphasized that the *qāḍī*s were usually a last resort, even for abandoned women. An abandoned wife would generally try to remarry quickly, even without going through the formality

to sexual intercourse – as is well illustrated in a case of abandonment from the medieval Maghrib studied by David Powers (Powers, "Women and Courts").

47 See an appointment decree issued in favor of the Ḥanbalī *qāḍī* in Damascus, ʿAlī b. Munajjā ʿAlāʾ al-Dīn al-Tanūkhī, in 732/1332 (al-Qalqashandī, *Ṣubḥ al-Aʿshā*, vol. XII, 57; al-Ṣafadī, *Aʿyān*, vol. III, 1285–86). See also similar appointment decrees in al-ʿUmarī, *Taʿrīf*, 122–23; al-Qalqashandī, *Ṣubḥ al-Aʿshā*, vol. XI, 95, 203.

48 Al-Suyūṭī, *Ḥāwī*, vol. I, 298 (a Shāfiʿī *qāḍī* grants judicial divorce after a year of absence); al-Anṣārī, *Iʿlām*, 268 (following a judicial divorce by a Shāfiʿī, the court discovers that the former husband owns property and allows the woman to claim it). For Ḥanafī doctrine, see Qāriʾ al-Hidāya, "al-Fatāwā al-Sirājiyya," fols. 14b–15a, 43a (case of a judicial divorce after an absence of fifteen years).

49 Al-Asyūṭī, *Jawāhir al-ʿUqūd*, vol. II, 125. See also al-ʿUthmānī, "*Kifāyat al-Muftiyyīn*," fol. 50b. For a concrete example, see Ḥaram document no. 609 (published in al-ʿAṣalī, *Wathāʾiq*, vol. II, 51 [no. 12]).

50 Ḥaram document no. 215. I was unable to decipher the woman's name. For a model document of this type of claim, see al-Ghazzī, "Adab al-Qaḍāʾ," fol. 84b.

51 Goitein, *A Mediterranean Society*, vol. III, 155, 189–205.

52 Ibn al-Ṣalāḥ, *Fatāwā*, 444 (no. 398), 450 (no. 411). In cases from the fifteenth century, the conditional divorce was to come into effect after a very short absence of two months or even ten days (al-Anṣārī, *Iʿlām*, 267; al-Suyūṭī, *Ḥāwī*, vol. I, 267). See also examples of conditional bills of divorce, and wives' strategic manipulation of these bills, from the medieval Maghrib (Powers, "Women and Divorce," 39–42; Powers, "Women and Courts").

53 Ibn Taymiyya, *Majmūʿ Fatāwā*, vol. XXXIII, 120; Qāriʾ al-Hidāya, "al-Fatāwā al-Sirājiyya," fol. 22b. See model documents for conditional bills of divorce in al-Jarawānī, "Mawāhib," fols. 92b–93a; al-Asyūṭī, *Jawāhir al-ʿUqūd*, vol. II, 147–49. For a conditional bill of divorce that takes effect after one month's absence and forfeiture of the *ṣadāq*, see al-Anṣārī, *Iʿlām*, 234, 267.

of terminating the first marriage. In a case put to Ibn Taymiyya, we hear about a wife who was left with no support for a year and "almost died of hunger." She eventually remarried, only to have this second marriage annulled on the grounds of her bigamy. The second husband continued to support the woman and their child.[54]

All divorcing couples came before the courts, or at least before notaries, but most did so only in order to register their divorces. Registration was necessary for future marriages as well as for confirming the financial settlements made by the couple.[55] At least until the end of the fourteenth century, court officials rarely had any say in the particulars of divorce settlements. Most often they saw themselves as an additional layer of mediators. There are plenty of stories about judges and notaries trying to reconcile couples just before writing the divorce deed. In one such anecdote the court officials tried unsuccessfully to talk a resolute wife back into the marriage.[56] A *qāḍī* would warn the wife against changing her husbands too frequently. When couples came before Ibn Qāḍī al-Ḥimāra (d. 788/1386), a Ḥanbalī judge in Damascus, he used to go to the lavatory and break his basin, and then come out showing great distress. When asked for the reason, he would explain that he was used to the old basin watching his private parts, and was ashamed to introduce them to a new basin. Supposedly, the lesson was not lost on any wife wishing to separate from her longtime husband.[57]

Prior to the fifteenth century, most domestic difficulties were solved through informal mediation rather than by formal litigation. Husbands who suspected their wives approached their in-laws; wives often preferred to appeal to neighbors and kin.[58] A couple could get marriage counseling from Sufi shaykhs, who were able to look into their followers' hearts. One shaykh, who realized that his disciple was distressed by a quarrel with his wife, told the man to go home, kiss her on the forehead and make peace.[59] The virtuous could expect the intervention of even higher authorities. After a saint by the name of Abū al-Faḍl al-Jawharī had a long fight with his wife, the Prophet came to each of them in their dreams and advised them to patch up their differences.[60] In 781/1379, a maltreated Cairene wife hid herself behind a wall and, speaking in the voice of a demon (*jinn*), warned her abusive husband of the punishments awaiting him in the afterlife.[61] It seems that the supernatural forces sometimes needed a bit of earthly assistance.

[54] Ibn Taymiyya, *Majmūʿ Fatāwā*, vol. XXXIV, 91–92. In a similar case, a woman married a second husband after her first husband went missing for six years (*ibid.*, vol. XXXII, 200).
[55] Ibn al-Ṣalāḥ, *Fatāwā*, 439 (no. 390); Ibn Taymiyya, *Majmūʿ Fatāwā*, vol. XXXII, 288.
[56] Al-Udfūwī, *al-Ṭāliʿ al-Saʿīd*, 542 (cited by several later authors, starting with al-Ṣafadī, *Aʿyān*, vol. IV, 547).
[57] Ibn al-Mibrad, *al-Jawhar al-Munaḍḍad*, 142. Ibn Baṭṭūṭa tells an anecdote about a judge from Mardin who preferred to reconcile a couple rather than separate them, in spite of the husband's repeated abuse (Ibn Baṭṭūṭa, *Riḥla*, vol. II, 87; Ibn Baṭṭūta, *Travels*, vol. II, 354).
[58] Ibn Taymiyya, *Majmūʿ Fatāwā*, vol. XXXII, 56–57.
[59] Al-Udfūwī, *al-Ṭāliʿ al-Saʿīd*, 396–97.
[60] Taylor, *In the Vicinity of the Righteous*, 163.
[61] Al-Maqrīzī, *Sulūk*, vol. III, 361–64.

## Divorce and the military courts

The timid attitude of the courts to the domestic sphere became much more assertive during the fifteenth century, mainly as a result of the expanding jurisdiction of the *maẓālim* courts headed by government officials. According to the traditional judicial organization in medieval Islam, the jurisdiction of the *maẓālim* courts was largely limited to administrative matters and to litigation involving the military, while most other matters, including matrimonial law, were under the exclusive jurisdiction of the *qāḍīs*. During the fifteenth century, however, the *maẓālim* courts headed by officers such as the chamberlain and the *dawādār* acquired a jurisdiction concurrent with that of the religious courts. As al-Maqrīzī notes, in his days the chamberlain was competent in all matters of commercial and matrimonial law, and attracted litigants from all walks of life, poor and rich, humble and noble.[62] The gates to the courts of the chamberlain and the *dawādār* were guarded by *naqībs* – formerly military policemen, but now effectively a regular police force, which was often called to intervene in domestic disputes.[63] Blamed by pious scholars for substituting God's law with man-made justice,[64] the courts of the military officials were in fact committed to implementing Islamic law. The sole exception was that the *maẓālim* courts were not bound by the same laws of procedure, and therefore more inclined to bypass legal niceties and complex rules of evidence – a method many found merely commonsensical.

The difference of approach between the religious and the military courts is well illustrated in a tragic case of child marriage, for which we have a firsthand testimony of a legal official. In 875/1470 the chronicler Ibn al-Ṣayrafī, who was employed as a deputy Ḥanafī *qāḍī*, received a petition from the maternal aunt of a twelve-year-old girl, whose parents were absent from the city. The aunt asked that the Ḥanafī deputy would save the girl from poverty by marrying her off to a suitable husband. In accordance with the request, Ibn al-Ṣayrafī married the girl to a soldier in the service of one of the royal *mamlūks*, negotiating a marriage gift of 7 gold dinars, and inserting a clause forbidding the man to consummate the marriage until the girl attained puberty. Despite this stipulation, the soldier raped the girl. He continued to beat her until she accepted a consensual divorce in which she forfeited her marriage gift. The husband even lodged a complaint against the girl with the

62 Al-Maqrīzī, *Khiṭaṭ*, vol. III, 80. These developments are summarized in E. Tyan, *Histoire de l'organisation judiciare en pays d'Islam*, 2nd edn. (Leiden: E. J. Brill, 1960), 490–92, 539–45. See also J. Nielsen, *Secular Justice in an Islamic State: Maẓālim under the Baḥrī Mamlūks, 662/1264–789/1387* (Leiden: Brill, 1985).

63 On the change in the role of the *naqībs*, see W. Popper, *Egypt and Syria under the Circassian Sultans 1382–1468 AD: Systematic Notes to Ibn Taghrî Birdî's Chronicles of Egypt* (Berkeley: University of California Press, 1956), 94; D. Ayalon, "Studies on the Structure of the Mamluk Army – III," *BSOAS* 16 (1954), 64.

64 Al-Maqrīzī, *Khiṭaṭ*, vol. III, 80, 88. For criticisms of the *siyāsa* administered in these courts, see also the sources cited in T. Khalidi, *Arabic Historical Thought in the Classical Period* (Cambridge: Cambridge University Press, 1994), 195–96.

police (*naqībs*), and she was fined a gold dinar for her supposed insubordination. When the girl returned home, her maternal aunt raised uproar in the neighborhood and appealed to the *dawādār* Yashbak min Mahdī. The *dawādār* found no fault in the deputy *qāḍī* 's conduct, but still ordered the soldier to be flogged, and asked the chief Ḥanafī *qāḍī*, Ibn al-Ṣayrafī's superior, to invalidate the divorce settlement. The soldier also had to pay the girl 4 dinars, about half of the promised marriage gift.[65] It seems that in this case, the more aggressive and interventionist approach of the military court was also the more just.

The military courts were also more resolute when dealing with husbands who failed to provide for their wives, and pushed the religious courts to extend the grounds for judicial divorce. In a case from Jerusalem, a local merchant by the name of Ibrāhīm b. Aḥmad al-ʿAjlūnī (d. 885/1480) failed to consummate his marriage. The bride's family then appealed to the chief military judge, the grand chamberlain Azbak al-Ẓāhirī, who set a deadline for the consummation of the marriage, and threatened to issue a judicial divorce unless the groom complied.[66] In 877/1473 Sitt al-Khulafā', the seventeen-year-old daughter of the caliph al-Mustanjid Yūsuf, appealed for a judicial divorce from her husband, an amir who was sent to Syria before he had a chance to consummate the marriage.[67] Upon the request of her father, the sultan convened a council of the chief *qāḍīs*, who eventually granted a judicial divorce in the following year. The grounds for the divorce were not only the husband's absence, but also the principle of equality in marriage (*kafā'ah*) and the right of minor brides to annul their marriages upon reaching puberty (*khiyār al-bulūgh*). Neither the right of equality in marriage and the right of annulment upon majority had previously been part of the judicial praxis of Mamluk courts, and their application in this case represents an important extension of the grounds for judicial divorce at the wife's initiative.

A more intrusive attitude towards the increasing monetization of marriage is also evident in a case involving two scions of the aristocratic Banū al-Bulqīnī. In 876/1471, Alif bt. ʿAlam al-Dīn al-Bulqīnī, daughter of the former chief Shāfiʿī *qāḍī*, appeared before the sultan and complained about her husband and cousin, Abū al-Saʿādāt al-Bulqīnī. Alif, who was also the supervisor of her family's endowment, claimed that she had given her husband a loan of 250 gold dinars, which he now refused to pay back. The sultan ordered the chief of police (*naqīb al-jaysh*) to send his men to the husband's house and threaten him. The matter was then brought

[65] Ibn al-Ṣayrafī, *Inbā' al-Haṣr*, 226–29. See translation and analysis by C. Petry, "Conjugal Rights Versus Class Prerogatives: A Divorce Case in Mamlūk Cairo," in Hambly (ed.), *Women in the Medieval Islamic World*, 227–40. My interpretation of the text is substantially different from Petry's, both in its details and its overall significance. According to Petry, the case demonstrates the prerogatives of the military elite.

[66] Al-Sakhāwī, *Ḍaw'*, vol. I, 12.

[67] The most detailed version of the case appears in al-Sakhāwī, *Wajīz al-Kalām*, vol. II, 847. See also al-Sakhāwī, *Ḍaw'*, vol. XII, 54–55 (no. 324) (Sitt al-Khulafā'), vol. III, 177 (no. 684) (husband). The case is also mentioned in Ibn Iyās, *Badā'iʿ*, vol. V, 85. The caliph was a descendant of the last Abbasid caliph in Baghdad and the titular head of state, but had no real power in the Mamluk political system.

before another government official, the privy secretary, Ibn al-Muzhir. Only at this stage did Ibn al-Muzhir decide to refer the case to a *qāḍī*, asking him to judge the case in accordance with Islamic law. The couple remained married throughout the litigation. Ibn al-Ṣayrafī concludes: "Behold the humiliation of *qāḍī*s and scholars, watch the cunning of women, and see how wretched and foolish this man is for not daring to repudiate his wife."[68]

Increasing intervention by the courts went both ways – and the most novel aspect of the increasing intervention was the phenomenon of husbands asking the court to discipline their wives. In 876/1471 ʿAbd al-ʿAẓīm Ibn al-Dirham wa'l-Niṣf, a wealthy government official, complained before the *dawādār* that a clerk in the Bureau of Escheats had seduced his wife. Ibn al-Dirham wa'l-Niṣf claimed that his marriage had collapsed as a result of this affair, that he had divorced his wife, and that the woman had now married her lover. The *dawādār* sent his *naqīb*s to bring the accused couple from their home. Following an intercession by the woman's relatives, the *dawādār* ruled that the couple should compensate the cuckolded husband with 1,000 dinars.[69]

By the late fifteenth century husbands came with similar complaints to the religious courts, especially before Mālikī *qāḍī*s. In 874/1469, a blacksmith complained before the Mālikī *qāḍī* that his wife had run away three days before, and asked the court to force her to come back. The woman, who had been hiding in the house of a merchant, made a counter-claim before a Ḥanafī *qāḍī*, who in turn sent for the husband. This domestic quarrel was settled only by a royal council and through the mediation of the sultan's wife.[70] In 876/1471–72, a junior officer complained before a Mālikī *qāḍī* that his wife was having an affair, and demanded financial restitution. This story ended tragically, for when the woman denied the allegations, the husband took out a knife and stabbed her to death in front of the court.[71]

As the military and religious courts strove to uphold patriarchal authority, the value of the threat of repudiation diminished. Husbands continued to threaten their wives with divorce in order to prevent them from leaving the conjugal home without permission, in order to limit their meetings with their families or neighbors, or simply as a disciplinary measure.[72] But the threat of repudiation was no longer as central an aspect of patriarchal authority. In one case a man swore on pain of divorce that if his wife left home without his permission, he would complain about her to the authorities (*siyāsa*) and bring the police to arrest her.[73] Obviously, the

[68] Ibn al-Ṣayrafī, *Inbāʾ al-Haṣr*, 365–66. On Alif and her economic activity as supervisor of the family endowment, see al-Sakhāwī, *Ḍawʾ*, vol. XII, 7.

[69] Ibn al-Ṣayrafī, *Inbāʾ al-Haṣr*, 124. [70] *Ibid.*, 153–56.

[71] Ibn al-Ṣayrafī laments that the murderer walked out undisturbed. See *ibid.*, 379; C. Petry, "'Quis Custodiet Custodes?' Revisited: The Prosecution of Crime in the Late Mamluk Sultanate," *MSR* 3 (1999), 16.

[72] Al-Anṣārī, *Iʿlām*, 235–36, 250, 253, 264; al-Suyūṭī, *Ḥāwī*, vol. I, 264, 266, 270; ʿAlī b. Yūsuf al-Buṣrawī, *Taʾrīkh al-Buṣrawī: Ṣafaḥāt Majhūlah min Taʾrīkh Dimashq fī ʿAṣr al-Mamālīk min Sanat 871 H li-Ghāyat 904 H*, ed. Akram Ḥasan al-ʿUlabī (Damascus: Dār al-Maʾmūn lil-Turāth, 1988), 53–54.

[73] Al-Anṣārī, *Iʿlām*, 246.

oath of divorce was used only to convey the husband's determination to appeal to the state authorities; it was not a threat in its own right. In a similar case, a husband swore on pain of divorce to complain about his wife, and then went out to fetch the local policemen. He was already on his way back home, accompanied by the *naqībs*, when a friend met him on the road and persuaded him to drop the matter and leave the police out of it.[74] Both cases show the involvement of non-religious authorities in the regulation of family life and in the application of family law. They also demonstrate a completely new attitude to divorce; in sharp contrast with past expectations, the threat of making a complaint in court was now considered more effective than the threat of repudiation.

## Divorce in fifteenth-century Cairo

In the absence of full court records, not to mention anything that resembles a census, it is usually necessary to reconstruct the patterns of divorce in medieval Muslim societies from anecdotal evidence. An exception can be made for late fifteenth-century Cairo, thanks to the work of the historian Muḥammad b. ʿAbd al-Raḥman al-Sakhāwī. The last volume of al-Sakhāwī's major historical work, the biographical collection entitled *Al-Ḍaw' al-Lāmiʿ li-Ahl al-Qarn al-Tāsiʿ*, is devoted to women. This is probably the largest single collection of biographies of women in pre-modern Islamic historiography.[75] It consists of 1,075 entries for contemporary women, many of them still alive when he completed the dictionary at the end of the fifteenth century. Included in the dictionary are daughters and wives of sultans, amirs and senior government officials. Some entries are copied from biographical dictionaries compiled in Mecca, but most are devoted to the female relatives of al-Sakhāwī himself, or of his friends among the merchants and scholars of Cairo. It is a mammoth collective profile of the propertied classes in Cairo during the second half of the fifteenth century.

Al-Sakhāwī's biographical dictionary is the closest we get to a significant sample of marriage and divorce in any medieval Muslim society.[76] Uniquely among medieval historians, al-Sakhāwī is quite diligent in recording the marriages and divorces of his female subjects, and takes great interest in the events leading to the breakdown of marriage. This is not a legal or a documentary source, and al-Sakhāwī is not recording court cases. He was essentially repeating the city gossip, and adding some of his own by putting out his family's dirty laundry. Obviously, this type of gossip is not always reliable. It is quite possible that al-Sakhāwī was not aware of all the marriages concluded by the thousands of subjects included in his biographical dictionary. Many marriages of short duration, terminating with a swift

74 *Ibid.*, 234.

75 For a comparative overview of women's representation in the genre, see Roded, *Women in the Islamic Biographical Dictionaries*; Musallam, "The Ordering of Muslim Societies," 189.

76 A point already made by Musallam, "The Ordering of Muslim Societies." See also Lutfi, "al-Sakhāwī's *Kitāb al-Nisā*"; Berkey, "Women and Islamic Education."

divorce, may have escaped his attention. Al-Sakhāwī's comments and interpretation are subjective and often vindictive, intent on settling scores with his academic and personal rivals. On the other hand, his record of marriage and divorce is set within the framework of fuller biographies. And while his comments should be always taken with a grain of salt, he allows us to go beyond the legal formalities, which may be misleading with regard to the true intentions and motivations of the divorcing spouses.

Al-Sakhāwī records the marital history of 168 fifteenth-century Cairene women, mentioning 287 marriages concluded by these women.[77] This is an average of almost two marriages per woman, although some were married four, five and six times. Among these 287 marriages, al-Sakhāwī mentions the cause of dissolution for 171 marriages. In the remaining 116, the cause of dissolution is not specified. Al-Sakhāwī often mentions a woman's successive husbands without dwelling on the fate of the marriages. For example, Zuhūr bt. Walī al-Dīn Aḥmad al-Bulqīnī was married six times, and was still alive when the work was completed. But there is no indication whether her frequent remarriages were a result of divorces or of the death of her husbands.[78] For the 171 marriages for which the cause of dissolution is known, al-Sakhāwī mentions 52 marriages dissolved through divorce and 119 marriages terminated by the death of one of the spouses.[79]

According to the data gathered from al-Sakhāwī's entries, three out of ten marriages among the propertied classes in fifteenth-century Cairo ended with divorce. It is probable that the actual rate of divorce among the general population of Cairo was higher. As noted above, al-Sakhāwī was not aware of all the marriages going on in the city, and some short-term unions may have escaped his attention. It is also probable that the rate of divorce among the lower classes was higher than among the elite, as was the case in the Jewish Geniza society. The prevalence of divorce is striking, and even more so if we keep in mind the high mortality rate, augmented in this period by the plague. Death at a young age meant that marriage, even without divorce, tended to be a much shorter affair than it is today.

In al-Sakhāwī's Cairo, divorce was omnipresent and pervasive, by no means limited to first marriages or childless marriages. It was almost as likely to occur in a woman's first marriage (28 out of 107) as in a marriage of a widow or a divorcée (24 out of 94). Sometimes divorce occurred before consummation or after less than a month,[80] but in other cases the spouses separated after the birth of children.

[77] The sample includes only women who were born in Egypt after 790/1388, or, if the date of birth is unknown, died after 853/1450 (including those still living when the final draft of the work was completed, shortly before the author's death in 902/1497). It excludes entries copied from earlier historical works, such as the hundreds of entries for Ḥijāzi women drawn from the biographical dictionaries composed by al-Fāsī (d. 832/1428) and Ibn Fahd (d. 885/1480).

[78] Al-Sakhāwī, *Ḍaw'*, vol. XII, 38 (no. 221).

[79] When a wife predeceased her husband, al-Sakhāwī notes that she "died married to him," or "died under his protection" (*mātat fī 'iṣmatihi, mātat taḥtahu*); a husband, on the other hand, "died on his wife" (*māta 'anhā*).

[80] See the biographies of Zaynab bt. Jalāl al-Dīn al-Bulqīnī (al-Sakhāwī, *Ḍaw'*, vol. XII, 41 [no. 243]); Umm al-Ḥasan bt. Badr al-Dīn al-Bulqīnī (*ibid.*, vol. X, 170 [no. 716], vol. XII, 137 [no. 847]); 'Ā'isha bt. Shams al-Dīn Ibn Suwayd (*ibid.*, vol. IX, 95, vol. XII, 80 [no. 492]).

Al-Sakhāwī notes the birth of children in 17 divorce cases, or about a third of all recorded divorces. It is almost certain that the actual figure was much higher, as al-Sakhāwī does not offer consistent data about children. The rate of divorce remains roughly the same when we examine endogamous marriages of cousins (9 out of 35).[81] Divorce rates are more or less equal across the military and civilian segments of the elite. It is also clear that divorce was not an obstacle for a woman who sought another match. The majority of divorcées remarried – women went on to another marriage in at least 34 of the divorce cases, about two-thirds of the sample.

Not surprisingly, judicial divorces represented only a very small proportion of divorces, despite their greater visibility in legal sources. Al-Sakhāwī reports only three dissolutions granted by a court without the consent of the husband. In one case, a distant female relative of al-Sakhāwī (the maternal granddaughter of his maternal aunt, to be precise) married a provincial deputy judge, who then decided to quit his job and to travel with his family to the Ḥijāz. He then continued to the Red Sea port of Suakin, probably in the hope of striking a fortune in commerce, but left his wife in Mecca without any marital support. After a while the woman "was tired of waiting" and had the marriage dissolved.[82] In a case from the 1460s, a deputy *qāḍī* by the name of Muḥammad b. Khalīl Ibn al-Muwaqqit granted Saʿādāt bt. Badr al-Dīn al-Simirbāʾī judicial divorce from her husband, an officer who was sent on duty to Mecca.[83]

In one solitary case, separation was not initiated by either of the spouses but was rather a result of a late discovery of a marriage impediment. Zaynab, second wife to the scholar and *qāḍī* Sirāj al-Dīn al-Bulqīnī, bore him two children before he found out that she had been suckled by his sister, and was therefore forbidden to him as a result of a milk relationship between them that is considered an impediment to marriage in Islamic law. The suckling relationship was revealed by the sister herself, who traveled to Cairo from their hometown of Bulqīna. When the husband was satisfied that the suckling did occur (and one must wonder about the motivations of the not-so-benevolent sister-in-law), he decided to avoid any sexual contact with her until his death ten years later. Formally, this case did not end in divorce.[84]

The vast majority of divorces reported by al-Sakhāwī were either repudiations (*ṭalāq*) or consensual separations (*khulʿ*). Revealingly, al-Sakhāwī makes no consistent distinction between repudiation and consensual separation, in sharp contrast to the emphasis of the legal sources. He denotes divorce by the use of the noun "separation" (*firāq*), or by commenting that the husband "divorced his wife" (*fāraqahā*)

[81] Including marriages of second and third cousins and affine relations. Al-Sakhāwī also mentions eleven cases of manumitted slaves marrying their masters' daughters; three of these marriages ended in divorce.

[82] *Ibid.*, vol. IV, 139.

[83] The validity of the judicial divorce was later contested in court. See *ibid.*, vol. XII, 63 (no. 379) (Saʿādāt), vol. III, 6 (first husband), vol. II, 100 (second husband), vol. VII, 236 (the deputy).

[84] *Ibid.*, vol. XII, 41 (no. 241). For a Meccan case of legal impediments to marriage, see *ibid.*, 99 (no. 625).

or "repudiated her" (*ṭallaqahā*). These two verbs are used interchangeably, and do not seem to indicate different forms of divorce.[85] The precise legal form of the divorce was perhaps unknown to al-Sakhāwī, and probably irrelevant. The divorce deed was only the end result of a negotiation process that took many factors into consideration, including money, custody of children, the wishes of the spouses' respective families and also, as al-Sakhāwī is keen to point out, the passions and desires of the spouses.

Commonly, it was the wife who initiated the divorce proceedings, as is demonstrated in the divorce between Fāṭima, daughter of Badr al-Dīn al-Saʿdī, the chief Ḥanbalī *qāḍī* of Cairo, and ʿIzz al-Dīn Muḥammad al-Jawjarī.[86] Born in 872/1467, Fāṭima was fifteen when she was married off to ʿIzz al-Dīn, the son of one of her father's deputies. We know that ʿIzz al-Dīn's academic achievements were less than impressive, but he had inherited teaching positions in several madrasas through his maternal grandfather, a renowned Ḥanbalī professor, and these secured him some sort of income. The marriage broke up after two years, when Fāṭima was seventeen. Al-Sakhāwī explains that "there was no compatibility," and fighting ensued.[87] In the divorce settlement ʿIzz al-Dīn received some financial compensation (*badhl*) for releasing Fāṭima, perhaps a sign that he did not initiate the divorce. ʿIzz al-Dīn's career after the divorce was rather sluggish. He remarried into a less prosperous scholarly family, and became a notary, the lowest rank in the scholarly vocation. Fāṭima married a certain Riḍā al-Isḥāqī, who was immediately appointed as an officer at the Ḥanbalī court presided over by his father-in-law, and then deputy to the Mālikī chief *qāḍī*. This was most probably the career ʿIzz al-Dīn would have had if his marriage to Fāṭima had lasted.

Al-Sakhāwī's biographical dictionary offers quite a few examples of wives pursuing a divorce against the wishes of their husbands. His own brother, Abū Bakr b. ʿAbd al-Raḥmān al-Sakhāwī, suffered greatly at the hands of his wife, who, in spite of his deteriorating health, never stopped pestering him. In order to appease her he agreed to move with her to another part of the city, far from al-Sakhāwī's overbearing family. Even when he became so ill as to be confined to his bed, she refused to accompany him to his family's quarters and kept asking for divorce. He eventually agreed to release her, and in return she acquitted him of any debts and even gave him financial compensation. He died shortly afterwards, in 893/1487, aged forty-eight.[88] Zaynab, daughter of the chief *qāḍī* Muḥibb al-Dīn Ibn al-Shiḥnah, "was not satisfied [with her husband] and they were divorced." The verb is used in the dual form, indicating a mutual action.[89] Another Zaynab, a descendant of the

85 *Ibid.*, 7 (no. 39), 125 (no. 765).
86 The following story is culled from several biographical entries. See *ibid.*, 104 (no. 657) (wife), vol. VI, 321 (no. 1052) (husband), vol. I, 349 (husband's father), vol. IX, 58–60 (wife's father), vol. IX, 239 (no. 584) (second husband).
87 Text: *lam yaḥṣul al-tiʾām*. It is unclear whether the marriage was consummated. In the husband's biography al-Sakhāwī mentions that the divorce took place before consummation, while in the entry for the husband's father he mentions that Fāṭima bore him a child.
88 *Ibid.*, vol. XI, 46.
89 Text: *lam taḥṣul ʿalā ṭāʾil wa-fāraqā* (*ibid.*, vol. XII, 49–50 [no. 292], vol. X, 264 [no. 1064]).

Banū al-Bārizī dynasty of civilian administrators, was widowed in 850/1446. She avoided remarriage for several years, until, at the request of her son, she concluded a marriage alliance with a senior government official. But she later pleaded with her new husband and he divorced her.[90]

For al-Sakhāwī divorce was almost always a decision taken by the couple, while the intervention of in-laws is rarely mentioned. The mother and brother of Qurrat al-ʿAyn bt. Abū Bakr al-Sakhāwī, the orphaned minor niece of al-Sakhāwī, were influential in causing her divorce from the husband chosen for her by al-Sakhāwī himself.[91] But al-Sakhāwī generally prefers to talk about love-marriages and about divorces caused by the absence of passion. After her divorce from her first husband and paternal cousin, the daughter of the chief Shāfiʿī *qāḍī* Jalāl al-Dīn al-Bulqīnī went on to marry an amir nicknamed ʿAddād al-Ghanam (Sheep Counter). Her first husband tried to talk her into coming back, but to no avail, as she fell "desperately in love" with her new husband.[92] Other women chose to marry their social inferiors. Fāṭima bt. Abī al-Khayr, widow of the renowned jurist Ibn al-Humām, married one of the porters on board a ship heading to Mecca in 898/1493. Al-Sakhāwī mischievously adds that it seems she was unable to control her desire and married him simply for sex.[93]

Among the many unstable marriages in fifteenth-century Cairo, polygamous marriages stand out as particularly so. A married man would often choose to conceal a second marriage from the public eye in order to avoid trouble with his first wife.[94] But when the first wife did find out, the man would often have to choose between the two. ʿAzīza bt. ʿAlī al-Zayyādī (d. 879/1475), the daughter of a Cairene scholar, married the Meccan scholar ʿAfīf al-Dīn al-Ījī when he visited Cairo. This marriage was kept secret from his first wife and paternal cousin, Ḥabībat Allāh bt. ʿAbd al-Raḥmān, who remained in Mecca. But when the Cairene wife accompanied her husband to Mecca, ʿAfīf al-Dīn was forced to divorce her after pressure from the first wife.[95] In other cases it was the second wife who gained the upper hand. Najm al-Dīn Ibn Ḥijjī preferred not to consummate his marriage with his young bride and relative, Fāṭima bt. ʿAbd al-Raḥmān Ibn al-Bārizī (d. 899/1494), because he had married a second and more mature woman. Al-Sakhāwī tells us that his second wife "took hold of his heart," and convinced him to divorce his cousin.[96]

90 *Ibid.*, vol. XII, 49 (no. 291) (Zaynab), vol. X, 252 (no. 1050) (Najm al-Dīn). See also Lutfi, "al-Sakhāwī's *Kitāb al-Nisāʾ*," 114.

91 Al-Sakhāwī, *Ḍawʾ*, vol. XII, 116 (no. 704). In a case from Syria, a marriage alliance of the Banū al-Shiḥnah and Banū al-Ṣawwāf did not materialize because of a fight between the womenfolk of the two households (*ibid.*, vol. III, 113–14).

92 Text: *tatahālaku fī al-tarāmī ʿalayhi* (*ibid.*, vol. XII, 41 [no. 243]). See also *ibid.*, vol. II, 188 (Walī al-Dīn), vol. II, 240 (ʿAddād al-Ghanam); and al-Sakhāwī, *al-Tibr al-Masbūk*, 236.

93 Text: *li-qaṣd al-mukhālaṭa wa-ʿadam imkān al-taḥarruz* (al-Sakhāwī, *Ḍawʾ*, vol. XII, 91 [no. 567]).

94 According to a contemporary legal manual, a clandestine marriage contract is like any other except that it is never made public. The presence of witnesses is required, but they take it upon themselves to keep the marriage secret (*kitmān al-nikāḥ*). The author explains that men have recourse to clandestine marriages when they take a second wife (al-Asyūṭī, *Jawāhir al-ʿUqūd*, vol. II, 89).

95 Al-Sakhāwī, *Ḍawʾ*, vol. XII, 82 (no. 505) (second wife), 19 (no. 102) (first wife). See also Lutfi, "al-Sakhāwī's *Kitāb al-Nisāʾ*," 114; Musallam, "The Ordering of Muslim Societies," 193–94.

96 For the second wife, Fāṭima bt. Kamāl al-Dīn al-Adhruʿī, see al-Sakhāwī, *Ḍawʾ*, vol. XII, 100 (no. 629). For the first wife, see *ibid.*, 94 (no. 589).

The negotiations over divorce were shaped by a legal system which was overwhelmingly poised in favor of husbands. A husband could repudiate his wife when it was to his financial advantage to do so. In a couple of cases, a husband divorced his wife on his deathbed in order to deprive her of a share in his inheritance. In both cases, the marriage had only been of short duration.[97] Despite the rising incidence of judicial divorces granted to deserted or abused wives, most wives who wanted to get out of marriage had to pay for it. The husband of Fāṭima bt. Abī al-Barakāt Ibn al-Jīʿān, a relative on her maternal side, "tormented her" until she released herself through financial compensation.[98]

The failed marriage of the scholar and historian Ibrāhīm b. ʿUmar al-Biqāʿī (809/1406–885/1480) to Saʿādāt bt. Nūr al-Dīn al-Būshī finely illustrates the interplay of personal, financial and legal pressures behind a divorce settlement. Al-Sakhāwī, who usually glosses over the legal and financial details of a marriage breakdown, makes an exception in this extraordinary biography of his bitter academic rival.[99] Al-Biqāʿī, a Syrian immigrant who settled in Cairo, first married the daughter of a perfume merchant, but divorced her when his luck changed for the better. In 858/1454, when he was in his late forties, he decided to marry Saʿādāt, the virgin daughter of the late shaykh of the *khānqāh* in Siryāqūs, Nūr al-Dīn al-Būshī (d. 856/1452). For al-Biqāʿī this was a chance to consolidate his status among the scholarly elite of Cairo. In his semi-autobiographical chronicle he shares with his readers his excitement and joy about the wedding. He cites from the Qur'ān the verse beginning with the words "This is the similitude of Paradise" (Q 43:67). He then relates that his bride had a dream about the wedding, in which she saw a man in fine white dress leading her and al-Biqāʿī to Paradise and asking them to take their clothes off.[100]

Whatever dreams Saʿādāt initially had, they were soon shattered. According to al-Sakhāwī, al-Biqāʿī's behavior towards Saʿādāt was abusive, in spite of mediation by friends and family. After less than five years, during which she gave birth to his child, she "could not take it any more" (*lam taḥtamil*) and asked for a divorce. Al-Biqāʿī agreed on condition that he would receive sole custody of the child. Furthermore, he demanded from Saʿādāt a pledge that should she attempt to take away the child or even attempt to see him, she would be subject to a penalty of 500 gold dinars. Although Saʿādāt consented, al-Biqāʿī had difficulty in confirming the validity of this pledge. He had to apply to a Mālikī *qāḍī*, since the Mālikī school allowed greater freedom of contract with regard to custody settlements.[101] But

97 See *ibid.*, vol. I, 325, vol. XII, 63 (no. 379), vol. IX, 98. In 853/1449, Cairo courts debated the validity of a divorce uttered by a husband on his deathbed, and the widow's right to a share of his estate (Jamāl al-Dīn Yūsuf Ibn Taghrī Birdī, *Ḥawādith al-Duhūr fī Madā al-Ayyām wa'l-Shuhūr*, ed. Muḥammad Kamāl al-Dīn ʿIzz al-Dīn, 2 vols. [Beirut: ʿĀlam al-Kutub, 1990], vol. I, 211).

98 Al-Sakhāwī, *Ḍaw'*, vol. XI, 270, vol. XII, 106 (no. 667).

99 *Ibid.*, vol. I, 101–10 (al-Biqāʿī), vol. XII, 105 (no. 664) (first wife), 62–63 (no. 377) (second wife), vol. V, 178 (Nūr al-Dīn al-Būshī). For a detailed biography, see Li Guo, "al-Biqāʿī's Chronicle: A Fifteenth Century Learned Man's Reflection on his Time and World," in Kennedy (ed.), *The Historiography of Islamic Egypt*, 121–48.

100 Guo, "al-Biqāʿī's Chronicle," 135.

101 Ibn Taymiyya, *Fatāwā al-Nisā'*, 288–89; Ibn Taymiyya, *Majmūʿ Fatāwā*, vol. XXXII, 353–54. See also Jackson, "Kramer Versus Kramer."

even the Mālikī *qāḍī* refused to approve the contract, describing it as unnatural.[102] It seems unlikely that al-Biqāʿī wanted the divorce. We are told that he "was about to die" when he learned that his ex-wife had married one of her father's students. The office of the shaykh of the *khānqāh* was taken over by another scholar, who married the late shaykh's widow.[103]

Marriage and, even more so, divorce were primarily a contract between two persons. It is striking that, according to the contemporary testimony of al-Sakhāwī, conjugal relations mattered much more than the extended household. Divorce was rarely a result of family pressure. Only a handful of marriages were dissolved as a result of a conflict between the spouses' respective kin groups. At the same time, conjugal relations were, to a large degree, shaped by a family law that privileged men with the right to unilateral repudiation. This right was a hallmark of patriarchy and a common threat against an insubordinate wife. But wives had also their legal recourses, especially towards the end of the fifteenth century, when the growing intervention of the military courts in domestic matters opened additional legal avenues for them. More than anything else, al-Sakhāwī's Cairene women stand out for their proactive and independent agency. The women described in al-Sakhāwī's biographies do not seem to have been intimidated by threats of divorce – which, in fact, are rarely mentioned; although men still held the unilateral right of repudiation, women appear to have initiated divorces as often as men.

102 Al-Sakhāwī, *Ḍaw'*, vol. IX, 113.
103 *Ibid.*, vol. XII, 7 (no. 36). See also al-Sakhāwī, *Wajīz al-Kalām*, vol. III, 962.

CHAPTER 5

# Repudiation and public power

In Mamluk society, divorce was not merely a domestic matter between a husband and a wife, nor even a dispute between two families. The absolute right of husbands to dissolve the marriage contract at will, together with the absolute right of a master to manumit his slave, were the ultimate symbols of patriarchal authority. In a society in which public status was seen to be derived from power over women, slaves and children, men were expected to use their patriarchal privileges to bolster their commitments in the public sphere. They did so through the legal mechanism of the oath on pain of divorce, a form of oath that makes repudiation of one's wife contingent on the non-fulfillment of the sworn undertaking. Since oaths could not always be respected and promises had to be broken, the violation of divorce oaths was an additional cause of the high divorce rate in Mamluk society. These separations were not directly initiated by either husband or wife, but were rather the result of men's failure to fulfill social pledges which went far beyond the domestic sphere.

According to its traditional interpretation, Islamic Sunni law grants special status to oaths on pain of divorce, along with oaths on pain of manumission.[1] They are considered conditional phrases, the act of divorce or manumission being contingent on the fulfillment of the condition. For example, when a man says "May my wife be repudiated if I enter this house," and then enters the house, divorce immediately follows. Oaths of divorce and manumission are therefore distinguished from oaths in the name of God. If a man says "By God, I will not enter this house," the oath is not judicially enforceable. The performance of an act of atonement (*kaffāra*) for violating the oath is left to the individual. When a man violates an oath on pain of divorce, on the other hand, no atonement is permitted.

[1] On oaths of divorce and manumission in the early compendia of Islamic law, see N. Calder, "*Ḥinth, Birr, Tabarrur, Taḥannuth*: An Inquiry into the Arabic Vocabulary of Oaths," *BSOAS* 51 (1989), 216–23. On divorce oaths in the Ottoman period see Peirce, "'She is Trouble'," 289–94; Tucker, *In the House of the Law*, 101–08; C. Imber, "Involuntary Annulment of Marriage and its Solutions in Ottoman Law," *Turcica* 25 (1993), 59–69. Calder, who studied the early Islamic legal doctrine on oaths, suggested translating the Arabic *ḥilf bi'l-ṭalāq* as "swearing on the basis of divorcing" ("*Ḥinth*," 215). For the purpose of this essay, I believe that "an oath on/under pain of divorce," or simply "divorce oath," reflect better the actual use of these phrases.

If he continues to have sexual relations with his wife, he would be committing adultery, and therefore liable to the punishments adulterers face.

Violation of an oath on pain of divorce does not mean eternal separation, since the couple could remarry, but Islamic law puts a limit on the number of consecutive divorces. After a man divorces his wife three times, the spouses are not allowed to remarry until the woman has contracted, consummated and been divorced from an intermediate marriage. Therefore, a man who wants to express resolve and determination should say: "May my wife be repudiated three times if I enter this house." By taking an oath on pain of triple divorce, the man is not only putting his marriage on the line. The oath means that, should he enter the house and violate the oath, he will not be able to remarry his wife until she has had sex with another man. At times, this second marriage would only be arranged with the intention and for the sole purpose of permitting the woman to her first husband, in which case it is called marriage of *taḥlīl* (making lawful) and the contracting man is called *muḥallil*.

Due to their special power, divorce oaths have had a long history in Muslim societies and, by the beginning of the Mamluk period, had come to be considered as the most solemn form of oath. Divorce oaths acquired political importance early on in Umayyad times, and were incorporated into the oath of allegiance (*bayʿa*) used by later medieval Muslim rulers, including the Mamluk sultans. During the Ayyubid and Mamluk periods divorce oaths became prevalent among all classes of society and were used in all sorts of financial, social and familial contexts. Under certain circumstances, men were even compelled to undertake divorce oaths as part of the judicial process. As the importance of the oaths of divorce grew, so did the number of legal stratagems devised to circumvent them, such as *taḥlīl* marriages.

The central role of divorce oaths to Mamluk society is highlighted by the challenge posed by Taqī al-Dīn Ibn Taymiyya to the validity of these oaths. Much has been written on Ibn Taymiyya's arrest and subsequent trials on account of his supposed anthropomorphism and attacks on the visiting of tombs.[2] Less well known are the trials for his views on oaths of divorce. In 718/1318 Ibn Taymiyya wrote a short treatise in which he argued that the legal rules that apply to oaths in the name of God apply also to oaths under pain of divorce. Against the established doctrine, which considered oaths on pain of divorce as conditional divorces, he reasoned that violation of a divorce oath requires an act of atonement, not the actual dissolution of marriage. After having been prohibited twice from issuing *fatwā*s on this subject, Ibn Taymiyya was eventually arrested.

The debate over Ibn Taymiyya's doctrines on divorce oaths allows us to finally appreciate the full importance of divorce as a public, and not merely private, institution. As the ultimate patriarchal prerogative, unilateral divorce was the basis

[2] The seminal studies on Ibn Taymiyya are H. Laoust, *Essai sur les doctrines sociales et politiques de Takī-d-Dīn Aḥmad b. Taimīya* (Cairo: Institut français d'archéologie orientale, 1939), and Muḥammad Abū Zahra, *Ibn Taymiyya: Ḥayātuhu wa-ʿAṣruhu – wa-Ārā'uhu al-Fiqhiyya* (Cairo: Dār al-Fikr al-ʿArabī, 1952). The trials of Ibn Taymiyya are described by Ḥasan Q. Murad, "Ibn Taymiya on Trial: A Narrative Account of his *Miḥan*," *Islamic Studies* 18 (1979), 1–32; and D. Little, "The Historical and Historiographical Significance of the Detention of Ibn Taymiyya," *IJMES* 4 (1973), 313–27 (reprinted in his *History and Historiography of the Mamlūks*).

for the most solemn and binding type of oath in Mamluk society, guarded by the Mamluk state as a cornerstone of the political order. Rather than laying the blame at the door of fickle husbands who used their powers indiscriminately, it was primarily the state authorities, in the interest of defending the medieval patriarchal system, who expected – or even demanded – men to effectively pawn their marriages. The use of divorce oaths diminished only towards the end of the Mamluk period, when an increasingly centralized state apparatus chose to rely on more formalized means of social control.

## The power of divorce oaths

For members of the Mamluk military elite, oaths of divorce superseded any other form of social commitment. In 711/1311–12, when the governor of Damascus, Sayf al-Dīn Karāy, started a campaign against bribery and theft, he undertook an oath on pain of divorce to inflict corporal punishment on those found guilty. Instead of issuing his new policy in the form of edicts, deriving authority from his official position as governor, Karāy backed up his threats with an oath on pain of divorce.[3] Karāy also declared that he had undertaken an oath of divorce not to accept any gifts during his tenure of office. When he later married the daughter of a former governor, he even refused to accept the customary wedding gifts. Urged by one of his *khushdāsh*es to accept his presents, Karāy declined, pointing out that breaking his oath would mean separation from his beloved wives and concubines.[4] The point of the story is that an oath on pain of divorce outweighed, at least for Sayf al-Dīn Karāy, the mutual friendship emanating from ties of *khushdāshiyya*.

Another example of the power attributed to divorce oaths comes from the biographies of the founder of the Mamluk state. In 661/1263, as Sultan al-Ẓāhir Baybars attempted to secure the surrender of al-Malik al-Mugīth, the Ayyubid ruler of Karak, Baybars promised, under an oath on pain of triple divorce, not to cause him any harm. Nonetheless, when al-Malik al-Mughīth agreed to meet Baybars outside the citadel of the city, he was immediately arrested and sent to Cairo, where he was duly executed. As he was put in chains, we are told by the Damascene chronicler Quṭb al-Dīn al-Yūnīnī, "signs of abhorrence appeared on the faces of several amirs, for he [Baybars] had undertaken forty oaths, including an oath on pain of triple divorce from [his wife] the mother of al-Malik al-Saʿīd. It has been said that she resorted to a *taḥlīl* marriage with a slave, who was afterwards murdered."[5] In

[3] Ismāʿīl b. ʿUmar Ibn Kathīr, *al-Bidāya wa'l-Nihāya*, 14 vols. (Cairo: n.p., 1932–39), vol. XIV, 66. See also H. Laoust, "Le hanbalisme sous les Mamlouks Bahrides (658–784/1260–1382)," *Revue d'études islamiques* 28 (1960), 27–29.

[4] Al-Ṣafadī, *Aʿyān*, vol. IV, 154–55.

[5] Al-Yūnīnī, *Dhayl*, vol. I, 532–33, vol. II, 192–94. There are several other versions of the events surrounding al-Mughīth's arrest. According to a particularly fantastic one, al-Mughīth had previously raped Baybars' wife, and was eventually executed by her maids. See A. A. Khowaiter, *Baibars the First, his Endeavors and Achievements* (London: Green Mountain, 1978), 31–34; P. Thorau, *The Lion of Egypt: Sultan Baybars I and the Near East in the Thirteenth Century*, trans. P. M. Holt (London: Longman, 1992), 136, 140 (n. 13), and the sources cited there.

spite of violating numerous other oaths, it was the violation of the oath on pain of divorce that most outraged the chronicler and Baybars' own allies.

Incorporated in the royal oath of allegiance, the oath on pain of divorce is the most frequently mentioned form of oath among the military and civilian elite. When chroniclers wish to emphasize the binding power of an oath, they refer either to the taking of an oath on a copy of the Qur'ān[6] or to an oath of divorce. The amir Mūsā b. ʿAlī b. Qalāwūn, when arrested by the sultan's officers, asked his captors to swear by God and on pain of triple divorce not to harm the person who gave him shelter.[7] In 735/1335, the government official Ibn Hilāl al-Dawla, under arrest and torture, denied on pain of triple divorce having any knowledge of the whereabouts of the money he was accused of embezzling.[8] Following the death of Sultan al-Nāṣir Muḥammad, the vice-regent Ṭuquztimur undertook an oath on pain of divorce not to remain in office under the new sultan.[9] In a question put to Ibn Taymiyya, an amir undertook, under pain of divorce, to collect extra taxes from a negligent peasant.[10] Significantly, the oath on pain of triple divorce was part of the oath of allegiance inaugurating the reign of every new Mamluk sultan. The person undertaking the oath of allegiance swore to divorce any wife he would ever marry should he violate the oath.[11]

Divorce oaths were used by commoners as well, and in a baffling variety of social contexts. Oaths were often connected with financial obligations. In a case put to Ibn al-Ṣalāḥ, a man had undertaken a divorce oath to make up for a debt by working for his creditor.[12] Divorce oaths were common in the marketplace. During a quarrel in the market, one tradesman swore on divorce to bring his opponent before the city's *muḥtasib*.[13] Ibn al-Ḥājj describes merchants who constantly swear to the quality of their merchandise, either by God or by divorce.[14] Men would use divorce oaths during quarrels with neighbors and relatives, taking an oath on pain

6 For an oath on a copy of the Qur'ān by an Ayyūbid ruler, see al-Yūnīnī, *Dhayl*, vol. II, 398–400; for an oath on a copy of the Qur'ān taken by a Mamlūk amir in 690/1291, see al-Ṣafadī, *Aʿyān*, vol. IV, 91.

7 Al-Ṣafadī, *Aʿyān*, vol. V, 480.

8 Al-Yūsufī, *Nuzhat al-Nāẓir*, 248. In 734/1334 the chief Shāfiʿī *qāḍī* of Damascus, Ibn Jumlah, denied charges of embezzlement by an oath of triple divorce (al-Jazarī, *Taʾrīkh*, vol. III, 674).

9 Shams al-Dīn al-Shujāʿī, *Taʾrīkh al-Malik al-Nāṣir Muḥammad b. Qalāʾūn al-Ṣāliḥ wa-Awlādihi*, ed. B. Schäfer, 2 vols. (Wiesbaden: Steiner, 1977–85), vol. I, 139.

10 Ibn Taymiyya, *Majmūʿ Fatāwā*, vol. XXX, 118.

11 See the text of the oath of allegiance given to Sultan Aḥmad in 742/1342 (al-Shujāʿī, *Taʾrīkh*, vol. I, 199). Fifteenth-century oaths of allegiance to new caliphs open with an oath on pain of divorce (al-Qalqashandī, *Ṣubḥ al-Aʿshā*, vol. IX, 312–13, 318–19). See also E. Tyan, "Bayʿa," *EI*[2]; H. Halm, "The Ismaʿili Oath of Allegiance (*ʿAhd*) and the 'Sessions of Wisdom' (*Majālis al-Ḥikma*) in Fatimid Times," in F. Daftary (ed.), *Mediaeval Ismaʿili History and Thought* (Cambridge: Cambridge University Press, 1996), 96.

12 Ibn al-Ṣalāḥ, *Fatāwā*, 687 (no. 1048). In another case a creditor undertook a divorce oath not to allow the release of his debtor from jail (*ibid.*, 445 [no. 399]). For more examples of the use of divorce oaths in commercial contexts, see Ibn Taymiyya, *Majmūʿ Fatāwā*, vol. XXX, 315–16.

13 Ibn Taymiyya, *Fatāwā al-Nisāʾ*, 252.

14 Ibn al-Ḥājj, *Madkhal*, vol. IV, 60. Al-Nawawī was asked about a master artisan who had sworn on pain of divorce that his apprentice knew how to perform a task assigned to him (al-Nawawī, *Fatāwā*, 140).

of divorce not to speak to someone or never to stay in someone's house.[15] Divorce oaths were often associated with gift giving, especially in popular literature. In an anecdote about ʿAlam al-Dīn Sanjar (d. 695/1296), chief of police in Cairo, it is told how he refused to receive a gift from a woman until her husband threatened to repudiate her; ʿAlam al-Dīn later insisted, by taking a divorce oath, on reciprocating the gift.[16]

In this period the use of divorce oaths in judicial processes became institutionalized, probably for the first time in the history of Islamic law. In a case from the end of the thirteenth century, the *qāḍī* of Damascus threatened to beat and shave the beard of a man brought in by the governor, unless the man swore on pain of triple divorce to renounce criminal activity.[17] The chief Ḥanafī *qāḍī* of Damascus, Najm al-Dīn al-Ṭarsūsī (d. 758/1357), gave judges permission to demand from litigants an oath on pain of divorce or manumission in lieu of a judicial oath. Al-Ṭarsūsī admits that this view has no precedent in legal literature, but comments that "in our days the *qāḍī* can do that, if he considers it in the public interest (*maṣlaḥa*)."[18] Indeed, according to the anonymous author of a fourteenth-century treatise on divorce oaths, Ḥanafī *qāḍī*s made litigants swear on pain of divorce as part of the judicial procedure. The author, most probably a Ḥanbalī scholar, also maintains that this was an unprecedented policy.[19] The report is confirmed by Ibn Qayyim al-Jawziyya, who states that *qāḍīs* demand from defendants a divorce oath as a condition for acquittal.[20]

Divorce oaths were invoked and violated so frequently as to blur the difference between an oath and a simple non-conditional repudiation. Some commoners believed that the mere pronouncing of a divorce oath necessarily led to divorce.[21] This confusion even crept into the notarial jargon. In al-Ṭarsūsī's legal manual the models for a divorce deed begin thus: "So-and-so acknowledged that he had violated [an oath] with regard to his wife . . . by a single divorce" (*aqarra fulān annahu ḥanitha fī zawjatihi . . . . bi-ṭalqa wāḥida*). Any translation here would do

15 For some examples, out of many, see Ibn al-Ṣalāḥ, *Fatāwā*, nos. 396, 399, 402; al-Nawawī, *Fatāwā*, 139, 140, 143, 145; al-Fazārī, "Fatāwā," fols. 92a, 94b; Ibn Taymiyya, *Fatāwā al-Nisāʾ*, 255, 256.

16 Badr al-Dīn al-ʿAynī, *ʿIqd al-Jumān fī Tāʾrīkh Ahl al-Zamān. ʿAṣr Salāṭīn al-Mamālīk*. ed. Muḥammad Muḥammad Amīn, 4 vols. (Cairo: al-Hayʾah al-Miṣriyya al-ʿĀmmah lil-Kitāb, 1987–92), vol. III, 340–42. A saint who would never accept charity was forced to take a gift of a robe from a man who swore to repudiate his wife – but then let it hang unused for thirty years (Taylor, *In the Vicinity of the Righteous*, 96).

17 Al-Fazārī, "Fatāwā," fol. 94a.

18 Guellil, *Damaszener Akten*, 276–77. Earlier treatises on judicial procedure make no mention of divorce oaths. Cf. Ibrāhīm b. ʿAbdallāh Ibn Abī al-Dam (d. 642/1244), *Kitāb Adab al-Qaḍāʾ*, ed. Muḥammad Muṣṭafā al-Zuhaylī (Damascus: Dār al-Fikr, 1982), 252–57 (Shāfiʿī); ʿAlī b. Muḥammad al-Simnānī, *Rawḍat al-Quḍāh*, ed. Ṣalaḥ al-Dīn al-Nāhī (Beirut: Muʾassasat al-Risāla, 1984), 282 (Ḥanafī).

19 Anonymous, "al-Radd ʿalā al-Taḥqīq fī Masʾalat al-Taʿlīq," Chester Beatty MS 3232, fol. 13b. The author was evidently a disciple of Ibn Taymiyya.

20 Ibn al-Qayyim even describes a legal subterfuge to circumvent this judicial divorce oath (*Iʿlām al-Muwaqqiʿīn*, vol. III, 248). There is no evidence of the use of divorce oaths in the Ḥaram court documents (Little, *Catalogue*, 47).

21 Ibn al-Ṣalāḥ, *Fatāwā*, 445.

injustice to this elliptical sentence, where the verb "*ḥanitha*," which signifies "to violate one's oath," is used as a substitute for the verb "*ṭallaqa*," "to divorce."[22]

Because divorce oaths were so widespread, they supported an industry of legal subterfuges intended to circumvent them. Many of the questions sent to jurists concern the permissibility of *taḥlīl* marriages, often performed by "professional" *muḥallils*.[23] As noted above, Baybars' wife allegedly contracted a *taḥlīl* marriage with one of his slaves. According to Ibn Taymiyya, this stratagem was common among elite households, for it protected the honor of the wife, and therefore of the household in general.[24] Ordinary couples would simply continue to cohabit, legitimizing their conduct by an odd variety of heterodox beliefs. Ibn Taymiyya states that some laymen instructed divorced couples to go to Mount ʿArafāt during the pilgrimage.[25] Others believed that having sexual intercourse above a roof or a staircase allowed the wife to return to her husband.[26] Some thought that if the wife gave birth to a male child, she was permitted to her husband with no further need of *taḥlīl*.[27] This was, apparently, a widely held belief, and one Sufi shaykh boasted of disseminating it all across the Syrian countryside.[28]

Besides *taḥlīl* marriage, other legal subterfuges specifically designed to circumvent the violation of divorce oaths were also in use. The most famous of these was "the iron chains." According to this method, when a husband says to his wife "when I repudiate you, you will have been repudiated three times in advance," he constructs a legal catch that prevents him from ever repudiating his wife.[29] Although most jurists rejected this method,[30] there are occasional references to

22 Note that this formula was used even when the divorce was not a result of the violation of an oath (Guellil, *Damaszener Akten*, 104 [no. 23], 181–82 [no. 76]).

23 Ibn Taymiyya, *Majmūʿ Fatāwā*, vol. XXXII, 97–101, 152–53; Ibn Taymiyya, *Fatāwā al-Nisāʾ*, 260; Shihāb al-Dīn al-Qarāfī, *Kitāb al-Iḥkām fī Tamyīz al-Fatāwā ʿan al-Aḥkām wa-Taṣarrufāt al-Qāḍī wa'l-Imām* (Aleppo: Maktabat al-Maṭbūʿāt al-Islāmiyya, 1967), 252–53.

24 Ibn Taymiyya, *Iqāmat al-Dalīl*, 243–44.

25 The reasoning for this practice was that, according to tradition, Adam and Eve met on Mount ʿArafāt. In another version of Ibn Taymiyya's account, the couple did not actually have to travel to Mecca. All the husband had to do was to daub his wife's head with oil, emulating the rites of the pilgrimage, in order for the couple to be permitted to each other (Ibn Taymiyya, *Ibid.*, 217; Ibn Taymiyya, *Majmūʿat Fatāwā*, vol. III, 65).

26 Unfortunately, this mysterious requirement is not explained (Ibn Taymiyya, *Iqāmat al-Dalīl*, 217; Ibn Taymiyya, *Majmūʿat Fatāwā*, vol. III, 65).

27 Ibn Taymiyya, *Fatāwā al-Nisāʾ*, 256.

28 Ibn Taymiyya reports that a friend of his, Abū al-Ḥakīm al-Nahrawānī, met a shaykh during a Sufi gathering (*ḥalqa*). The shaykh asked Abū al-Ḥakīm whether giving birth to a male child permits a triply divorced woman to her husband. When Abū al-Ḥakīm vehemently denied this, the shaykh told him that he issued *fatwā*s in support of this practice "from here to al-Buṣrā" (Ibn Taymiyya, *Iqāmat al-Dalīl*, 217).

29 The "iron chains" method (*masʾalat al-dūr al-ḥadīdiyya*) was so called because the husband loses his power to divorce his wife altogether, as if he is bound by chains. It was also called "*al-masʾala al-Surayjiyya*," after the Shāfiʿī scholar Ibn Surayj (d. 306/918) to whom it is attributed (J. Schacht, "Ibn Suraydj," *EI*[2]). According to Ibn Ḥajar al-ʿAsqalānī, this method had gained followers in Egypt only by the middle of the twelfth century (*Rafʿ al-Iṣr ʿan Quḍāt Miṣr*, ed. ʿAlī Muḥammad ʿUmar [Cairo: Maṭbaʿat al-Khānjī, 1998], 323).

30 Ibn al-Ṣalāḥ, *Fatāwā*, 438; Ibn Taymiyya, *Majmūʿat Fatāwā*, vol. III, 378. Taqī al-Dīn al-Subkī initially gave his approval to the method, but later changed his mind (*Fatāwā*, vol. I, 297–303, 313–14). Later Shāfiʿī jurists rejected it and Shāfiʿī *qāḍī*s were not allowed to confirm it (al-ʿUthmānī, *Raḥmat al-Umma*, 414; al-Asyūṭī, *Jawāhir al-ʿUqūd*, vol. II, 152–55; al-Anṣārī, *Iʿlām*, 251–52).

its use. ʿImād al-Dīn ʿAlī b. Yaʿqūb al-Mawṣilī (d. 682/1283–84), a scholar from Damascus, had imposed on himself "iron chains" never to repudiate his wife, and had the subterfuge confirmed with a judge.[31] Another subterfuge was the retroactive invalidation of the original marriage contract. When a couple that had been separated by triple divorce could prove that their marriage was voidable due to a major defect in the original contract, it meant that the husband did not have the legal capacity to issue a divorce. For this reason, we find spouses retroactively claiming that, at the time of the marriage contract, the bride's father was in the habit of drinking wine or of not attending prayers. According to some jurists, grossly impious behavior by the bride's guardian could have counted as the desired major defect in marriage.[32]

The most popular method of circumventing a divorce oath was a form of consensual divorce known as *khulʿ al-yamīn*. Under this legal device, the husband and wife agree on a consensual divorce (*khulʿ*) just before the husband is about to violate an oath he has undertaken. When the oath is then violated, the spouses are no longer married, and the triple divorce that should follow the breach of the oath cannot take place. The spouses are therefore allowed to remarry immediately. This is probably the explanation behind the consensual divorce concluded between the notary Shihāb al-Dīn Ibn Ṭawq and his wife, mentioned at the beginning of this book. As the debt-ridden Shihāb al-Dīn records in his diary, he had recently sworn on triple divorce not to ask for more credit. It seems that he and his wife then arranged for a *khulʿ al-yamīn* consensual divorce in order to allow him to request another loan without invoking the triple repudiation. Following the *khulʿ* divorce the couple were able to remarry immediately. Couples preferred to register their *khulʿ al-yamīn* divorces with a Ḥanbalī *qāḍī*, since the Ḥanbalī doctrine allows for repetition of the legal device as many times as is necessary.[33]

As much as all this may seem like legalistic hair-splitting, it mattered a great deal to commoners as well as to scholars. The Damascene historian al-Jazarī tells of an evening spent in his suburban orchard with the Shāfiʿī jurist Kamāl al-Dīn Ibn Qāḍī Shuhba (d. 726/1326). The main topic of discussion that night was the various methods of circumventing divorce oaths, such as the "iron chains" and *khulʿ al-yamīn*. In the course of the discussion, the Shāfiʿī scholar digressed to tell how, once upon a time, Abū Ḥanīfa had helped Hārūn al-Rashīd to block a legal subterfuge intended to circumvent the caliphal oaths of allegiance. Seeing that his loyal jurist had saved his kingdom, Hārūn al-Rashīd ordered all the scholars

31 Al-Fazārī, "Fatāwā," fol. 96a. On this man, see al-Ṣafadī, *Aʿyān*, vol. III, 357. A trace of this method can also be found in a Jewish marriage contract from the beginning of the twelfth century, in which a husband undertook never to divorce his wife (Goitein, *A Mediterranean Society*, vol. III, 271).

32 Al-Fazārī, "Fatāwā," fols. 85b–86b, 95a; Ibn Taymiyya, *Iqāmat al-Dalīl*, 243–46.

33 According to most schools of law, *khulʿ* separations count as divorces; therefore, if this legal device is repeated three times, a triple divorce ensues. Ḥanbalī doctrine, on the other hand, considers *khulʿ* separations as dissolutions (*faskh*) which do not count as divorce and can be repeated more than three times. See Ibn Abī al-Dam, *Kitāb Adab al-Qaḍāʾ*, 671–74; Ibn al-Ṣalāḥ, *Fatāwā*, 443 (no. 395); al-Nawawī, *Fatāwā*, 136, 139; Ibn al-Qayyim, *Iʿlām al-Muwaqqiʿīn*, vol. III, 280; al-ʿUthmānī, *Raḥmat al-Umma*, 413. For model documents of *khulʿ al-yamīn* as preformed by a Ḥanbalī judge, see al-Asyūṭī, *Jawāhir al-ʿUqūd*, vol. II, 121; al-Jarawānī, "Mawāhib," fol. 86b.

to follow the opinions of Abū Ḥanīfa.[34] Al-Jazarī's Damascene audience readily recognized the allegory; during the 1320s, a very similar story was unfolding in their own city.

## Ibn Taymiyya on divorce oaths

In 718/1318, Ibn Taymiyya wrote a short epistle, entitled *al-Ijtimāʿ wa'l-Iftirāq fī al-Ḥilf bi'l-Ṭalāq* (The Meeting and Parting of Ways concerning Oaths on Pain of Divorce).[35] In this work he proposed a novel doctrine regarding divorce oaths, contradicting not only the established doctrine but also his own earlier views on the subject. The main argument of the treatise was that conditional divorces and oaths on pain of divorce form two distinct legal categories. Divorce oaths should be equated with oaths in the name of God, and therefore should have the same legal consequences. Since an oath in the name of God required expiation, a violation of a divorce oath requires a similar act of atonement, not the actual dissolution of marriage. In the following years, Ibn Taymiyya composed many more treatises and *fatwā*s on this issue, which seems to have occupied him until his final arrest in 726/1326.[36]

The crux of Ibn Taymiyya's argument was his broad definition of intention. In his view, intentions supersede the explicit or formal meanings conveyed in speech. When a man says "May my wife be repudiated if I enter this house," his intention is merely to assert his determination, as in the sentence "By God, I shall not enter this house." The same applies to testimonies about past events, such as "May my wife be repudiated if I stole this money," which conveys the same intention as "By God, I did not steal this money." Ibn Taymiyya argues that when a man has the intention of either deterring (*manʿ*) or inciting (*ḥathth*) himself or someone else from or to a certain action, or attesting (*taṣdīq*) or contesting (*takdhīb*) a certain piece of information, he is in fact undertaking an oath. As proof, he makes an analogy with vows of pilgrimage and charity, such as "May I give all my property

34 Al-Jazarī, *Ta'rīkh*, vol. II, 172–73.

35 Ibn Taymiyya, *al-Ijtimāʿ wa'l-Iftirāq fī al-Ḥilf bi'l-Ṭalāq*, ed. Muḥammad ʿAbd al-Razzāq Ḥamza (Cairo: Maktabat Anṣār, 1346/1927–28). The manuscript used for the published edition contains an *ijāza* by Ibn Taymiyya, dated 27 Rabīʿ I 718 (May 10, 1318), and it can be assumed that he completed the treatise shortly prior to that date. See also H. Laoust's translation of this treatise, which he prefaced with a short introduction ("Une risāla d'Ibn Taimīya sur le serment de répudiation," *Bulletin d'études orientales* 7–8 [1937–38], 215–36), and the discussions of Ibn Taymiyya's views on divorce oaths in Laoust, *Essai*, 424–34; Abū Zahra, *Ibn Taymiyya*, 414–37.

36 The most elaborate, and probably the latest, work by Ibn Taymiyya on oaths of divorce is found in the fifth and final chapter of his *Bayān al-ʿUqūd* (The Elucidation of Contracts), devoted to oaths and vows (in Ibn Taymiyya, *Majmūʿat Fatāwā*, vol. III, 349–84). A shorter treatise, called *Lamḥat al-Mukhtaṭif fī al-Farq bayna al-Ṭalāq wa'l-Ḥilf* (A Quick Glance at the Difference between Divorces and Oaths), as well as several *fatwā*s on the subject, were published in *Majmūʿat Fatāwā*, vol. III, 2–8, 27 ff. Ibn Taymiyya's biographers mention at least ten additional works on this subject (Ibn ʿAbd al-Hādī, *al-ʿUqūd al-Durriyya fī Manāqib Shaykh al-Islām Aḥmad Ibn Taymiyya*, ed. Muḥammad Ḥāmid al-Fiqī [Cairo: Maṭbaʿat al-Ḥijāzī, 1938], 214). Ibn Qayyim al-Jawziyya's eloquent exposition of his master's views on divorce oaths is found in his *Iʿlām al-Muwaqqiʿīn*, vol. III, 50–80, vol. IV, 97–118; *Ighāthat al-Lahfān*, vol. II, 87–97.

to charity if I enter this house." Most Sunni scholars agree that these vows are not simple conditional sentences, and categorize them as oaths. Thus, when a man violates a vow of pilgrimage, he is not required to actually go to Mecca.

Ibn Taymiyya then argues that if the intention is that of an oath, the laws of oaths should apply. God commanded men to respect their valid oaths to the utmost of their ability, but also gave permission to violate oaths as long as proper atonement is performed. The acts of atonement prescribed in the Qur'ān are the feeding and clothing of the indigent, the manumission of a slave, or three days of fasting. The divine legislation, argues Ibn Taymiyya, must apply to all oaths, including oaths on pain of divorce. Therefore, violation of an oath on pain of divorce, like the violation of any other oath, should be expiated, not punished.[37] Ibn Taymiyya did not object to oaths as such. On the contrary, he considered it a moral duty to abide by one's oaths, and even more so with regard to an oath of allegiance to the sultan. But oaths, whatever their form, should never supersede the obedience due to God.[38]

Closely related to Ibn Taymiyya's views on divorce oaths was his doctrine on the invalidity of triple repudiation. He argued that repudiation is only valid if it is made in the way recommended by the Prophet, the so-called *sunnī* divorce. In Islamic law, a distinction is made between a *sunnī* divorce – that is, a single revocable repudiation uttered when the wife is in a state of purity – and *bid'ī* divorces – that is, acts of divorce made in any other way, including the single utterance of a triple repudiation. While *sunnī* divorces are preferable, all the orthodox schools recognize the validity of both *sunnī* and *bid'ī* divorces. Ibn Taymiyya, however, argued that *bid'ī* divorces do not bind at all. For example, when a man says "You are repudiated thrice," the established view is that triple divorce follows; but Ibn Taymiyya ruled that the result is only one single, revocable divorce, as the two other repudiations are *bid'ī* divorces.[39] In effect this was another attempt to mitigate the power of divorce oaths, as the implication of Ibn Taymiyya's position was that a violation of an oath taken on pain of triple repudiation causes only a single, and revocable, divorce.

Ibn Taymiyya's doctrines regarding conditional divorces were almost certainly original. There was no precedent to his positions among the Sunni schools, and the established doctrine he wished to overturn relied on a consensus (*ijmā'*) of the jurists.[40] Ibn Taymiyya himself claimed that several contemporary North African

[37] Ibn Taymiyya, *al-Ijtimā' wa'l-Iftirāq*, 14 ff.; Ibn Taymiyya, *Majmū'at Fatāwā*, vol. III, 364–69, 381.

[38] Ibn Taymiyya, *Majmū'at Fatāwā*, vol. III, 28, 53, 351, 375; Ibn al-Qayyim, *I'lām al-Muwaqq i'īn*, vol. III, 73–80; Laoust, *Essai*, 287–88.

[39] Ibn Taymiyya, *Majmū'at Fatāwā*, vol. III, 13–27; Ibn Taymiyya, *Majmū'at al-Rasā'il al-Kubrā*, 2 vols. (Cairo: Maṭba'at al-'Āmira, 1905–06), vol. II, 203–16. See also Ibn Qayyim al-Jawziyya, *Zād al-Mi'ād fī Hady Khayr al-'Ibād*, ed. Shu'ayb and 'Abd al-Qādir al-Arnā'ūṭ, 5 vols. (Beirut: Mu'assasat al-Risāla, 1979), vol. V, 218–71; Ibn al-Qayyim, *I'lām al-Muwaqqi'īn*, vol. III, 30–50. For a lucid summary of Ibn Taymiyya's arguments, see Abū Zahra, *Ibn Taymiyya*, 414–27.

[40] On the existence of *ijmā'* in support of the established doctrine on divorce oaths, see Muwaffaq al-Dīn Ibn Qudāma (d. 620/1223), *al-Mughnī*, 14 vols. (Beirut: Dār al-Fikr, 1984), vol. XI, 220–21; Muḥammad Ibn Rushd al-Qurṭūbī, *Bidāyat al-Mujtahid wa-Nihāyat al-Muqtaṣid*, 4 vols. (Beirut: Dār al-Ma'rifa, 1985), vol. I, 411.

Mālikī jurists, whose names he lists, shared his view on the expiable nature of divorce oaths.[41] The first name on this list, Abū Yaḥyā al-Haskūrī, may be identified with the jurist Mūsā b. Yawmīn al-Haskūrī, who was convicted of fornication in Fez during the 1310s, and whose case has been studied by David Powers. Al-Haskūrī, who divorced his wife three times and then remarried her without *taḥlīl*, argued in his defense that two of his divorces were *khul'* consensual separations, which, according to a minority view, do not count as divorces.[42] The mention of North African jurists brings to mind the doctrine of the Ẓāhirīs, who maintain that oaths on pain of divorce are invalid. But the Ẓāhirī argument is based on a fundamental rejection of any conditional divorces, a methodology Ibn Taymiyya did not follow.[43]

Another source of influence on Ibn Taymiyya – naturally unacknowledged – may have been the Shī'ī Imāmī doctrine that rejects both conditional divorces and the utterance of triple repudiation.[44] Unlike Sunnis, Shī'ī Imāmīs were not bound by oaths on pain of divorce, and this marked a major difference between the two communities. The conversion of the Mongol Īlkhān Öljeitü to the Shī'ī creed in 709/1310, only ten years before Ibn Taymiyya composed his first treatise on divorce oaths, has been attributed to his exasperation with the Sunni divorce law. When the Īlkhān wanted to remarry a wife he had previously repudiated thrice, the Sunni jurists offered him no solution except a *taḥlīl* marriage. The Shī'ī scholar al-Ḥillī, on the other hand, allowed him to take back his wife.[45] The account is apocryphal, but Sunni–Shī'ī rivalry may have contributed to the development of Ibn Taymiyya's doctrines on divorce oaths.

Ibn Taymiyya often evokes the age of the Prophet in order to justify his views, but he does so in a utilitarian fashion, as a means of defending himself against the established consensus. For example, he claims that divorce oaths were unknown

41 Ibn Taymiyya, *al-Ijtimā' wa'l-Iftirāq*, 24. See also Ibn Taymiyya, *Majmū'at Fatāwā*, vol. III, 10; Ibn Taymiyya, *Majmū' Fatāwā*, vol. XX, 13. Ibn Qayyim al-Jawziyya makes a more specific reference to a work by the Cordovan *qāḍī* Abū al-Walīd Hishām b. 'Abdallāh al-Azdī (d. 606/1209), entitled *al-Mufīd li'l-Ḥukkām*. Ibn al-Qayyim claims that in this book Abū al-Walīd makes a systematic distinction between oaths and divorces (*Ighāthat al-Lahfān*, vol. II, 92–94).

42 In the published edition the name appears as Abū Yaḥyā al-Haskūrī from Miltāna (Ibn Taymiyya, *al-Ijtimā' wa'l-Iftirāq*, 24). The place name is probably a corruption of Milyāna, a town in western Tūnis; Abū Yaḥyā is possibly a misspelling of Abū al-Najā, a *kunya* that goes well with the personal name Mūsā. On the case, see D. Powers, *Law, Society, and Culture in the Maghrib, 1300–1500* (Cambridge: Cambridge University Press, 2002), 39–54. Triple divorces have been the subject of bitter scholarly debates in eleventh-century al-Andalus (D. Serrano, "Legal Practice in an Andalusī–Maghribī Source from the Twelfth Century CE: The *Madhāhib al-Ḥukkām fī Nawāzil al-Aḥkām*," *ILS* 7/2 [2000], 225–28).

43 'Alī b. Muḥammad Ibn Ḥazm, *al-Muḥallā bi'l-Āthār*, ed. 'Abd al-Ghaffār Sulaymān al-Bindārī, 10 vols. (Beirut: Dār al-Kutub al-'Ilmiyya, 1988), vol. IX, 476–79 (no. 1965). Unlike Ibn Taymiyya, Ibn Ḥazm accepted the validity of triple repudiation (*ibid.*, 384–401).

44 On the non-Sunni doctrines on divorce oaths, see Abū Zahra, *Ibn Taymiyya*, 419, 427. For Ibn Taymiyya's own view on the differences between his doctrines and those of the Ẓāhirīs and Shi'ī Imāmīs, see *Majmū'at Fatāwā*, vol. III, 8–9.

45 S. Schmidtke, *The Theology of al-'Allāma al-Ḥillī (d. 726/1325)* (Berlin: K. Schwarz, 1991), 23–25. For other variants of this story, see M. al-'Āmilī, *A'yān al-Shī'ah*, ed. Ḥasan al-Amīn, 11 vols. (Beirut: Dār al-Ta'āruf, 1986), vol. V, 399.

at the time of the Prophet, and that the practice itself is an innovation (*bid'a*).[46] He also argues, on the basis of a tradition attributed to Ibn 'Abbās (d. 68/687), that the first Muslims considered triple repudiation as only a single, revocable divorce. The same tradition also attributes the change in law to the second caliph, 'Umar b. al-Khaṭṭāb, who wanted to deter Muslim men from taking divorce too lightly. According to Ibn Taymiyya, just as 'Umar changed the laws of divorce in the interest of the community, jurists must now revert to the practice of the Prophet in order to combat the evil practice of *taḥlīl*.[47] For Ibn Taymiyya going back to the practices of the Prophet was not an end in itself, at least not in this case. It was a tool, used to defend his heterodox doctrine against the prevailing orthodoxy.[48]

The primary motivation for Ibn Taymiyya's radical re-thinking of the divorce oath was his entrenched opposition to legal subterfuges, and in particular to *taḥlīl* marriages. Ibn Taymiyya was not, of course, the first to criticize these legal stratagems. Al-Ghazālī warned husbands against pronouncing triple repudiations, as a man might regret it and would be compelled to have a *muḥallil* marry his former wife.[49] Ibn Taymiyya's attack, however, is accompanied by a sense of urgency and a deep apprehension about the spread of legal subterfuges in his days.[50] *Taḥlīl* marriages, in particular, he regarded as the most abominable of the legal devices, denigrating the image of Islam in the minds of commoners. They were also mocked by the Jews, who branded the Muslims "*mamzīrīm*" (*sic*), the Hebrew word for bastards, on account of this practice.[51] Ibn Taymiyya accused *muḥallil*s of contracting simultaneous marriages with more than four women, and of incestuous marriage to a daughter and her mother. *Taḥlīl* marriages were tantamount to adultery because they were often kept secret from the woman's legal guardian, whose consent is necessary for the validity of the contract. In some cases, Ibn Taymiyya claims, *taḥlīl* caused infanticide, as women killed children born from their disgraceful intercourse with the *muḥallil*.[52] Ibn Taymiyya shared this apprehension with other contemporary scholars. Sulaymān b. 'Abd al-Qawī al-Ṭūfī (d. 716/1316) was also

46 Ibn Taymiyya, *Majmū'at Fatāwā*, vol. III, 53, 59–60, 375; Ibn al-Qayyim, *I'lām al-Muwaqqi'īn*, vol. III, 54.

47 Ibn Taymiyya, *Majmū'at Fatāwā*, vol. III, 22–3; Ibn Taymiyya, *Majmū'at al-Rasā'il*, 206; Ibn al-Qayyim, *I'lām al-Muwaqqi'īn*, vol. III, 30–50; Ibn al-Qayyim, *al-Ṭuruq al-Ḥukmiyya*, 16–17.

48 For another example of Ibn Taymiyya's positioning of the age of the Prophet against prevailing orthodoxy, see Shahab Ahmed, "Ibn Taymiyyah and the Satanic Verses," *SI* 87 (1998), 111.

49 Al-Ghazālī argues that *taḥlīl* marriages cause the wife to become disenchanted with her first husband (Madeleine Farah, *Marriage and Sexuality in Islam. A Translation of al-Ghazali's Book on the Etiquette of Marriage from the* Iḥyā' [Salt Lake City: Utah University Press, 1984], 117–18).

50 According to Ibn Taymiyya, in his days even Mālikī and Ḥanbalī jurists were counseling commoners to use legal subterfuges (*Iqāmat al-Dalīl*, 68).

51 Ibn al-Qayyim, *Ighāthat al-Lahfān*, vol. II, 344. Jewish law allows a man to remarry his ex-wife only if she did *not* marry another man in the meantime; thus, in Jewish law a *taḥlīl* marriage has the opposite effect of making the wife forbidden, rather than permitted, to her first husband. Intriguingly, however, two twelfth-century documents from the Geniza refer to oaths on pain of divorce undertaken by Jewish men, undoubtedly influenced by the prevailing Muslim practice (Goitein, *A Mediterranean Society*, vol. III, 156).

52 Ibn Taymiyya, *Iqāmat al-Dalīl*, 216–18.

known for his vociferous opposition to legal subterfuges.[53] Contemporary moralists, such as Ibn al-Ḥājj and Ibn Baydakīn, described the corrupting effect of *taḥlīl* marriages in similar terms.[54]

For Ibn Taymiyya, the perils of *taḥlīl* furnish the ultimate confirmation of his doctrines. His reasoning is as follows: Let us concede, for the sake of the argument, that the evidence in the Qur'ān and the Ḥadīth is contradictory and ambiguous. In that case, the correct analogy must lead us to support the expiability of divorce oaths, for this is in the interest (*maṣlaḥa*) of the Muslims. Otherwise, as happens in our day, the believers find themselves in a quagmire, having no way out other than *taḥlīl* marriages or other types of legal subterfuges.[55]

In one of his later works, summarizing all his doctrines on divorce, Ibn Taymiyya explains:

> When the innovation of oaths on pain of divorce was introduced, many jurists believed that they were binding upon violation, with no possibility of atonement; subsequently, many jurists believed that forbidden (*muḥarram*) divorces were valid, and some thought that it was even permissible to utter triple divorces . . . People have come to believe that divorces occur [in these cases], in spite of the immense harm and corruption, both in religious and in temporal affairs, which are the result of the separation of a husband from his wife.
>
> Faced with divorces resulting from these controverted legal questions, men were divided into two groups. One group consisted of those who prohibited *taḥlīl*, in accordance with the example of the Prophet and the Companions, while at the same time also prohibiting what the Prophet himself did not [with regard to these questions of divorce]. Their legal rulings imposed heavy burdens and yokes and immense oppression, which lead to corruption in religious and temporal affairs, not least the apostasy of those who are told by a *muftī* that [their pronouncement of divorce] is binding, shedding of innocent blood, loss of sanity, enmity between people, replacement of Islamic law with a multitude of sins, as well as many other evils of this kind.
>
> The other group consisted of those who thought that they would remove this immense oppression by using legal subterfuges to allow a wife to return to her husband. First, the marriage of *taḥlīl* was introduced, and some jurists even believed that God rewards those who contract *taḥlīl* marriages, for they permit the wife to her husband and remove the cause of corruption. This legal subterfuge was then used to circumvent all other forms of binding divorce. Later, other legal subterfuges were introduced with regard to oaths [of divorce] . . . However, all past authorities and men of knowledge have denounced these legal subterfuges and their likes, regarding them as nullifying the wisdom of the Divine law and the true essence of the verses of the Qur'ān, and as nothing less than derision and mockery of the Divine word.[56]

Thus, Ibn Taymiyya justified his opposition to legal subterfuges and divorce oaths through his reading of Islamic history. At the time of the Prophet, he argues, the Divine law must have been interpreted correctly. But once rigid and formalistic interpretations of the law led to the innovation of the divorce oath, believers became

[53] Laoust, "Le hanbalisme," 62–63.
[54] Ibn al-Ḥājj, *Madkhal*, vol. II, 61; Lutfi, "Manners," 106; Ibn Baydakīn, *Kitāb al-Luma'*, 160.
[55] Ibn Taymiyya, *Majmū'at Fatāwā*, vol. III, 5, 29, 375–78. [56] *Ibid.*, 54–55.

burdened with shackles and fetters which could not have come from God. Well-meaning jurists then devised legal subterfuges in order to relieve the community of these burdens. But, since God could not have prohibited something and then allowed it through trickery and deceit, these legal subterfuges are of no use, adding to the sources of corruption rather than reducing them. The problem, according to Ibn Taymiyya, is not the legal subterfuges themselves, for they are but a symptom. The legal subterfuges would not have been introduced to Muslim society if God's laws had been interpreted correctly – that is, through the understanding of their divine cause rather than according to their formal meaning.

## Ibn Taymiyya on trial

As soon as Ibn Taymiyya began circulating his views on the expiable nature of oaths on pain of divorce, they were quickly refuted by leading jurists in Damascus and Cairo, most notably by the Egyptian Shāfiʿī jurist Taqī al-Dīn al-Subkī.[57] Al-Subkī composed his first refutation of Ibn Taymiyya's doctrine on divorce oaths shortly after the appearance of *al-Ijtimāʿ wa'l-Iftirāq*, and later authored at least four more treatises about divorce oaths and triple divorces.[58] His refutations of Ibn Taymiyya paved his way to higher office: he was eventually appointed chief Shāfiʿī *qāḍī* of Damascus in 739/1338, gradually acquiring several other offices in the city, many of which he was able to pass on to his sons. Compared to Ibn Taymiyya, al-Subkī, as a Shāfiʿī Egyptian who amassed official appointments, represents the opposite end of the social spectrum of Mamlūk *ʿulamāʾ*. Unlike the ever-celibate Ibn Taymiyya, al-Subkī was married to several wives, divorcing the first, who was also his paternal cousin, at the age of fifteen.[59]

Central to al-Subkī's refutation was his equation of divorce oaths with conditional divorces. Al-Subkī admits that laymen refer to conditional divorces as oaths, a term that was even accepted into the jargon of the jurists (*ʿurf al-fuqahāʾ*). The jurists, however, do not use the term in a literal sense, and it has no bearing on

[57] On al-Subkī's relationship with Ibn Taymiyya, see al-Ṣafadī, *Aʿyān*, vol. III, 429; al-Subkī, *Ṭabaqāt*, vol. VI, 168. On a treatise by Ibn al-Zamlakānī refuting Ibn Taymiyya's doctrine on divorce, see al-Ṣafadī, *Aʿyān*, vol. IV, 630; S. Jackson, "Ibn Taymiyya on Trial in Damascus," *Journal of Semitic Studies* 39 (1994), 48–49. Another refutation of Ibn Taymiyya was written by the Ḥanafī jurist Aḥmad b. ʿUthmān Ibn al-Turkumānī (d. 744/1343) (al-Ṣafadī, *Aʿyān*, vol. I, 284).

[58] Al-Subkī's first treatise on divorce oaths was *al-Taḥqīq fī Masʾalat al-Taʿlīq* (The Determination of Truth in Conditional Phrases), of which apparently only extracts survive in a Damascus manuscript. A second treatise, *Naqd al-Ijtimāʿ wa'l-Iftirāq fī Masāʾil al-Aymān wa'l-Ṭalāq* (published in al-Subkī, *Fatāwā*, vol. II, 303–09), was completed on 20 Ramaḍān 718 (November 15, 1318). At a later date, al-Subkī added a more detailed treatise, *al-Durra al-Muḍiyya fī al-Radd ʿalā Ibn Taymiyya* (The Shining Pearl on the Refutation of Ibn Taymiyya), which dealt with triple divorces as well as with divorce oaths. These last two, together with another short treatise on divorce oaths completed in Muḥarram 725/January 1325, were published in Taqī al-Dīn al-Subkī, *al-Rasāʾil al-Subkiyya fī al-Radd ʿalā Ibn Taymiyya wa-Tilmīdhihi Ibn Qayyim al-Jawziyya* (Beirut: ʿĀlam al-Kutub, 1983), 151–91. An abridgment, entitled "Masʾalat al-Ṭalāq al-Muʿallaq" (On Conditional Divorces), is found in the Princeton Manuscripts Collection (Yahuda 878, fols. 135a–139a).

[59] The most detailed biography of Taqī al-Dīn al-Subkī was composed by his son, Tāj al-Dīn (*Ṭabaqāt*, vol. VI, 146–227). See also J. Schacht and C. E. Bosworth, "al-Subkī," *EI*[2].

the legal rules that apply to this action.[60] Even if, like Ibn Taymiyya, one assumes the primacy of the speaker's intention, this intention could only be inferred from social practice. And as is well known, the praxis is that no expiation is allowed in divorce oaths. Therefore, argues al-Subkī, a man who undertakes a divorce oath consciously commits himself to a divorce upon violation of his oath; otherwise he would not have taken the oath in the first place.[61] Al-Subkī also refutes Ibn Taymiyya's analogy between divorce oaths and vows of pilgrimage. He argues that pilgrimage vows are similar to oaths in the name of God, and therefore expiable, because they are made with the intention of seeking God's favor. Divorce, on the other hand, cannot be considered a pious act, and the analogy of divorce oaths with pilgrimage vows does not stand.[62] Al-Subkī then accuses Ibn Taymiyya of sloppy research as well as of deliberate misquotation.[63] In contrast to the weak traditions presented by Ibn Taymiyya, al-Subkī quotes a multitude of traditions in support of the established view – a veritable *ijmāʿ*.[64]

By the time al-Subkī was writing his refutations of Ibn Taymiyya, the state had already started to exert its coercive power. In Jumādā al-Ūlā 718/July 1318, no more than a couple of months after the completion of his first treatise on divorce oaths, an edict of the sultan arrived from Cairo prohibiting Ibn Taymiyya from issuing *fatwā*s on the subject.[65] We are told that the matter was brought to the sultan's attention by his chief Ḥanafī *qāḍī*, the Syrian-born Shams al-Dīn al-Ḥarīrī. By this time the chief Ḥanbalī *qāḍī* of Damascus had already approached Ibn Taymiyya and asked him to discontinue his *fatwā*s on divorce. The chroniclers suggest that Ibn Taymiyya complied with the sultan's edict for more than a year, but then returned to the subject, claiming that he was not permitted to conceal true knowledge. Ibn Taymiyya received another royal reprimand in Ramaḍān 719/November 1319, and a council of the leading amirs and jurists summoned by the local governor confirmed the earlier prohibition.[66]

In Rajab 720/August 1320, Ibn Taymiyya was summoned again to the governor's palace, this time to be finally arrested. The unpublished and relatively unknown chronicle of al-Fayyūmī contains a unique eyewitness account of this council.[67] In the presence of the governor, *qāḍī*s and notables of the city, Ibn Taymiyya denied having issued any *fatwā*s after the promulgation of the royal ban. Several

60 Al-Subkī, *al-Rasāʾil*, 179, 190; al-Subkī, "Masʾalat al-Ṭalāq," fols. 136b–137a.

61 Al-Subkī, *al-Rasāʾil*, 155, 171, 190.

62 *Ibid.*, 166–71; al-Subkī, "Masʾalat al-Ṭalāq," fol. 138b.

63 Al-Subkī demonstrates that "this heretic" (*al-mubtadiʿ*), i.e., Ibn Taymiyya, quoted only the first part of a tradition on the expiability of oaths, omitting its second part which excludes oaths of divorce and manumission from the general rule (al-Subkī, *al-Rasāʾil*, 158, 160; al-Subkī, "Masʾalat al-Ṭalāq," fols.135b–136a, 139a).

64 Al-Subkī, *al-Rasāʾil*, 156–57. For lists of Followers who held that divorce oaths are binding, see *ibid.*, 159–61; al-Subkī, "Masʾalat al-Ṭalāq," fols. 136a–136b. Al-Subkī concedes that oaths of divorce were not common at the time of the Prophet, and that it is difficult to find traditions of the Companions in support of the orthodox doctrine ("Masʾalat al-Ṭalāq," fol. 137a).

65 Murad, "Ibn Taymiya," 21–23. See also Ibn ʿAbd al-Hādī, *ʿUqūd*, 214–16; Ibn Kathīr, *Bidāya* (Cairo), vol. XIV, 93, 97–98; al-Ṣafadī, *Aʿyān*, vol. I, 237; Laoust, *Essai*, 143–45.

66 Ibn ʿAbd al-Hādī, *ʿUqūd*, 214–16.

67 ʿAlī b. Muḥammad al-Fayyūmī, "Nathr al-Jumān fī Tarājim al-Aʿyān," Chester Beatty MS 4113, 134b–135a. On al-Fayyūmī and his work, see D. Little, *An Introduction to Mamlūk Historiography* (Wiesbaden: F. Steiner, 1970), 40–42.

witnesses then testified that they saw a butcher by the name of Qamar arrive in the orchard of the Ḥanbalī family of the Banū al-Munajjā in order to receive a *fatwā* on divorce from Ibn Taymiyya. When members of the Banū al-Munajjā rose to deny the allegation, the Shāfiʿī chief *qāḍī*, Najm al-Din Ibn Ṣaṣrā, dismissed their objections as partisan. Ibn Taymiyya was then told to sign a statement declaring that he would refrain from delivering any sort of *fatwā*. He apparently consented, but Najm al-Din Ibn Ṣaṣrā still ordered his detention in the citadel of Damascus. He remained in prison for five months, until his release through a royal amnesty on the Day of ʿĀshūrāʾ 721/January 1321.

Contemporary chroniclers and modern scholars emphasize the personal dimension of the conflict between Ibn Taymiyya and the state authorities. Ibn Qayyim al-Jawziyya explains that his shaykh's enemies "found no way to refute his doctrines other than petitioning the sultan."[68] Most modern scholars concur, suggesting that the coercive power of the state was more or less manipulated by Ibn Taymiyya's personal enemies among the *ʿulamāʾ*. Henri Laoust argues that the trials of Ibn Taymiyya on the issues of divorce and visitation were a result of scholarly factionalism.[69] According to Eliyahu Ashtor-Strauss, the alliance between the military and the scholarly elite required the former to act against any threat to the spiritual domination of their allies.[70] Donald Little, more cautiously, notes that contemporary chronicles stress the rivalry among the *ʿulamāʾ* as the leading factor in the arrests of Ibn Taymiyya.[71] Michael Chamberlain suggests that in the trials of Ibn Taymiyya, as in other contemporary heresy trials, scholars fought each other over the right to determine true knowledge; the specific issue at hand was of secondary importance.[72]

In our case, however, it appears that Ibn Taymiyya's trials were about his ideas, not about his personality. Most of his detractors in 718/1318 had stood by his side during previous trials. The Ḥanafī *qāḍī* Shams al-Dīn al-Ḥarīrī, who instigated the royal reprimand of 718/1318, had been deposed from his offices in 705/1305–06 because of his alleged support for Ibn Taymiyya.[73] Their acquaintance went back even further. In 702/1302, they were both accused of corresponding secretly with the recently repelled Mongols, together with another future detractor of Ibn Taymiyya, Kamāl al-Dīn Ibn al-Zamlakānī.[74] Ibn al-Zamlakānī, who would write a refutation of Ibn Taymiyya's doctrine on divorce oaths, was previously known as an admirer and close associate of the Ḥanbalī jurist. He even wrote verses of admiration for Ibn Taymiyya's unrivaled learning and intelligence.[75] Several years earlier Ibn al-Zamlakānī had been summoned to Cairo to be reprimanded

[68] *Iʿlām al-Muwaqqiʿīn*, vol. III, 62, vol. IV, 114. [69] Laoust, *Essai*, 477.

[70] E. Ashtor-Strauss, "L'Inquisition dans l'état mamlouk," *Rivista degli Studi Orientali* 25 (1950), 14.

[71] Little, "The Detention," 323–27. [72] Chamberlain, *Knowledge*, 167–73.

[73] At the time, al-Ḥarīrī was the chief Ḥanafī *qāḍī* in Damascus (Murad, "Ibn Taymiya," 14).

[74] The accusations arose after the discovery of a letter written by the three jurists and directed to one of the Mongol generals. Later, however, the letter was proved to be a forgery (Murad, "Ibn Taymiya," 4; Ibn Kathīr, *Bidāya* [Cairo], vol. XIV, 22).

[75] Ibn ʿAbd al-Hādī, *ʿUqūd*, 7–8; ʿAbd al-Raḥmān b. Aḥmad Ibn Rajab, *Dhayl ʿalā Ṭabaqāt al-Ḥanābila*, ed. Muḥammad Ḥāmid al-Fiqī, 2 vols. (Cairo: Maṭbaʿat al-Sunna al-Muḥammadiyya, 1952), vol. II, 391.

for his ties with Ibn Taymiyya, and eventually dismissed from his position as the administrator of the city's hospital.[76] The reigning sultan, al-Nāṣir Muḥammad, not only released Ibn Taymiyya from his earlier imprisonment in Cairo, but also reportedly befriended Ibn Taymiyya during the latter's sojourn in Egypt. Now, it is possible to speculate about shifts in factional politics that transformed allies into enemies.[77] But it makes much more sense to assume that al-Ḥarīrī, Ibn al-Zamlakānī and the sultan himself were averse to Ibn Taymiyya's views on divorce rather than to any of his personal faults.

So why did Ibn Taymiyya's views on divorce provoke such a reaction? According to Ibn Qayyim al-Jawziyya, three specific accusations led to Ibn Taymiyya's arrest. First, the state authorities persecuted Ibn Taymiyya for his breach of the jurists' consensus on questions of divorce.[78] Concern over Ibn Taymiyya's breach of the *ijmāʿ* is echoed in other contemporary accounts.[79] Violating the *ijmāʿ* was not merely a methodological error, but also a threat to the uniformity of the judicial system. Al-Subkī especially bemoaned the spread of Ibn Taymiyya's "vile views" among the Bedouins, peasants and the inhabitants of the peripheral lands, where *qāḍī*s were scarce and the interpretation of the law was in the hands of local *muftī*s or shaykhs.[80] Commoners, such as Qamar the butcher, could come to Ibn Taymiyya in order to circumvent their oaths of divorce, and thus also to bypass the state's judicial system. By breaching the consensus of the jurists, Ibn Taymiyya posed a threat to the legal order, in which both the state and the scholars had a stake.

Ibn Taymiyya was also accused of encouraging adultery. Al-Subkī warned that Ibn Taymiyya's doctrines would lead laymen to disregard the laws of divorce and live in a state of sin.[81] In that sense, al-Subkī felt he was protecting the children of Muslims from the stigma of illegitimate birth. His friend, the historian and encyclopedist Ibn Faḍl Allāh al-ʿUmarī (d. 749), believed that one of al-Subkī's lasting achievements was safeguarding lineage and noble descent from the danger posed by the doctrines of Ibn Taymiyya.[82] Ibn al-Qayyim, defending Ibn Taymiyya, notes that "the lowly and sheepish people who belittled him [Ibn Taymiyya], claimed that he prevented Muslims from divorcing their wives, and caused the number of bastards to grow. And those who have but a whiff of sense in them said that he prohibited conditional divorces altogether."[83]

But the most severe accusation was the suspicion of giving license to political insubordination. Ibn Qayyim al-Jawziyya says that Ibn Taymiyya's opponents told

[76] On Ibn al-Zamlakānī's dismissal from this office as a result of his support (*intimāʾ*) for Ibn Taymiyya, see Ibn Kathīr, *Bidāya* (Cairo), vol. XIV, 41, 48–99; Murad, "Ibn Taymiya," 18; Jackson, "Ibn Taymiyya on Trial," 48–49; Ibn Ḥajar, *Durar*, vol. IV, 193.

[77] The historian al-Ṣafadī speculated that Ibn al-Zamlakānī allied himself with Ibn Taymiyya against his rival Shāfiʿī jurist and *qāḍī* Ibn al-Wakīl (*Aʿyān*, vol. I, 247).

[78] Ibn al-Qayyim, *Iʿlām al-Muwaqqiʿīn*, vol. III, 62.

[79] Ibn Rajab remarks that the jurists objected to Ibn Taymiyya's support of weak opinions against the dominant opinions of the schools (*Dhayl*, vol. II, 394). See also al-Ṣafadī, *Aʿyān*, vol. I, 235; Abū Zahra, *Ibn Taymiyya*, 79–82, 437–38, 451; Little, "The Detention," 326.

[80] Al-Subkī, *al-Rasāʾil*, 151–52. [81] *Ibid.*, 152.

[82] Al-Subkī, *Ṭabaqāt*, vol. VI, 151. [83] Ibn al-Qayyim, *Iʿlām al-Muwaqqiʿīn*, vol. IV, 115.

their patrons that "he has released those who had undertaken the oath of allegiance to the sultan from their obligations."[84] To Ibn Taymiyya's contemporaries, oaths of divorce were the principal way by which a man could be made accountable for his sworn undertakings. The oath of allegiance was the most important sworn undertaking in the political sphere, and Ibn Taymiyya's doctrines, intentionally or not, posed a threat to this central symbol of the regime. If his views were to be accepted, a violation of the oath of allegiance would require the violator only to perform an act of atonement. Al-Subkī may be hinting at the political ramifications of the debate when he comments that "Ibn Taymiyya began his innovation with this issue [i.e., oaths of divorce]. But his intention was to achieve, if he were to succeed, a further goal."[85]

## Divorce oaths and the medieval state

The Sunni doctrine on divorce oaths withstood Ibn Taymiyya's attack. His position never gained wide acceptance among the jurists, nor even spread much beyond the Ḥanbalī stronghold in the al-Ṣāliḥiyya quarter in Damascus. In part, this was due to the efforts of the state authorities, which continued to suppress his doctrines long after his death. Yūsuf b. Mājid al-Mardāwī (d. 783/1381) was arrested several times because he endorsed Ibn Taymiyya's positions on divorce.[86] In 789/1387, Shams al-Dīn al-Ḥarīrī, the leader of a Ḥanbalī mosque in Damascus, was flogged and paraded on a donkey around the city on account of his views on divorce oaths.[87] ʿAlī b. ʿAbd al-Muḥsin al-Dawālibī, the shaykh of the Abū ʿUmar madrasa in al-Ṣāliḥiyya, suffered a similar fate some sixty years later. As he was led on the donkey, a court official proclaimed: "This is the punishment for anyone who adopts Ibn Taymiyya's doctrine on triple divorce."[88] Other Ḥanbalī scholars who issued *fatwā*s in accordance with Ibn Taymiyya's views were reproached by the chief *qāḍī*s.[89] By the end of the fifteenth century even Ḥanbalī support had petered out. Ibn al-Mibrad, writing in 870/1465, admitted that only a handful of scholars still adhered to the doctrines of Ibn Taymiyya on the issue of divorce.[90]

Ibn Taymiyya not only failed to cause his fellow jurists to change their minds; his views seem to have had limited impact on social practices. Throughout the

[84] Text: *hādhā ḥalla bayʿat al-sulṭān min aʿnāq al-ḥālifīn* (*ibid.*, 115).
[85] Al-Subkī, *al-Rasāʾil*, 156.
[86] Ibn Qāḍī Shuhba, *Taʾrīkh*, vol. I, 79; Ibn Ḥajar, *Inbāʾal-Ghumr*, vol. I, 252.
[87] Ibn Qāḍī Shuhba, *Taʾrīkh*, vol. I, 91, 215; al-Maqrīzī, *Durar al-ʿUqūd*, vol. I, 291; Ibn Ḥajar, *Inbāʾ al-Ghumr*, vol. I, 260; Laoust, *Essai*, 499. According to Ibn al-Mibrad, the background was petty factionalism among the Ḥanbalī community in the city (*Sayr al-Ḥāthth ilā ʿIlm al-Ṭalāq al-Thalāth*, ed. Muḥammad b. Nāṣir al-ʿAjamī (Beirut: Dār al-Bashāʾir al-Islāmiyya, 1997), 56).
[88] Ibn al-Ḥimṣī, *Ḥawādith*, vol. I, 141; al-Sakhāwī, *Ḍawʾ*, vol. V, 256.
[89] Yūsuf b. Aḥmad Ibn al-ʿIzz (d. 798/1396), another *imām* of the Abū ʿUmar madrasa, was reproved for his *fatwā*s on divorce (Ibn Ḥajar, *Inbāʾ al-Ghumr*, vol. I, 251). Ibn Ḥajar personally reproached a Ḥanbalī shaykh by the name of Muḥammad al-Qabāqibī (d. 826/1423) for the same offense (*ibid.*, vol. III, 322). On the persecution of Ibn Taymiyya's disciples in general, see Laoust, "Le hanbalisme," 66–71.
[90] Ibn al-Mibrad, *Sayr al-Ḥāthth*, 35 ff.

second half of the fourteenth century we find members of the military and civilian elite using divorce oaths to cement alliances and express commitments.[91] The practice of *taḥlīl* remained sufficiently widespread to capture the attention and the imagination of European travelers. During his 1384 visit to Egypt, the Italian merchant Sigoli reported that when a husband divorced his wife three times, the *qāḍī* would send three blind men to have intimate relations with her for a whole day, and only after this could the couple remarry. His fellow traveler Frescobaldi added that some people blinded themselves in order to become eligible for the job.[92] The Ḥaram documents provide additional examples of the use of divorce oaths in the late fourteenth century, including a record of what appears to be a *taḥlīl* marriage. On 13 Rabīʿ al-Awwal 783 (June 9, 1381), Ulfiyya(?) bt. Jibrīl from the city of Ramla, a divorcée, married a certain Khiḍr b. Kamāl al-Nabulsī in Jerusalem. This turned out to be an extremely short marriage, as Khiḍr repudiated her on the following day. From their marriage contract we learn that her previous husband, ʿAlī al-Ramlī, divorced her by a triple repudiation. It seems likely that Ulfiyya's marriage in Jerusalem was intended to allow her Ramlan husband to take her back.[93]

Commoners continued using divorce oaths in their daily life. Ibn Ṭawq records several instances in which he himself pronounced oaths on pain of divorce. In one case he swore by triple divorce from his wife that he did not steal a letter he was supposed to deliver. In another case he swore on pain of divorce not to take more loans as long as he was still in debt. This oath, as we have seen, was probably the reason for his actual divorce from his wife three weeks later.[94] In fifteenth-century collections of *fatāwā* we still find men swearing on pain of divorce not to allow a daughter to marry a certain suitor, not to sell a certain property, or not to enter the

[91] In 776/1374, the sultan al-Ashraf Shaʿbān took an oath on pain of divorce not to accept the resignation of the chief *qāḍī* Burhān al-Dīn Ibn Jamāʿa (Ibn Ḥajar, *Inbāʾ al-Ghumr*, vol. I, 73; al-Maqrīzī, *Sulūk*, vol. III, 242). The *qāḍī* Badr al-Dīn al-Subkī denied an allegation of embezzlement by taking an oath of triple divorce (Ibn Qaḍī Shuhba, *Taʾrīkh*, vol. I, 219). In 791/1389 the governor of al-Karak swore on pain of divorce not to harm the deposed sultan Barqūq (Ibn al-Ṣayrafī, *Nuzhat al-Nufūs*, vol. I, 250). In 800/1398, the ruler of Mardin claimed that Tamerlane had forced him to swear allegiance on pain of divorce, and that therefore he had no choice but to lend support to the conqueror's armies (al-Maqrīzī, *Sulūk*, vol. III, 898). In 804/1402 the amirs Baybars and Nawrūz pledged friendship by taking mutual oaths on pain of divorce (Ibn Ḥajar, *Inbāʾ al-Ghumr*, vol. II, 203; Ibn al-Ṣayrafī, *Nuzhat al-Nufūs*, vol. III, 142).

[92] Frescobaldi et al., *Visit*, 49, 164.

[93] Ḥaram document no. 623. There are two other references to divorce oaths in the Ḥaram documents. In 795/1392, Yaʿqūb b. Yūsuf acknowledged violating an oath on pain of one single revocable divorce from his wife Fāṭima. The couple remarried immediately afterwards (Ḥaram document no. 321). In 774/1373, the amir Urmanjī, an officer in the *ḥalqa* corps, appeared with his wife Khadīja bt. Badr al-Dīn al-Ṣūfī before a Ḥanbalī deputy in Jerusalem. The couple asked the judge to authorize their *khulʿ* separation according to Ḥanbalī doctrine. Since the couple remarried soon afterwards, this was probably a case of the legal stratagem of *khulʿ al-yamīn*; Urmanjī was about to violate a divorce oath, and he circumvented the oath by a temporary consensual separation (Ḥaram document no. 47, published in al-ʿAsalī, *Wathāʾiq*, vol. I, 254–57). As mentioned above, by registering the temporary separation with a Ḥanbalī official, a couple could repeat the subterfuge several times. The Ḥaram records show that Urmanjī and Khadīja separated and remarried on at least one other occasion.

[94] Ibn Ṭawq, *Taʿlīq*, 442 (3/3/889).

house of their in-laws.[95] Divorce oaths were frequently a form of collateral. The Shāfiʿī jurist al-Samhūdī devoted a treatise to the question of a man who swears on pain of divorce to pay a debt, and then claims bankruptcy. Al-Samhūdī maintained that the court should not dissolve the debtor's marriage, since an oath of divorce serves to express his intention to exert his utmost efforts; if he did try to pay his debts, he should not be penalized.[96]

During the fifteenth century, however, divorce oaths were not as widespread, especially in the political sphere, and their use appears to have gradually declined. As far as we can judge from contemporary chronicles, fifteenth-century members of the elite resorted to divorce oaths only infrequently.[97] Even the value of oaths of allegiance was increasingly questioned. When Qānṣūh al-Ghawrī introduced periodic oath-takings by his troops, the historian Ibn Iyās dismissed them as hollow ceremonies with little meaning.[98] The chroniclers sometimes even take what appears to be a tongue-in-cheek approach. Al-Sakhāwī, for example, tells that Aḥmad b. Sulayman Ibn ʿAwjān, a corrupt Māliki *qāḍī* from Jerusalem, appeared posthumously in a friend's dream and swore on pain of triple divorce that God had forgiven him.[99] Although al-Sakhāwī occasionally mentions the undertaking of divorce oaths, he does not refer even once to an actual divorce caused by such an oath.

As a means of social control divorce oaths were overshadowed by the *qasāma*, a sworn undertaking registered in court at the instigation of the authorities. In Islamic law the term *qasāma* denotes an archaic form of compurgation, but D. S. Richards has already demonstrated that the word had acquired a different meaning in the post-classical period.[100] In the Ḥaram collection the term is found in eleven documents dating from the beginning and the end of the fourteenth century. Most of these documents register village headmen's sworn obligations to cultivate their land and keep the peace. One is the *qasāma* of a group of Jewish butchers who solemnly undertake not to sell meat to Muslims. According to the

95 Al-Anṣārī, *Iʿlām*, 234, 241–42, 246, 248–50, 254; al-Suyūṭī, *Ḥāwī*, vol. I, 264, 268; Ibn Quṭlubughā, "Fatāwā," MS Princeton Yahuda 3393, fol. 114a.

96 Al-Samhūdī, "al-Fawāʾid al-Jamma fī al-Masāʾil al-Thalāth al-Muhimma," MS Princeton Yahuda 321, fols. 50b–61b. The treatise was composed in 897/1492. Similarly, al-Anṣārī and al-Suyūṭī ruled that a man who swears on pain of divorce to pay a debt could exempt himself by claiming bankruptcy (Al-Anṣārī, *Iʿlām*, 235, 244; al-Suyūṭī, *Ḥāwī*, vol. I, 265).

97 The jurist Ibn al-Dayrī swore on divorce that his rival al-Harawī had circulated an erroneous *fatwā* (Ibn Ḥajar, *Inbāʾ al-Ghumr*, vol. III, 166). After his removal from the chief *qāḍī*ship in 851/1447, Ibn Ḥajar was ready to swear on pain of divorce that he was no longer interested in the job (al-Sakhāwī, *al-Jawāhir waʾl-Durar*, vol. II, 630). ʿAlī b. Mūsā al-Buḥayrī swore on pain of divorce never to speak again with a fellow scholar (al-Sakhāwī, *Ḍawʾ*, vol. VI, 43, 260). Muḥammad b. ʿAlī Ibn al-Mughayribī (d. 869/1464) swore on pain of divorce not to accept a certain teaching position (al-Sakhāwī, *Ḍawʾ*, vol. VIII, 164).

98 Petry, *Protectors or Praetorians*, 90. See also Ibn al-Ḥimṣī, *Ḥawādith*, vol. II, 46, 172. These sources do not specifically mention divorce oaths, but rather refer vaguely to "binding oaths." For oaths taken by troops for fifteenth-century sultans, see Ibn Taghrī Birdī, *Nujūm*, vol. XIII, 190, vol. XV, 240, vol. XVI, 219.

99 Al-Sakhāwī, *Ḍawʾ*, vol. I, 307.

100 D. S. Richards, "The Qasāma in Mamlūk Society: Some Documents from the Ḥaram Collection in Jerusalem," *AI* 25 (1991), 245 ff.

phrasing of these documents, the individuals concerned had to swear by God and by the "*qasāma* of the Sultan" to keep their obligations. In case of non-fulfillment, the penalty was either payment of a sum of money to the treasury or the vaguely described "[penalty] for violation of an oath."

The *qasāma* became common practice during the fifteenth century, and is often mentioned in contemporary chronicles. In 808/1405 the deposed *muḥtasib* Ibn al-Jabbās undertook a *qasāma* not to dress like a scholar.[101] In 811/1409 Cairene merchants were required to undertake a *qasāma* not to accept gold coins.[102] References to the *qasāma* become very frequent in the last quarter of the fifteenth century: dealers in women's clothes swear to obey the sumptuary regulations; men swear that they will not work again as *qāḍī*s, notaries or brokers; and wardens in prisons swear not to extort money from the prisoners.[103] By this time the *qasāma* had become sufficiently widespread to be discussed in legal manuals.[104] The term also appears in a group of late fifteenth-century and early sixteenth-century documents from St. Catherine's monastery. In one of the clearest examples, Sultan Qānṣūh al-Ghawrī orders a certain individual to swear a *qasāma* not to disrupt the public peace, setting a penalty of 2,000 dirhams for violation.[105]

A comparison between the *qasāma* and divorce oaths is instructive, as it contrasts the formality of the former with the patriarchal nature of the latter. As Richards insightfully notes, both were means of conveying commitments, and they existed side by side throughout the Mamluk period. But there are also important differences, and these differences may explain the increasing references to the *qasāma* in the fifteenth century. First, unlike the divorce oath, the *qasāma* developed into a formalized written document registered in court. Second, the oath on pain of divorce was, at least theoretically, a private act, while the *qasāma* was, by definition, instigated by state authorities and bore the sultan's name. A third and crucial difference was the type of penalty incurred upon violation. Monetary fines replaced the humiliation involved in a triple divorce. Last but not least, the *qasāma* could be administered to non-Muslims and even to women. In 886/1481 the popular singer Khadīja al-Ruḥābiyya had to swear a *qasāma* that she would discontinue her appearances because of the danger she posed to public morality.[106]

It is obvious, but nonetheless worth stating: only men could undertake an oath on pain of divorce. It is not a coincidence that oaths on pain of divorce and manumission have a special status in Islamic law, different from any other oath. A man could effect changes in status in those members of his household who were under his authority. Divorce and manumission were an extreme manifestation of patriarchal authority, as well as its symbols, precisely because they severed the

[101] Ibn Ḥajar, *Inbā' al-Ghumr*, vol. II, 322.
[102] Richards, "Qasāma," 245–46, and the sources cited there.
[103] In addition to the examples cited by Richards from the chronicle of Ibn Iyās (*ibid.*, 246), see also Ibn al-Ṣayrafī, *Inbā' al-Haṣr*, 207, 261, 321, 408.
[104] Al-Jarawānī, "Mawāhib," fol. 140a; al-Asyūṭī, *Jawāhir al-'Uqūd*, vol. II, 318, 374.
[105] Richards, "Qasāma," 247; H. Ernst, *Die mamlukischen Sultansurkunden des Sinai-Klosters* (Wiesbaden: O. Harrassowitz, 1960), 246–49 (no. LXXI).
[106] Ibn Iyās, *Badā'i'*, vol. III, 185–86; cited in Richards, "Qasāma," 246.

ties that held a household together. The most frequently invoked example of a divorce oath is that of a husband threatening his wife, "If you leave the house without my permission, you are divorced." In this example, the husband warns his wife against transgressing the spatial boundaries of the household, physical boundaries that serve also as a symbol of his authority. The warning is accompanied by a threat to use the ultimate manifestation of this authority, the power of repudiation.

In Mamluk society the household was the locus of social power; it was also the prototype for a variety of relations in the public sphere. Michael Chamberlain has identified the central place of the terminology of love and intimacy, originating in the domestic sphere, for cementing alliances and loyalties among the military and civilian elites.[107] Divorce oaths too had their roots in domestic practices, but were invoked to express authority and power rather than amity and alliance. When the governor of Damascus issued his anti-bribery campaign in the form of a divorce oath, he backed up his threats with the power invested in him as head of household rather than deriving his authority from his official position as governor. The same logic extended to the use of divorce oaths in commercial or social contexts. When a man made a commitment on pain of divorce, he was evoking the patriarchal power granted to him as the head of a domestic unit.

Like divorce itself, divorce oaths seem to have been a distinctive trait of Near Eastern societies. In medieval Latin Europe, the institution that bears the closest resemblance is the oath on pain of excommunication.[108] Divorce, unlike excommunication, was not "social death." But it was a harsh punishment, which we should not underestimate. Triple divorce, requiring a *taḥlīl* marriage, was an extreme humiliation. The trials of Ibn Taymiyya can only be explained through the central place of divorce oaths in the political, commercial and domestic spheres – indeed, as a crucial means of effecting social bonds. By allowing expiation in divorce oaths, Ibn Taymiyya questioned the most common and solemn form of social commitment, and one that was part of the oath of allegiance inaugurating the rule of every new sultan. The state retaliated by suppressing his doctrines, and continued to do so for more than a century after his death.

The trial of Ibn Taymiyya is not only a fascinating aspect of his biography, but also an important chapter in the history of gender in medieval Islam. Because repudiation was a key symbol of patriarchy, the oath on pain of repudiation became the most solemn and binding type of oath in the Mamluk period – and also the cause of many unwanted divorces. Ibn Taymiyya's attempt to reform the Sunni law

[107] Chamberlain, *Knowledge*, 113–16.

[108] F. Pollock and F. W. Maitland, *The History of English Law before the Time of Edward I*, 2nd edn., 2 vols. (Cambridge: Cambridge University Press, 1968), vol. II, 189–92; L. Kolmer, *Promissorische Eide im Mittelalter* (Kallm unz Opf.: M. Lassleben, 1989), 335–50. In Islamic law, oaths on pain of apostasy, such as "If I shall do such-and-such, I am a Christian or a Jew," are not considered binding. From a legal point of view, these are not valid oaths since the name of God or one of his attributes is not mentioned (see Ibn Rushd, *Bidāyat al-Mujtahid*, vol. I, 410–11). In any case, excommunication is an elusive category in Islamic law, probably as a result of the absence of a centralized religious authority comparable to the Church.

on divorce oaths, an attempt which landed him and his followers in jail, highlights the inextricable link between the patriarchal order of the domestic sphere and the patriarchal values at the heart of the political and social order. Perhaps more than any individual story of failed marriage, the reaction of the Mamluk state to the ideas of Ibn Taymiyya demonstrates the crucial role of the institution of divorce within medieval Islamic society.

# Conclusion

Compared to other medieval matrimonial regimes, such as those of Latin Europe or of Sung China, the most distinctive feature of marriages in medieval urban Islam was the ubiquity of divorce. Polygamy and concubinage, as in other medieval societies, appear to have been limited in scope. In Near Eastern marriages, as in contemporary marriages in Europe or China, the dowry brought by the bride, rather than the marriage gift of the groom, was the significant gift at marriage.[1] But, while Chinese or European marriages were relatively stable affairs, for the most part ending with the death of one of the spouses, a very large number of marriages in medieval Cairo, Damascus and Jerusalem ended in divorce. Conjugal units of medieval urban Islamic society, already hit by high mortality, were further broken up and dispersed. By their very nature, the high rates of divorce severely and institutionally undermined the ideal patriarchal order, in which society was imagined as composed of households led by men who exercised control over their wives, children and slaves.

Given the destabilizing impact of divorce, this book has attempted to explain why divorces were, nonetheless, so common. As is the case with the soaring rates of divorce in Western societies in the latter half of the twentieth century, the answer cannot be simple or one-dimensional. A decision about divorce involved – as it does today – anxieties about the fate of children and of family ties, about economic security, and about one's sense of status and place in society at large. The preceding discussion of divorce in a medieval Islamic society has brought out, I hope, the complex uncertainties of separation, then as now. At the same time, it also highlighted two rather contradictory features of medieval Islamic society that had contributed, perhaps more than others, to the prevalence of divorce: On the one hand, the value of divorce as a uniquely patriarchal privilege, and, on the other hand, the degree of women's economic independence, both of their husbands and of their natal families.

[1] On the matrimonial regime of Sung China, see Ebrey, *The Inner Quarters*. On marriage and dowries in medieval Europe see, among others, G. Duby, *Love and Marriage in the Middle Ages*, trans. J. Dunnett (Chicago: University of Chicago Press, 1994); J. Goody, *The European Family* (Oxford: Blackwell, 2000); D. Herlihy, *Medieval Households* (Cambridge, MA: Harvard University Press, 1985); Howell, *The Marriage Exchange*.

In a paradoxical way, high divorce rates were partly due to the value of unilateral repudiation as a key symbol of patriarchal authority. Because divorce was seen as the ultimate privilege of a husband over his wife, it was routinely evoked in order to keep a wife in her place. It was also extended to the public sphere, as husbands put their marriages on the line as a guarantee for fulfilling social obligations that went far beyond their relations with their wives. By evoking divorce so frequently, by making divorce the hallmark of patriarchy, husbands were endangering the stability of their marriages and their households. But it would be facile to accuse medieval Muslim husbands of being reckless or whimsical. As is demonstrated by Ibn Taymiyya's failed reform of Islamic divorce law, it was primarily the medieval state that defended and exploited oaths on pain of divorce as a crucial means of social control well into the fifteenth century. The Gordian knot that linked divorce with the patriarchal political order was not easily unraveled.

In spite of the value of repudiation as a unilateral and patriarchal privilege, actual divorce tended to be a much more balanced event. In fact, while a husband's prerogative of unilateral repudiation was often invoked as a threat, the majority of divorces in Mamluk society were consensual separations. Husbands' right of divorce left them with substantial leverage power during the negotiations preceding formal separation, and they were quite often able to impose a settlement favorable to their interests. But, in spite of the simplicity of the legal act of repudiation, most husbands were deterred by the financial costs of divorce. Upon unilateral repudiation husbands were expected to pay all their remaining financial obligations, including the late and due portions of the marriage gift, any arrears in payments of support and clothing, and other debts they might have incurred during the marriage. Wives were able to use their husbands' financial obligations as a bargaining chip in divorce negotiations, as they were in a position to give up some, or all, of their financial rights in return for release from an unwanted marriage. As can be seen in the majority of the individual cases of divorce mentioned in this book, breaking up a marriage was rarely a one-sided affair.

Besides highlighting the value of divorce as a patriarchal privilege, this book has also argued that the high rates of divorce in Mamluk society could not have been sustained without a considerable degree of economic independence for women. Among the elite, this economic independence has been founded upon the institution of the dowry – the importance of which has been underestimated by historians. Dowries, delivered in the form of trousseaux, gender-specific items of personal property, functioned as a form of pre-mortem inheritance reserved exclusively for daughters. Usually much larger than the marriage gifts of the groom, the dowries were a substantial portion of a family's patrimony. Once donated by the bride's parents, the dowry remained under the woman's exclusive ownership and control throughout marriage, and then again through widowhood and divorce. Depending on circumstances, women used their dowries to invest in real estate or in exclusively female savings associations, or to derive income from interest-bearing loans.

Another key aspect of medieval women's economic independence, often overlooked by both medieval writers and modern historians, was the widespread female participation in the production of textiles. Female spinners, seamstresses and embroiderers were of crucial importance to the textile industry as a whole, and when that industry expanded in the thirteenth and fourteenth centuries, so did women's economic opportunities. Examples drawn from chronicles and *fatwā* collections demonstrate that the remuneration women received for their work was often sufficient to support them, even if at a modest level. Some women, such as the seamstress Ḍayfa bt. ʿUmar, were able to support entire families, including their husbands. Through their wages, many women, and not necessarily elite women, were able to remain single for long periods of time. Some of them found refuge in exclusively female religious houses, the *ribāṭ*s, built with the purpose of providing them with their own moral and physical space within the male public sphere.

The patterns of Mamluk divorce also highlight medieval women's independence of their natal families, thereby qualifying the usefulness of the agnatic principle as an explanation of frequent divorces in traditional Muslim societies.[2] It is true that in Mamluk society blood often mattered more than marriage. Women normally retained their birth identity throughout life, using the support of kin to guarantee their rights within marriage. Yet it is striking that all types of medieval sources – whether the marriage contracts of Zumurrud or the gossipy narratives of al-Sakhāwī – tend to depict divorce as a profoundly conjugal affair, arising from the incompatibility of husband and wife, not from a conflict between two households. In most cases, wives are seen as acting on their own initiative, directly negotiating with their husbands or approaching the court in person. Moreover, the demographic realities of an urban medieval society must have also circumscribed the dominance of agnatic lineage. As is well attested by the proliferation of female *ribāṭ*s, high mortality rates and high mobility often meant that divorced women did not have a kin group to return to.

The value of repudiation as a source of authority over wives diminished towards the end of the middle ages, in line with wider social and economic developments in Mamluk society. Since our sources do not allow for meaningful statistical comparisons, it is not possible to trace changes in the rate of divorce over time. But the medieval sources do point to a growing monetization of marriage, i.e., an increasing tendency among husbands and wives to attach a cash value to various aspects of the relationship. As wives acquired the right to demand the payment of their marriage gifts at any time during marriage, expected a daily cash allowance, a 'bed-fee' or a separate clothing budget, or even asked their spouses to pay them rent, more and more of husbands' obligations acquired pecuniary value. This monetization meant, first of all, that wives held a better bargaining position in divorce negotiations. On an ideological level, the intrusion of cash contracts typical of the

[2] N. Tapper, *Bartered Brides: Politics, Gender and Marriage in an Afghan Tribal Society* (Cambridge: Cambridge University Press, 1991), 16; L. Abu Lughod, *Veiled Sentiments. Honor and Poetry in a Bedouin Society* (Berkeley: University of California Press, 1986), 54; D. Eickelman, *The Middle East: An Anthropological Approach*, 2nd edn. (Englewood Cliffs, NJ: Prentice Hall, 1989), 163; Goitein, *A Mediterranean Society*, vol. III, 1–2.

marketplace fundamentally challenged the patriarchal ideal of an autonomous and hierarchical household.

Another reason for the erosion in the value of divorce as a patriarchal privilege was the increasing intervention of the courts in family affairs. Throughout medieval Islam, *qāḍī*s appear to have been reluctant to intervene in matrimonial disputes, and most often saw themselves as an additional layer of mediators. During the fifteenth century, however, the courts turned much more assertive, mainly as a result of the expanding jurisdiction of administrative courts headed by military officials. Since these courts were not bound by the stringent procedure required by Islamic law, they could act more resolutely against husbands who had abused their wives or had failed to provide for them. On the other hand, judges were now ready to entertain husbands' complaints about the insubordination of their wives. As a by-product of this more intrusive attitude by the courts, the threat of repudiation had lost its value as a central tenet of patriarchal authority. Fifteenth-century *fatwā*s demonstrate that the common threat against a disobedient wife was no longer repudiation, but rather the summoning of the police.

Because we so seldom hear the voice of medieval Muslim women, we often mistake medieval normative and legal texts for descriptive accounts of gender relations in medieval Islam. It is often still assumed that women were in a state of complete dependence on their husbands and their fathers. The high incidence of divorce, however, exposes the exhortations of the moralists for what they were – attempts to mold society into a particular ideological framework, and to provide justification for the domination of men over women. Women have always challenged this domination. When medieval Muslim women attained economic independence, or when they brought their husbands to court, and, ultimately, when they opted out of marriage, they were testing and, quite literally, dismembering the patriarchal utopia. Medieval marriage was therefore a domain of conflicting interests, an unstable and fragile realm where power was constantly negotiated, never the domestic haven imagined by the scholars. Nevertheless, medieval Muslim wives and husbands also helped define a legacy that was – compared to hollow accounts of male privilege – far more balanced, far more complex and, ultimately, far more enduring.

# Bibliography

## Medieval works


Abū Shāma, Shihāb al-Dīn ʿAbd al-Raḥmān b. Ismāʿīl. *Tarājim Rijāl al-Qarnayn al-Sādis wa'l-Sābiʿ al-Maʿrūf bi'l-Dhayl ʿalā al-Rawḍatayn*, ed. M. Zāhid al-Kawtharī. Cairo: Dār al-Kutub al-Malikiyya, 1947.

al-ʿĀmilī, M. *Aʿyān al-Shīʿah*, ed. Ḥasan al-Amīn, 11 vols. Beirut: Dār al-Taʿāruf, 1986.

Anon. (fifteenth century). A Shāfiʿī treatise on marriage. MS Chester Beatty 4665.

Anon. (fourteenth century). "Al-Radd ʿalā al-Taḥqīq fī Mas'alat al-Taʿlīq." MS Chester Beatty 3232.

al-Anṣārī, Zakariyā. *Al-Iʿlām wa'l-Ihtimām bi-Jamʿ Fatāwā Shaykh al-Islām Abī Yaḥyā Zakariyā al-Anṣārī*, ed. Aḥmad ʿUbayd. Beirut: ʿĀlam al-Kutub, 1984.

— "*ʿImād al-Riḍā bi-Bayān Adab al-Qaḍā'*." MS Chester Beatty 3420 (1).

al-Aqfahsī, ʿImād al-Dīn. "Tawqīf al-Ḥukkām ʿalā Ghawāmiḍ al-Aḥkām." MS Chester Beatty 3328.

al-Asyūṭī, Shams al-Dīn Muḥammad al-Minhājī. *Jawāhir al-ʿUqūd wa-Muʿīn al-Quḍāh wa'l-Muwaqqiʿīn wa'l-Shuhūd*, 2 vols. Cairo: Maṭbaʿat al-Sunnah al-Muḥammadiyyah, 1955.

al-ʿAynī, Badr al-Dīn. *ʿIqd al-Jumān fī Tā'rīkh Ahl al-Zamān. ʿAṣr Salāṭīn al-Mamālīk*, ed. Muḥammad Muḥammad Amīn, 4 vols. Cairo: al-Hay'ah al-Miṣriyya al-ʿĀmmah lil-Kitāb, 1987–92.

al-Buṣrawī, ʿAlī b. Yūsuf. *Ta'rīkh al-Buṣrawī: Ṣafaḥāt Majhūlah min Ta'rīkh Dimashq fī ʿAṣr al-Mamālīk min Sanat 871 H li-Ghāyat 904 H*, ed. Akram Ḥasan al-ʿUlabī. Damascus: Dār al-Ma'mūn lil-Turāth, 1988.

Casola, P. *Canon Pietro Casola's Pilgrimage to Jerusalem in the Year 1494*, trans. M. Newett. Manchester: Manchester University Press, 1907.

al-Dhahabī, Shams al-Dīn. *Siyar Aʿlām al-Nubalā'*, ed. Shuʿayb al-Arnā'ūṭ and Ḥusayn al-Asad, 25 vols. Beirut: Mu'assasat al-Risāla, 1981–88.

— *Tar'īkh al-Islām wa-Wafayāt al-Mashāhīr wa'l-Aʿlām*, ed. ʿUmar ʿAbd al-Salām Tadmurī. Beirut: Dār al-Kitāb al-ʿArabī, 1987–.

al-Fayyūmī, ʿAlī b. Muḥammad. "Nathr al-Jumān fī Tarājim al-Aʿyān." MS Chester Beatty 4113.

al-Fazārī, 'Abd al-Raḥmān b. al-Firkāḥ b. Ibrāhīm. "Fatāwā al-Fazārī." MS Chester Beatty 3330.

Foggibonsi, Nicolá da. *A Voyage Beyond the Seas, 1346–1350*, trans. T. Bellorini and E. Hoade. Jerusalem: Franciscan Press, 1945.

Frescobaldi, Leonardo, Giorgio Gucci and Simone Sigoli. *Visit to the Holy Places of Egypt, Sinai, Palestine, and Syria in 1384*, trans. T. Bellorini and E. Hoade. Jerusalem: Franciscan Press, 1948.

al-Ghazzī, 'Isā b. 'Uthmān. "Adab al-Qaḍā'." MS Chester Beatty 3763.

al-Ghazzī, Najm al-Dīn. *Al-Kawākib al-Sā'ira bi-A'yān al-Mi'ah al-'Āshirah*, ed. Jibrīl Sulaymān Jabbūr, 3 vols. Beirut: American University Press, 1945–59.

Harff, Arnold von. *The Pilgrimage of the Knight Arnold von Harff*, trans. M. Letts. London: Hakluyt, 1946.

al-Ḥazrajī, Shihāb al-Dīn al-Ḥijāzī. *Al-Kunnas al-Jawārī fī al-Ḥisān min al-Jawārī*, ed. Riḥāb al-'Akkāwī. Beirut: Dār al-Ḥarf al-'Arabī, 1998.

Ibn 'Abd al-Hādī. *Al-'Uqūd al-Durriyya fī Manāqib Shaykh al-Islām Aḥmad Ibn Taymiyya*, ed. Muḥammad Ḥāmid al-Fiqī. Cairo: Maṭba'at al-Ḥijāzī, 1938.

Ibn 'Abd al-Salām. "Al-Qawā'id al-Kubrā." MS British Museum Or. 3102.

Ibn Abī al-Dam, Ibrāhīm b. 'Abdallāh. *Kitāb Adab al-Qaḍā'*, ed. Muḥammad Muṣṭafā al-Zuhaylī. Damascus: Dār al-Fikr, 1982.

Ibn Bassām, Muḥammad b. Aḥmad. *Kitāb Nihāyat al-Rutba fī Ṭalab al-Ḥisba*, ed. Ḥusām al-Dīn al-Samarrā'ī. Baghdad: Maṭba'at al-Ma'ārif, 1968.

Ibn Baṭṭūṭa. *Riḥlat Ibn Baṭṭūṭa al-Musammā Tuḥfat al-Nuẓẓār fī Gharā'ib al-Amṣār wa-'Ajā'ib al-Asfār*, ed. 'Abd al-Hādī al-Tāzī, 5 vols. Rabat: Akādimiyat al-Mamlaka al-Maghribiyya, 1997.

— *The Travels of Ibn Baṭṭūṭa, AD 1325–1354*, trans. H. A. R. Gibb, 2 vols. Cambridge: Hakluyt Society, 1958–62.

Ibn Baydakīn al-Turkumānī. *Kitāb al-Luma' fī al-Ḥawādith wa'l-Bida'*, ed. Ṣubḥī Labīb. Wiesbaden: F. Steiner Verlag, 1986.

Ibn Daniyāl, Muḥammad. *Kitāb Ṭayf al-Khayāl*, ed. Paul Kahle; with a critical apparatus by D. Hopwood. Cambridge: Trustees of the E. J. W. Gibb Memorial, 1992.

Ibn Ḥajar al-'Asqalānī, Shihāb al-Dīn Aḥmad. *Al-Durar al-Kāmina fī A'yān al-Mi'ah al-Thāminah*, 4 vols. Hyderabad: Dā'irat al-Ma'ārif, 1929–32.

— *Inbā' al-Ghumr bi-Abnā' al-'Umr*, ed. Ḥasan Ḥabashī, 3 vols. Cairo: Lajnat Iḥyā' al-Turāth al-'Arabī, 1971–76.

— *Raf' al-Iṣr 'an Quḍāt Miṣr*, ed. 'Alī Muḥammad 'Umar. Cairo: Maṭba'at al-Khānjī, 1998.

Ibn al-Ḥājj, Muḥammad b. Muḥammad. *Al-Madkhal ilā Tanmiyat al-A'māl bi-Taḥsīn al-Niyyāt*, 4 vols. Cairo: al-Maṭba'ah al-Miṣriyyah, 1929–32.

Ibn Ḥazm, 'Alī b. Muḥammad. *Al-Muḥallā bi'l-Āthār*. ed. 'Abd al-Ghaffār Sulaymān al-Bindārī, 10 vols. Beirut: Dār al-Kutub al-'Ilmiyya, 1988.

Ibn al-Ḥimṣī, Aḥmad b. Muḥammad. *Ḥawādith al-Zamān wa-Wafayāt al-Shuyūkh wa'l-Aqrān*, ed. 'Umar 'Abd al-Salām al-Tadmurī, 3 vols. Sayda: al-Maktaba al-'Aṣriyya, 1999.

Ibn Iyās, Abū al-Barakāt. *Badā'i' al-Zuhūr fī Waqā'i' al-Duhūr*, ed. M. Muṣṭafā, 5 vols. Wiesbaden: F. Steiner, 1975–92.

Ibn Kathīr, Ismā'īl b. 'Umar. *Al-Bidāya wa'l-Nihāya*, 14 vols. Cairo: n.p. 1932–39.

— *Al-Bidāya wa'l-Nihāya*, ed. Aḥmad Abū Mulḥim et al., 14 vols. Beirut: Dār al-Kutub al-'Ilmiyya, 1994.

Ibn al-Mibrad, Jamāl al-Dīn Yūsuf. *Akhbār al-Nisā' al-Musammā al-Rusā lil-Ṣāliḥāt min al-Nisā'*, ed. Māhir Muḥammad 'Abd al-Qādir. Homs: Dār al-Ma'ārif, 1993.

— *Al-Jawhar al-Munaḍḍad fī Ṭabaqāt Muta'akhkhirī Aṣḥāb Aḥmad,* ed. 'Abd al-Raḥmān al-'Uthaymīn. Cairo: Maktabat al-Khānjī, 1987.

— *Sayr al-Ḥāthth ilā 'Ilm al-Ṭalāq al-Thalāth*, ed. Muḥammad b. Nāṣir al-'Ajamī. Beirut: Dār al-Bashā'ir al-Islāmiyya, 1997.

— *Thimār al-Maqāṣid fī Dhikr al-Masājid*. ed. Muḥammad As'ad Ṭalas. Beirut: Institut Français de Damas, 1943.

Ibn Qāḍī Shuhba, Abū Bakr b. Aḥmad. *Tar'īkh Ibn Qāḍī Shuhba*, ed. 'Adnān Darwīsh, 3 vols. Damascus: Institut Français de Damas, 1977–1994.

Ibn Qayyim al-Jawziyya. *Ighāthat al-Lahfān min Maṣā'id al-Shayṭān*, ed. Muḥammad Ḥāmid al-Fiqī, 2 vols. Cairo: Maṭba'at Muṣṭafā al-Bābī al-Ḥalabī, 1939.

— *I'lām al-Muwaqqi'īn 'an Rabb al-'Ālamīn*, ed. Ṭāhā 'Abd al-Ra'ūf Sa'd, 4 vols. Beirut: Dār al-Jīl, 1964.

— *Al-Ṭuruq al-Ḥukmiyya fī al-Siyāsa al-Shar'iyya*. Cairo: Maṭba'at al-Adāb, 1317/1898–99.

— *Zād al-Mi'ād fī Hady Khayr al-'Ibād*, ed. Shu'ayb and 'Abd al-Qādir al-Arnā'ūṭ, 5 vols. Beirut: Mu'assasat al-Risāla, 1979.

Ibn Qudāma, Muwaffaq al-Dīn. *Al-Mughnī*, 14 vols. Beirut: Dār al-Fikr, 1984.

Ibn Quṭlubughā. "Fatāwā." MS Princeton Yahuda 3393.

Ibn Rajab, 'Abd al-Raḥmān b. Aḥmad. *Dhayl 'alā Ṭabaqāt al-Ḥanābila*, ed. Muḥammad al-Fiqī, 2 vols. Cairo: Maṭba'at al-Sunna al-Muḥammadiyya, 1952.

Ibn Rushd al-Qurṭūbī, Muḥammad. *Bidāyat al-Mujtahid wa-Nihāyat al-Muqtaṣid*, 4 vols. Beirut: Dār al-Ma'rifa, 1985.

Ibn al-Ṣalāḥ al-Shahrazūrī, *Fatāwā wa-Masā'il Ibn al-Ṣalāḥ*, ed. 'Abd al-Mu'ṭī Qal'ajī. Beirut: Dār al-Ma'rifa, 1986.

Ibn al-Ṣayrafī, al-Khaṭīb al-Jawharī. *Inbā' al-Haṣr bi-Abnā' al-'Aṣr*, ed. Ḥasan Ḥabashī. Cairo: Dār al-Fikr al-'Arabī, 1970.

— *Nuzhat al-Nufūs wa'l-Abdān fī Tawārīkh al-Zamān*, ed. Ḥasan Ḥabashī, 4 vols. Cairo: al-Hay'ah al-Miṣriyya al-'Āmmah li'l-Kitāb, 1970–94.

Ibn al-Suqā' ī, Faḍlallāh b. Abī al-Fakhr. *Tālī Kitāb Wafayāt al-A'yān*, ed. J. Sublet. Damas: Institut Français de Damas, 1974.

Ibn Taghrī Birdī, Jamāl al-Dīn Yūsuf. *Ḥawādith al-Duhūr fī Madā al-Ayyām wa'l-Shuhūr*, 2 vols. Beirut: 'Ālam al-Kutub, 1990.

— *Al-Manhal al-Ṣāfī wa'l-Mustawfā Ba'd al-Wāfī*, ed. Muḥammad Muḥammad Amīn. Cairo: al-Hay'ah al-Miṣriyya al-'Āmmah li'l-Kitāb, 1984–.

— *Al-Nujūm al-Zāhira fī Mulūk Miṣr wa'l-Qāhirah*, 16 vols. Cairo: [various publishers], 1929–72.

Ibn Ṭawq. *Al-Ta'līq. Yawmiyyāt Shihāb al-Dīn Aḥmad Ibn Ṭawq (834/1430–915/1509): Mudhakkirāt Kutibat bi-Dimashq fī Awākhir al-'Ahd al-Mamlūkī, 885/1480–908/1502*, ed. Ja'far al-Muhājir, vol. I (885/1480–890/1485). Damascus: Institut Français de Damas, 2000.

Ibn Taymiyya. *Fatāwā al-Nisā'*, ed. Ibrāhīm Muḥammad al-Jamal. Cairo: Maktabat al-Qur'ān, 1987.

— *Al-Ijtimā' wa'l-Iftirāq fī al-Ḥilf bi'l-Ṭalāq*, ed. Muḥammad 'Abd al-Razzāq Ḥamza. Cairo: Maktabat Anṣār, 1346/1927–28.

— *Iqāmat al-Dalīl fī Ibṭāl al-Taḥlīl*. Published as part of the third volume of *Majmū'at Fatāwā*.

— *Majmū' Fatāwā Shaykh al-Islām Aḥmad Ibn Taymiyya*, ed. 'Abd al-Raḥmān b. Muḥammad al-'Āṣimī al-Najdī, 35 vols. Riyadh: Maṭba'at Riyāḍ, 1381–86/1961–66.

— *Majmū'at Fatāwā Shaykh al-Islām Taqī al-Dīn Ibn Taymiyya*, 5 vols. Cairo: Maṭba'at Kurdistān, 1326–29/1908–11.

— *Majmū'at al-Rasā'il al-Kubrā*, 2 vols. Cairo: Maṭba'at al-'Āmira, 1905–06.

Ibn Ṭūlūn, Muḥammad b. 'Alī. *Al-Fulk al-Mashḥūn fī Aḥwāl Muḥammad Ibn Ṭūlūn*, ed. Muḥammad Khayr Ramaḍān Yūsuf. Beirut: Dār Ibn Ḥazm, 1996.

— *Mufākahat al-Khīlān fī Ḥawādith al-Zamān*, ed. Muḥammad Muṣṭafā, 2 vols. Cairo: al-Mu'assasah al-Miṣriyyah al-'Āmmah li'l-Ta'līf wa'l-Tarjamah wa'l-Tibā'ah wa'l-Nashīr, 1962–64.

— *Al-Thaghr al-Bassām fī Dhikr Man Wuliyya Qaḍā' al-Shām*, ed. Ṣalāḥ al-Dīn al-Munajjid. Damascus: Maṭbū'āt al-Majma' al-'Ilmī al-'Arabī, 1956.

Ibn al-Ukhuwwa. *Ma'ālim al-Qurba fī Aḥkām al-Ḥisba*, ed. R. Levy. London: Luzac & Co., 1938.

Ibn Zufar al-Irbilī. *Madāris Dimashq wa-Rubuṭihā wa-Jawāmi'uhā wa-Ḥammāmatihā*, ed. Muḥammad Aḥmad Duhmān. Damascus: Maṭba'at al-Taraqqī, 1947.

al-Jarawānī, Abū 'Abdallāh Muḥammad b. 'Abdallāh al-Ḥasanī. "Al-Mawāhib al-Ilāhiyya wa'l-Qawā'id al-Mālikiyya." MS Chester Beatty 3401.

al-Jazarī, Muḥammad b. Ibrāhīm. *La chronique de Damas d'al-Jazari, années 689–698 H*, ed. J. Sauvaget. Paris: Librairie ancienne H. Champion, 1949.

— *Ta'rīkh Ḥawādith al-Zamān wa-Anbā'ihi wa-Wafayāt al-Akābir wa'l-A'yān min Abnā'ihi. Al-Ma'rūf bi-Tā'rīkh Ibn al-Jazarī*, ed. 'Umar 'Abd al-Salām Tadmurī, 3 vols. Sayda: al-Maktabah al-'Aṣriyya, 1998.

al-Maqrīzī, Taqī al-Dīn. *Durar al-'Uqūd al-Farīdah fī Tarājim al-A'yān al-Mufīdah*, ed. 'Adnān Darwīsh and Muḥammad al-Miṣrī, 2 vols. Damascus: Wizārat al-Thaqāfah, 1995.

— *Kitāb al-Mawā'iẓ wa'l-I'tibār fī Dhikr al-Khiṭaṭ wa'l-Āthār al-Ma'rūf bi'l-Khiṭaṭ al-Maqrīziyya*, ed. Muḥammad Zaynhum and Madīḥa al-Sharqāwī, 3 vols. Cairo: Maktabat al-Madbūlī, 1998.

— *Kitāb al-Sulūk li-Ma'rifat al-Duwal wa'l-Mulūk*, ed. Muḥammad Muṣṭafā Ziyādah and Sa'īd 'Abd al-Fattāḥ 'Āshūr, 4 vols. Cairo: Dār al-Kutub al-Miṣriyya, 1934–72.

Meshūllam of Volterra. *Massa' Meshūllam mi-Volterra be-Erets Yisra'el (1481)*, ed. Avraham Ya'arī. Jerusalem: Mosad Byalik, 1948.

al-Nawawī, Yaḥyā b. Sharaf. *Fatāwā al-Imām al-Nawawī al-Musammā bi'l-Masā'il al-Manthūra*, ed. 'Alā' al-Dīn Ibn al-'Aṭṭār. Beirut: Dār al-Kutub al-'Ilmiyya, 1982.

al-Nu'aymī, 'Abd al-Qādir b. Muḥammad. *Al-Dāris fī Ta'rīkh al-Madāris*. ed. Ja'far al-Ḥusaynī, 2 vols. Damascus: Maṭba'at al-Taraqqī, 1948–51.

al-Nuwayrī, Muḥammad Ibn al-Qāsim. *Kitāb al-Ilmām bi'l-I'lām fīmā Jarat bihi al-Aḥkām wa'l-Umūr al-Muqḍiyya fī Waq'at al-Iskandriyya*, ed. A. S. Atiyya, 7 vols. Hyderabad: Dā'irat al-Ma'ārif, 1968–1976.

al-Nuwayrī, Shihāb al-Dīn Aḥmad. *Nihāyat al-Arab fī Funūn al-Adab*. Cairo: Dār al-Kutub al-Miṣriyya; al-Hay'ah al-Miṣriyya al-'Āmmah li'l-Kitāb, 1923–.

Obadiah Bertinoro. *Me-Italyah li-Yerūshalayim. Igrōtav shel R. Ovadyah mi-Bartenūra me-Erets Yisrael*, ed. A. David and M. Hartom. Ramat Gan: Bar Ilan University, 1997.

Piloti, E. *L'Egypte au commencement du quinzième siècle, d'après le traité d'Emmanuel Piloti de Crète, incipit 1420*, ed. P.-H. Dopp. Cairo: Imp. Université Fouad 1er, 1950.

al-Qalqashandī, Aḥmad b. 'Abdallāh. *Ṣubḥ al-A'shā fī Ṣinā'at al-Inshā'*, 14 vols. Cairo: Dār al-Kutub al-Miṣriyya, 1913–18.

al-Qarāfī, Shihāb al-Dīn. *Kitāb al-Iḥkām fī Tamyīz al-Fatāwā 'an al-Aḥkām wa-Taṣarrufāt al-Qāḍī wa'l-Imām*. Aleppo: Maktabat al-Maṭbū'āt al-Islāmiyya, 1967.

Qāri' al-Hidāya, 'Umar b. 'Alī al-Qaṭṭānī. "Al-Fatāwā al-Sirājiyya." MS British Library Or. 5781.

Al-Rāfi'ī, 'Abd al-Karīm b. Muḥammad. *Al-'Azīz Sharḥ al-Wajīz*. ed. 'Alī Muḥammad Mu'awwaḍ and 'Ādil Aḥmad 'Abd al-Mawjūd, 14 vols. Beirut: Dār al-Kutub al-'Ilmiyya, 1997.

al-Ṣafadī, Ṣalāḥ al-Dīn Khalīl b. Aybak. *A'yān al-'Aṣr wa-A'wān al-Naṣr*, ed. 'Alī Abū Zayd, Nabīl Abū 'Amasha, Muḥammad al-Maw'id and Maḥmūd Sālim Muḥammad, 6 vols. Damascus: Dār al-Fikr, 1998.

al-Sakhāwī, Muḥammad b. 'Abd al-Raḥmān. *Al-Ḍaw' al-Lāmi' li-Ahl al-Qarn al-Tāsi'*, ed. Ḥusām al-Qudsī, 12 vols. Cairo: Maṭba'at al-Quds, 1934–36.

— *Al-Jawāhir wa'l-Durar fī Tarjamat Shaykh al-Islām Ibn Ḥajar*, ed. Ibrāhīm Bājis 'Abd al-Majīd, 3 vols. Beirut: Dār Ibn Ḥazm, 1999.

— *Kitāb al-Tibr al-Masbūk fī Dhayl al-Sulūk*. Būlāq: al-Maṭbū'āt al-Amiriyya, 1896.

— *Wajīz al-Kalām fī al-Dhayl 'alā Duwal al-Islām*, ed. Bashshār 'Awwād Ma'rūf, 'Iṣām Fāris al-Ḥarastānī and Aḥmad al-Khutaymī, 3 vols. Beirut: Mu'assasat al-Risāla, 1995.

al-Samhūdī. "Al-Fawā'id al-Jamma fī al-Masā'il al-Thalāth al-Muhimma." MS Princeton Yahuda 321, fols. 44a–66b.

al-Sarūjī. *Kitāb Adab al-Qaḍā'*, ed. Ṣ. Yāsīn. Beirut: Dār al-Bashā'ir al-Islāmiyya, 1997.

al-Shayzarī, 'Abd al-Raḥmān b. Naṣr. *Nihāyat al-Rutba fī Ṭalab al-Ḥisba*, ed. al-Sayyid al-Bāz al-'Arīnī. Cairo: Maṭba'at Lajnat al-Ta'līf wa'l-Tarjama wa'l-Nashr, 1946.

al-Shujā'ī, Shams al-Dīn. *Ta'rīkh al-Malik al-Nāṣir Muḥammad b. Qalā'ūn al-Ṣāliḥ wa-Awlādihi*, ed. B. Schäfer, 2 vols. Wiesbaden: Steiner, 1977–85.

Sibṭ Ibn al-'Ajamī. *Kunūz al-Dhahab fī Ta'rīkh Ḥalab*, ed. Shawqī Sha'ath and Fāliḥ al-Bakkūr, 2 vols. Aleppo: Dār al-Qalam al-'Arabī, 1996–97.

al-Simnānī, 'Alī b. Muḥammad. *Rawḍat al-Quḍāh*, ed. Ṣalaḥ al-Dīn al-Nāhī. Beirut: Mu'assasat al-Risāla, 1984.

al-Subkī, Tāj al-Dīn. *Kitāb Mu'īd al-Ni'am wa-Mubīd al-Niqam*. Beirut: Dār al-Ḥadāthah, 1983.

— *Ṭabaqāt al-Shāfi'iyya al-Kubrā*, 6 vols. Cairo: Maṭba'at al-Ḥusayniyya, 1906.

al-Subkī, Taqī al-Dīn. *Kitāb al-Fatāwā*, 2 vols. Cairo: Maṭba'at al-Qudsī, 1937.

— "Mas'alat al-Ṭalāq al-Mu'allaq." MS Princeton Yahuda 878, fols. 135a–139a.

— *Al-Rasā'il al-Subkiyya fī al-Radd 'alā Ibn Taymiyya wa-Tilmīdhihi Ibn Qayyim al-Jawziyya*. Beirut: 'Ālam al-Kutub, 1983.

Suriano, Francesco. *Treatise on the Holy Land*, trans. T. Bellorini and E. Hoade. Jerusalem: Franciscan Press, 1949.

al-Suyūṭī, Jalāl al-Dīn. *Al-Ḥāwī lil-Fatāwā fī al-Fiqh wa-'Ulūm al-Tafsīr wa'l-Ḥadīth wa'l-Uṣūl wa'l-Naḥw wa'l-I'rāb wa-Sā'ir al-Funūn*, 2 vols. Cairo: Idārat al-Ṭibā'a al-Munīriyya, 1352/1933.

— *Nuzhat al-Julasā' fī Ash'ār al-Nisā'*, ed. Ṣalāḥ al-Dīn al-Munajjid. Beirut: Dār al-Makshūf, 1958.

al-Ṭarsūsī, Najm al-Dīn. *Al-Fatāwā al-Ṭarsūsiyya aw Anfa' al-Wasā'il ilā Taḥrīr al-Masā'il*, ed. Muṣṭafā Muḥammad Khafājī. Cairo: Maṭba'at al-Sharq, 1926.

— *Kitāb Tuḥfat al-Turk*, ed. M. Minasri. Damascus: Institut Français de Damas, 1997.

al-Udfūwī, Ja'far b. Tha'lab. *Al-Ṭāli' al-Sa'īd al-Jāmi' li-Asmā' al-Fuḍalā' wa'l-Ruwāt bi-A'lā al-Ṣa'īd*. Cairo: al-Dār al-Miṣriyya li'l-Ta'līf wa'l-Tarjamah, 1966.

al-'Ulaymī, Mujīr al-Dīn. *Al-Uns al-Jalīl bi-Ta'rīkh al-Quds wa'l-Khalīl*, 2 vols. Najaf: al-Maṭba'a al-Ḥaydariyya, 1969.

al-'Umarī, Ibn Faḍl Allāh. *Al-Ta'rīf bi'l-Muṣṭalaḥ al-Sharīf*. Cairo, 1312/1894.

al-'Uthmānī, Muḥammad b. 'Abd al-Raḥmān. "Kifāyat al-Muftiyyīn wa'l-Ḥukkām fī al-Fatāwā wa'l-Aḥkām." MS Chester Beatty 4666.

— *Raḥmat al-Umma fī Ikhtilāf al-A'immah*, ed. 'Alī al-Sharbajī and Qāsim al-Nūrī. Beirut: Mu'assasat al-Risāla, 1994.

al-Yūnīnī, Quṭb al-Dīn. *Dhayl Mir'āt al-Zamān*, 2 vols. Hyderabad: Dār al-Ma'ārif, 1954–55.

al-Yūsufī, Mūsā b. Muḥammad. *Nuzhat al-Nāẓir fī Sīrat al-Malik al-Nāṣir*, ed. Aḥmad Ḥuṭayṭ. Beirut: ʿĀlam al-Kutub, 1986.

## Modern works

Abbott, N. *Two Queens of Baghdad: Mother and Wife of Harun al-Rashid*. Chicago: University of Chicago Press, 1946.

ʿAbd al-Rāziq, Aḥmad. "ʿAqdā Nikāḥ min ʿAṣr al-Mamālīk al-Baḥriyya," *al-Majallah al-ʿArabiyya liʾl-ʿUlūm al-Insāniyya* (Kuwait) 6 (1986), 68–88.

— "Un document concernant le mariage des esclaves au temps des mamlūks," *JESHO* 13 (1970), 309–14.

— *La femme au temps des Mamlouks en Egypte*. Cairo: Institut français d'archéologie orientale, 1973.

— "Al-Mamālīk wa-Mafhūm al-Usrah Ladayhum," *Majallat Kulliyat al-Āthār* (Cairo) 2 (1977), 188–207.

— "Trois foundations féminines dans l'Egypte mamlouke," *Revue d'études islamiques* 41 (1973), 95–126.

Abdal-Rehim, A. A. "The Family and Gender Laws in Egypt during the Ottoman Period," in El-Azhary Sonbol (ed.), *Women, Family and Divorce Laws*, 96–111.

Abu-Lughod, L. "Feminist Longings and Postcolonial Conditions," in L. Abu Lughod (ed.), *Remaking Women. Feminism and Modernity in the Middle East* (Princeton: Princeton University Press, 1998), 3–32.

— *Veiled Sentiments. Honor and Poetry in a Bedouin Society*. Berkeley: University of California Press, 1986.

Abū Zahra, Muḥammad. *Ibn Taymiyya: Ḥayātuhu wa-ʿAṣruhu – wa-Ārāʾuhu al-Fiqhiyya*. Cairo: Dār al-Fikr al-ʿArabī, 1952.

Adler, Elkan (ed.). *Jewish Travelers*. London: Routledge, 1930.

Afifi, Mohamed. "Reflections on the Personal Laws of Egyptian Copts," in El-Azhary Sonbol (ed.), *Women, Family and Divorce Laws*, 202–15.

Ahmed, L. *Women and Gender in Islam: Historical Roots of a Modern Debate*. New Haven: Yale University Press, 1992.

Ahmed, Shahab. "Ibn Taymiyyah and the Satanic Verses," *SI* 87 (1998), 67–124.

Amīn, M. M. *al-Awqāf waʾl-Ḥayāh al-Ijtimāʿiyya fī Miṣr, 648–923 H/1250–1517 M*. Cairo: Dār al-Nahḍa al-ʿArabiyya, 1980.

— *Fihrist Wathāʾiq al-Qāhirah ḥattā Nihāyat ʿAṣr al-Mamālīk. Catalogue des doucments d'archives du Caire de 239/853 á 922/1516*. Cairo: Institut français d'archéologie orientale, 1981.

Ardener, S. and S. Burman (eds.). *Money-go-rounds: The Importance of Rotating Savings and Credit Associations for Women*. Oxford: BERG, 1995.

al-ʿAṣalī, K. *Wathāʾiq Maqdisiyya Taʾrīkhiyya*, 3 vols. Amman: n.p., 1983–85.

Ashtor-Strauss, E. *Histoire des prix et des salaires dans l'Orient médiéval*. Paris: SEVPEN, 1969.

— "L'Inquisition dans l'état mamlouk," *Rivista degli Studi Orientali* 25 (1950), 11–26.
— "Levantine Sugar Industry in the Later Middle Ages – an Example of Technological Decline," *Israel Oriental Studies* 7 (1977), 226–80.
— *Les metaux précieux et la balance des payements du Proche-Orient à la basse époque*. Paris: SEVPEN, 1971.
— *A Social and Economic History of the Near East in the Middle Ages*. Berkeley: University of California Press, 1976.
— *Tōldōt ha-Yehūdīm be-Mitzrayim ve-Sūryah taḥat Shilṭōn ha-Mamlūkīm*, 3 vols. Jerusalem: Mossad ha-Rav Kuk, 1944–70.
— "Venetian Cotton Trade in Syria in the Later Middle Ages," *Studi Medievali* 17 (1976), 677–81.
ʿĀshūr, S. ʿA. *Al-Mujtamaʿ al-Miṣrī fī ʿAṣr Salāṭīn al-Mamālīk*. Cairo: Dār al-Nahda al-ʿArabiyya, 1962.
Ayalon, David. "The Great Yāsa of Chingiz Khān. A Re-examination," *SI* 33 (1971), 97–140.
— "Studies on the Structure of the Mamluk Army – III," *BSOAS* 16 (1954), 57–90.
El-Azhary Sonbol, Amira (ed.). *Women, Family and Divorce Laws in Islamic History*. Syracuse: Syracuse University Press, 1996.
Becker, G. *A Treatise on the Family*. Cambridge, MA: Harvard University Press, 1981.
Behrens-Abouseif, D. *Fatḥ Allāh and Abū Zakariyā': Physicians under the Mamluks*. Cairo: Institut français d'archéologie orientale, 1987.
— *Islamic Architecture in Cairo: An Introduction*. Leiden: Brill, 1989.
— "Patterns of Urban Patronage in Cairo: A Comparison between the Mamluk and the Ottoman Periods," in Phillip and Haarman (eds.), *The Mamluks in Egyptian Politics and Society*, 224–34.
Berkey, Jonathan. *Transmission of Knowledge in Medieval Cairo*. Princeton: Princeton University Press, 1992.
— "Women and Islamic Education in the Mamluk Period," in Keddie and Baron (eds.), *Women in Middle Eastern History*, 143–57.
Botticini, M. and Aloysius Siow. "Why Dowries?" *American Economic Review* 93/4 (2003), 1385–98.
Brustad, Kristen. "Imposing Order: Reading the Conventions of Representation in al-Suyūṭī's Autobiography," *Edebiyât: Special Issue – Arabic Autobiography* 7/2 (1997), 327–44.
Calder, Norman. "*Ḥinth, Birr, Tabarrur, Taḥannuth*: An Inquiry into the Arabic Vocabulary of Oaths," *BSOAS* 51 (1989), 214–39.
Chamberlain, Michael. *Knowledge and Social Practice in Medieval Damascus, 1190–1350*. Cambridge: Cambridge University Press, 1994.
Chapoutot-Remadi, M. "Une grand crise à la fin du XIIIe siècle en Egypte", *JESHO* 26 (1983), 217–45.
Coles, Catherine and B. Mack (eds.), *Hausa Women in the Twentieth Century*. Madison: University of Wisconsin Press, 1991.

Cornell, Laurel L. "Peasant Women and Divorce in Pre-industrial Japan," *Signs* 15 (1990), 710–32.

Cornell, Rkia E. *Early Sufi Women.* Dhikr al-Niswa al-Muta'abbidāt aṣ-Ṣūfiyyāt *by Abū 'Abd ar-Raḥmān as-Sulamī.* Louisville, KY: Fons Vitae, 1999.

Darāwsheh, Qāsim. "Celebrations and Social Ceremonies in Egypt during the Mamluk Period, 648/1250–923/1517" (in Hebrew) (MA dissertation, Hebrew University, 1986).

Davis, N. "Women and the Crafts in Sixteenth-Century Lyon," in B. Hanawalt (ed.), *Women and Work in Pre-industrial Europe* (Bloomington: Indiana University Press, 1986).

Denoix, S. "Pour une exploitation d'ensemble d'un corpus: Les waqf mamelouks du Caire," in R. Deguilhem (ed.), *Le Waqf dans l'espace islamique: outil de pouvoir socio-politique* (Damascus: Institut français d'études arabes de Damas, 1995), 29–44.

Diem, W. "Vier arabische Rechtsurkunden aus Ägypten des 14. und 15. Jahrhunderts," *Der Islam* 72 (1995), 193–257.

Dietrich, A. "Eine arabische Eheurkunde aus der Aiyūbidenzeit," in J. Fück (ed.), *Documenta Islamica Inedita* (Berlin: Akademie Verlag Berlin, 1952), 121–54.

Dols, M. *The Black Death in the Middle East.* Princeton: Princeton University Press, 1977.

Duby, G. and P. Ariés (eds.). *A History of Private Life*, vol. II: *Revelations of the Medieval World*, trans. A. Goldhammer. Cambridge, MA: Harvard University Press, 1988.

— *Love and Marriage in the Middle Ages*, trans. J. Dunnett. Chicago: University of Chicago Press, 1994.

Early, Evelyn A. *Baladi Women of Cairo. Playing with an Egg and a Stone.* Boulder: Lynne Rienner, 1993.

Ebrey, Patricia. *The Inner Quarters. Marriage and the Lives of Chinese Women in the Sung Period.* Berkeley: University of California Press, 1993.

Eddé, Anne-Marie. *La principauté ayyoubide d'Alep (579/1183–658/1260).* Stuttgart: Franz Steiner Verlag, 1999.

Eickelman, Dale. *The Middle East: An Anthropological Approach*, 2nd edn. Englewood Cliffs, NJ: Prentice Hall, 1989.

Ernst, H. *Die mamlukischen Sultansurkunden des Sinai-Klosters.* Wiesbaden: O. Harrassowitz, 1960.

Escovitz, J. "The Establishment of Four Chief Judgeships in the Mamluk Empire," *JAOS* 102 (1982), 529–31.

— *The Office of Qadî al-Qudât in Cairo under the Bahrî Mamlûks.* Berlin: Klaus Schwarz, 1984.

— "Patterns of Appointment to the Chief Judgeship of Cairo during the Baḥrī Mamlūk Period," *Arabica* 30 (1983), 147–68.

Fadel, M. "The Social Logic of *Taqlīd* and the Rise of the *Mukhtaṣar*," *ILS* 3 (1996), 193–233.

Farah, Madeleine. *Marriage and Sexuality in Islam. A Translation of al-Ghazali's Book on the Etiquette of Marriage from the* Iḥyā' (Salt Lake City: Utah University Press, 1984).

Fay, Mary Ann. "Women and Waqf: Toward a Reconsideration of Women's Place in the Mamluk Household," *IJMES* 29 (1997), 33–51.

Fernandes, L. *The Evolution of a Sufi Institution in Mamluk Egypt: The Khânqâh*. Berlin: K. Schwarz, 1988.

Friedman, M. A. "Ransom Divorce," *Israel Oriental Studies* 6 (1976), 288–307.

— *Ribūi Nashīm be-Yisrael: Mekōrōt Ḥadashīm mi-Genīzat Kahīr*. Jerusalem: Mosad Byalik, 1986.

Garcin, J.-C. and M. A. Taher. "Enquête sur le financement d'un *waqf* Egyptien du XV$^{e}$ siècle: Les comptes de Jawhār Lālā," *JESHO* 38 (1995), 262–304.

Gervres, Veronica. "Weavers, Tailors and Traders. A New Collection of Medieval Islamic Textiles in the Royal Ontario Museum, Toronto," *Hali* 2 (1979), 125–32.

Giladi, A. *Infants, Parents and Wet Nurses: Medieval Islamic Views on Breast-feeding and their Social Implications*. Leiden: Brill, 1999.

Goitein, S. D. *A Mediterranean Society. The Jewish Communities of the Arab World as Portrayed in the Documents of the Geniza*, 6 vols. Berkeley: University of California Press, 1967–93.

Goode, William J. *World Changes in Divorce Patterns*. New Haven: Yale University Press, 1993.

Goody, J. "Bridewealth and Dowry in Africa and Euroasia," in J. Goody and S. J. Tambiah (eds.), *Bridewealth and Dowry* (Cambridge: Cambridge University Press, 1973).

— *The Development of the Family and Marriage in Europe*. Cambridge: Cambridge University Press, 1983.

— *The European Family*. Oxford: Blackwell, 2000.

Gottheil, R. and W. H. Worrell. *Fragments from the Cairo Genizah in the Freer Collection*. New York: Macmillan, 1927.

Grohmann, A. *Arabic Papyri in the Egyptian Library*, 6 vols. Cairo: Egyptain Library Press, 1934–62.

— "Arabische Papyri aus den Staatlische Museen zu Berlin," *Der Islam* 22 (1935), 1–68.

— "Einige arabische Ostraka und ein Ehevertrag aus der Oase Baḥriya," in *Studi in onore di Aristide Calderini e Roberto Paribeni*, 3 vols. (Milan: Ceshina, 1957), vol. II, 499–509.

Guellil, G. *Damaszener Akten des 8./14. Jahrhunderts nach at-Tarsusis* Kitāb al-I'lām. *Eine Studie zum arabischen Justizwesen*. Bamberg: Aku, 1985.

Guo, Li. "Al-Biqā'ī's Chronicle: A Fifteenth Century Learned Man's Reflection on his Time and World," in Kennedy (ed.), *The Historiography of Islamic Egypt*, 121–48.

— "Mamluk Historiographic Studies: The State of the Art," *MSR* 1 (1997), 15–43.

Haarmann, U. "Joseph's Law – the Careers and Activities of Mamluk Descendants before the Ottoman Conquest of Egypt," in Phillip and Haarmann (eds.), *The Mamluks in Egyptian Politics and Society*, 55–84.

— "The Sons of Mamluks as Fief-holders in Late Medieval Egypt," in T. Khalidi (ed.), *Land Tenure and Social Transformation in the Middle East* (Beirut: American University of Beirut, 1984), 141–68.

Hallaq, Wael. *Authority, Continuity and Change in Islamic Law*. Cambridge: Cambridge University Press, 2001.

Halm, H. *Ägypten nach den mamlukischen Lehensregistern*, 2 vols. Wiesbaden: Reichert, 1979–80.

— "The Isma'ili Oath of Allegiance (*'Ahd*) and the 'Sessions of Wisdom' (*Majālis al-Ḥikma*) in Fatimid Times," in F. Daftary (ed.), *Mediaeval Isma'ili History and Thought* (Cambridge: Cambridge University Press, 1996), 91–115.

Hambly, Gavin (ed.). *Women in the Medieval Islamic World: Power, Patronage, Piety*. London: Curzon Press, 1999.

al-Harithy, Howyda. "Female Patronage of Mamluk Architecture in Cairo," *Harvard Middle Eastern and Islamic Review* 1 (1994), 152–74.

al-Hassan, Ahmed Y. and Donald R. Hill. *Islamic Technology: An Illustrated History*. Cambridge: Cambridge University Press, 1986.

Hathaway, Jane. "Marriage Alliances among the Military Households of Ottoman Egypt," *AI* 29 (1995), 134–49.

Hecker, Y. "The Immigration of Spanish Jews to Palestine, 1391–1492" (Hebrew), *Cathedra* 36 (1985), 3–35.

Herlihy, D. *Medieval Households*. Cambridge, MA: Harvard University Press, 1985.

— "The Medieval Marriage Market," *Medieval and Renaissance Studies* 6 (1976), 1–27.

— *Opera Muliebria. Women and Work in Medieval Europe*. New York: McGraw-Hill, 1990.

Holt, P. M. "An-Nāṣir Muḥammad b. Qalāwūn (684–741/1285–1341): His Ancestry, Kindred and Affinity," in U. Vermeulen and D. De Smet (eds.), *Egypt and Syria in the Fatimid, Ayyubid and Mamluk Eras* (Leuven: Uitgeverij Peeters, 1995), 313–24.

Homerin, T. Emil. "'I've stayed by the Grave'. A Nasīb for Nuḍār," in Mustansir Mir (ed.), *Literary Heritage of Classical Islam. Arabic and Islamic Studies in Honor of James A. Bellamy* (Princeton: Princeton University Press, 1993), 107–18.

— "Reflections on Arabic Poetry in the Mamluk Age," *MSR* 1 (1997), 63–85.

— "Saving Muslim Souls: The Khānqāh and the Sufi Duty in Mamluk Lands," *MSR* 3 (1999), 59–84.

Howell, Martha. *The Marriage Exchange. Property, Social Place and Gender in Cities of the Low Countries, 1300–1500*. Chicago: University of Chicago Press, 1998.

Humphreys, R. S. *From Saladin to the Mongols*. Albany: State University of New York Press, 1977.

— "Women as Patrons of Religious Architecture in Ayyubid Damascus," *Muqarnas* 11 (1994), 35–54.

Idris, H. R. "Le mariage en Occident musulman d'après un choix de fatwàs médiévales extraites du Mi'yār d'al-Wanšarīsī," *SI* 32 (1970), 157–67.

— "Le mariage en Occident musulman. Analyse de fatwàs médiévales extraites du Mi'yār d'al-Wanšarīsī," *Revue de l'Occident Musulman et de la Méditerranée* 12 (1972), 45–62; 17 (1974), 71–105; 25 (1978), 119–38.

Imber, C. "Involuntary Annulment of Marriage and its Solutions in Ottoman Law," *Turcica* 25 (1993), 59–69.

Irwin, Robert. "'Alī al-Baghdādī and the Joy of Mamluk Sex," in Kennedy (ed.), *The Historiography of Islamic Egypt*, 45–57.

— "Iqta' and the End of the Crusader States," in P. M. Holt (ed.), *The Eastern Mediterranean Lands in the Period of the Crusades* (Warminster: Aris & Phillips, 1977), 62–77.

— *The Middle East in the Middle Ages: The Early Mamluk Sultanate, 1250–1382*. London: Croom Helm, 1986.

Ivanova, S. "The Divorce between Zubaida Hatun and Essaied Osman Aga: Women in the Eighteenth-Century Shari'a Court of Rumelia," in El-Azhary Sonbol (ed.), *Women, Family and Divorce Laws*, 112–125.

Jackson, Sherman. "Ibn Taymiyya on Trial in Damascus," *Journal of Semitic Studies* 39 (1994), 41–85.

— "Kramer Versus Kramer in a Tenth/Sixteenth Century Egyptian Court: Post-Formative Jurisprudence Between Exigency and Law," *ILS* 8 (2001), 27–51.

— "The Primacy of Domestic Politics: Ibn Bint al-A'azz and the Establishment of the Four Chief Judgeships in Mamluk Egypt," *JAOS* 115 (1995), 52–65.

Jennings, R. "Divorce in the Ottoman Sharia Court of Cyprus, 1580–1640," *SI* 77–78 (1993), 155–68.

Jones, Gavin W. "Modernization and Divorce: Contrasting Trends in Islamic Southeast Asia and the West," *Population and Development Review* 23 (1997), 95–114.

Jordan, William Chester. *Women and Credit in Pre-industrial and Developing Societies*. Philadelphia: University of Pennsylvania Press, 1992.

Keddie, N. "Problems in the Study of Middle Eastern Women," *IJMES* 10 (1979), 225–40.

Keddie, N. and B. Baron (eds.). *Women in Middle Eastern History: Shifting Boundaries in Sex and Gender*. New Haven: Yale University Press, 1992.

Kennedy H. (ed.). *The Historiography of Islamic Egypt (c. 950–1800)*. Leiden: Brill, 2000.

Khalidi, T. *Arabic Historical Thought in the Classical Period*. Cambridge: Cambridge University Press, 1994.

Khoury, Nuha N. "The Autobiography of Ibn al-ʿAdīm as Told to Yāqūt al-Rūmī," *Edebiyât: Special Issue – Arabic Autobiography* 7/2 (1997), 289–311.

Khowaiter, A. A. *Baibars the First, his Endeavors and Achievements*. London: Green Mountain, 1978.

Kolmer, L. *Promissorische Eide im Mittelalter*. Kallm unz Opf.: M. Lassleben, 1989.

Kramer, Joel. "Women's Letters from the Cairo Genizah: A Preliminary Study" (in Hebrew), in Yael Atzmon (ed.), *Eshnav le-Ḥayehen shel Nashīm be-Ḥevrōt Yehūdiyōt* (Jerusalem: Merkaz Zalman Shazar, 1995), 161–81.

Lamm, Carl J. *Cotton in Mediaeval Textiles of the Near East*. Paris: P. Geuthner, 1937.

Lamdan, R. *A Separate People: Jewish Women in Palestine, Syria, and Egypt in the Sixteenth Century*. Leiden: Brill, 2000.

Laoust, H. *Essai sur les doctrines sociales et politiques de Takī-d-Dīn Aḥmad b. Taimīya*. Cairo: Institut français d'archéologie orientale, 1939.

— "Le hanbalisme sous les Mamlouks Bahrides (658–784/1260–1382)," *Revue d'études islamiques* 28 (1960), 1–71.

— "Une risāla d'Ibn Taimīya sur le serment de répudiation," *Bulletin d'études orientales* 7–8 (1937–38), 215–36.

Lapidus, Ira. "The Grain Economy of Mamluk Egypt," *JESHO* 12 (1969), 1–15.

— *Muslim Cities in the Later Middle Ages*. Cambridge, MA: Harvard University Press, 1967.

Largueche, D. "Confined, Battered and Repudiated Women in Tunis since the Eighteenth Century," in El-Azhary Sonbol (ed.), *Women, Family and Divorce Laws*, 259–76.

el-Leithy, Tamer. "Of Bodies Chang'd to Various Forms . . . : Hermaphrodites and Transsexuals in Mamluk Society" (unpublished paper, Princeton University, 2001).

Levanoni, Amalia, and M. Winter (eds.). *The Mamluks in Egyptian and Syrian Politics and History*. Leiden: Brill, 2004.

Little, Donald P. *A Catalogue of the Islamic Documents from al-Ḥaram aš-Šarīf in Jerusalem*. Beirut and Wiesbaden: F. Steiner, 1984.

— "Documents Related to the Estates of a Merchant and his Wife in Late Fourteenth Century Jerusalem," *MSR* 3 (1999), 93–177.

— "Ḥaram Documents Related to the Jews of Late Fourteenth-Century Jerusalem," *Journal of Semitic Studies* 30 (1985), 227–64.

— "The Ḥaram Documents as Sources for the Arts and Architecture of the Mamluk Period," *Muqarnas* 2 (1984), 61–72.

— "The Historical and Historiographical Significance of the Detention of Ibn Taymiyya," *IJMES* 4 (1973), 313–27.

— "Historiography of the Ayyūbid and the Mamlūk Epochs," in Petry (ed.), *The Cambridge History of Egypt*, 421–32.

— *History and Historiography of the Mamlūks*. London: Variorum, 1986.

— *An Introduction to Mamlūk Historiography*. Wiesbaden: F. Steiner, 1970.

— "The Nature of *Khānqāhs*, *Ribāṭs* and *Zāwiyas* under the Mamlūks", in W. Hallaq and D. Little (eds.), *Islamic Studies Presented to Charles J. Adams.* Leiden: Brill, 1991, 91–107.

— "Notes on the Early *Naẓar al-khāṣṣ*," in Phillip and Haarmann (eds.), *The Mamluks in Egyptian Politics and Society*, 235–53.

— "Six Fourteenth Century Purchase Deeds for Slaves from al-Ḥaram Aš-Šarīf," *Zeitschrift der Deutschen Morgenländischen Gesellschaft* 131 (1981), 297–337.

Lopez, Robert, Harry Miskimin and Abraham Udovitch. "England to Egypt: 1350–1500: Long-Term Trends and Long-Distance Trade," in M. Cook (ed.), *Studies in the Economic History of the Middle East* (London: Oxford University Press, 1970), 93–128.

Lowry, Joseph. "Time, Form and Self: The Autobiography of Abū Shāma," *Edebiyât: Special Issue – Arabic Autobiography* 7/2 (1997), 313–25.

Lutfi, Huda. "Manners and Customs of Fourteenth-Century Cairene Women: Female Anarchy Versus Male Sharʿī Order in Muslim Prescriptive Treatises," in Keddie and Baron (eds.), *Women in Middle Eastern History*, 99–121.

— *Al-Quds al-Mamlûkiyya: A History of Mamlûk Jerusalem Based on the Ḥaram Documents*. Berlin: K. Schwarz, 1985.

— "Al-Sakhāwī's *Kitāb al-Nisā'* as a Source for the Social and Economic History of Muslim Women during the Fifteenth Century AD," *Muslim World* 71 (1981), 104–24.

— "A Study of Six Fourteenth-Century *Iqrārs* from al-Quds Relating to Muslim Women," *JESHO* 26 (1983), 246–94.

Mackie, L. "Towards an Understanding of Mamluk Silks: National and International Considerations," *Muqarnas* 2 (1984), 127–46.

Māhir, Suʿād. *al-Nasīj al-Islāmī*. Cairo: al-Jihāz al-Markazī li'l-Kutub al-Jāmiʿiyya wa'l-Madrasiyya wa'l-Wasā'il al-Taʿlīmiyya, 1977.

— "ʿUqūd al-Zawāj ʿalā al-Mansūjāt al-Athariyya," in *al-Kitāb al-Dhahabī li'l-Iḥtifāl al-Khamsīnī bi'l-Dirāsāt al-Athariyya bi-Jāmiʿat al-Qāhira*, 3 vols. Cairo: al-Jihāz al-Markazī li'l-Kutub al-Jāmiʿiyya wa'l-Madrasiyya wa'l-Wasā'il al-Taʿlīmiyya, 1978.

Mann, J. *Texts and Studies in Jewish History and Literature*, 2 vols. Cincinnati: Hebrew Union College Press, 1931–35.

Marcus, Abraham. *The Middle East on the Eve of Modernity: Aleppo in the Eighteenth Century*. New York: Columbia University Press, 1989.

Marmon, Shaun. *Eunuchs and Sacred Boundaries in Islamic Society*. New York: Oxford University Press, 1995.

Martel-Thoumian, B. *Les civils et l'administration dans l'état militaire mamlūk (ix[e]/xv[e] siècle)*. Damascus: Institut français de Damas, 1991.

Marzouk, M. *History of the Textile Industry in Alexandria, 331 BC–1517 AD* Alexandria: Alexandria University Press, 1955.

Masson, Jacques. "Histoire des causes du divorce dans le tradition canonique copte (des origins au XIIIè siècle)," *Studia Orientalia Christiana. Collectanea* 14 (1970–71), 163–250; 15 (1972–73), 181–294.

Mayer, L. A. *Mamluk Costume: A Survey*. Geneva: A. Kundig, 1952.

Mazzaoui, Maureen F. *The Italian Cotton Industry in the Later Middle Ages, 1100–1600*. Cambridge: Cambridge University Press, 1981.

Meriwether, M. *The Kin Who Count. Family and Society in Ottoman Aleppo, 1770–1840*. Austin: University of Texas Press, 1999.

Michel, N. "Les *rizaq iḥbāsiyya*, terres agricoles en mainmorte dans l'Egypte mamelouke et ottomane. Etude sur les *Dafātir al-Aḥbās* ottomans," *AI* 30 (1996), 105–98.

Milwright, M. "Pottery in the Written Sources of the Ayyubid–Mamluk period (c. 567–923/1171–1517)," *BSOAS* 62 (1999), 505–18.

Murad, Ḥasan Q. "Ibn Taymiya on Trial: A Narrative Account of his *Miḥan*," *Islamic Studies* 18 (1979), 1–32.

Murk-Jansen, S. *Brides in the Desert: The Spirituality of the Beguines*. Maryknoll, NY: Orbis Books, 1998.

Murray, Stephen O. "Male Homosexuality, Inheritance Rules and the Status of Women in Medieval Egypt: The Case of the Mamluks," in S. Murray and W. Roscoe, *Islamic Homosexualities: Culture, History and Literature* (New York: New York University Press, 1997), 161–73.

Musallam, Basim. "The Ordering of Muslim Societies," in F. Robinson (ed.), *The Cambridge Illustrated History of the Islamic World*. Cambridge: Cambridge University Press, 1996, 186–97.

— *Sex and Society in Islam: Birth Control before the Nineteenth Century*. Cambridge: Cambridge University Press, 1983.

Neel, C. "The Origins of the Beguines," in Judith M. Bennett, Elisabeth A. Clark, Jean F. O'Barr, B. Anne Vilen and Sarah Westpahl-Wihl (eds.), *Sisters and Workers in the Middle Ages* (Chicago: University of Chicago Press, 1989), 240–60.

Nielsen, J. *Secular Justice in an Islamic State: Maẓālim under the Baḥrī Mamlūks, 662/1264–789/1387*. Leiden: Brill, 1985.

— "Sultan al-Ẓāhir Baybars and the Appointment of Four Chief Qāḍīs, 663/1265," *SI* 60 (1984), 167–76.

Olsowy-Schlanger, Judith. *Karaite Marriage Documents from the Cairo Geniza. Legal Tradition and Community Life in Mediaeval Egypt and Palestine*. Leiden: Brill, 1998.

Opitz, Claudia. "Life in the Late Middle Ages," in Georges Duby and Michelle Perrot (eds.), *A History of Women in the West* (Cambridge, MA: Harvard University Press, 1992), vol. II: *Silences of the Middle Ages*, 267–317.

Peirce, L. "'She is Trouble and I will Divorce Her': Orality, Honor and Divorce in the Ottoman Court of 'Aintab," in Hambly (ed.), *Women in the Medieval Islamic World*, 269–300.

Petry, Carl (ed.), *The Cambridge History of Egypt*, vol. I: *Islamic Egypt, 640–1517*. Cambridge: Cambridge University Press, 1998.

— "Class Solidarity Versus Gender Gain: Women as Custodians of Property in Later Medieval Egypt," in Keddie and Baron (eds.), *Women in Middle Eastern History*, 122–42.

— "Conjugal Rights Versus Class Prerogatives: A Divorce Case in Mamlūk Cairo," in Hambly (ed.), *Women in the Medieval Islamic World*, 227–40.
— "Disruptive 'Others' as Depicted in the Chronicles of the Late Mamlūk Period," in Kennedy (ed.), *The Historiography of Islamic Egypt*, 167–94.
—"The Estate of al-Khuwand Fāṭima al-Khāṣṣbakiyya: Royal Spouse, Autonomous Investor," in Levanoni and Winter (eds.) *The Mamluks in Egyptian and Syrian Politics and History*, 277–94.
— *Protectors or Praetorians? The Last Mamlūk Sultans and Egypt's Waning as a Great Power*. Albany: State University of New York Press, 1994.
— "'Quis Custodiet Custodes?' Revisited: The Prosecution of Crime in the Late Mamluk Sultanate," *MSR* 3 (1999), 13–30.
Phillip, Thomas and Ulrich Haarman (eds.). *The Mamluks in Egyptian Politics and Society*. Cambridge: Cambridge University Press, 1998.
Phillips, R. *Untying the Knot. A Short History of Divorce*. Cambridge: Cambridge University Press, 1991.
Pollock, F. and Maitland, F. W. *The History of English Law before the Time of Edward I*, 2nd edn., 2 vols. Cambridge: Cambridge University Press, 1968.
Popper, W. *Egypt and Syria under the Circassian Sultans 1382–1468 AD: Systematic Notes to Ibn Taghrî Birdî's Chronicles of Egypt*. Berkeley: University of California Press, 1956.
Pouzet, L. *Damas au VII<sup>e</sup>/XIII<sup>e</sup> siècle. Vie et structures religieuses d'une métropole Islamique*. Beirut: Dar el-Machreq Sarl, 1988.
Powers, David. "*Fatwās* as Sources for Social and Legal History: A Dispute over Endowment Revenues from Fourteenth-Century Fez," *al-Qanṭara* 11 (1990), 295–341.
— *Law, Society, and Culture in the Maghrib, 1300–1500*. Cambridge: Cambridge University Press, 2002.
— "The Mālikī Family Endowment: Legal Norms and Social Practices," *IJMES* 25 (1993), 379–406.
— "Parents and their Minor Children: Familial Politics in the Middle Maghrib in the Eighth/Fourteenth Century," *Continuity and Change* 16/2 (2001), 177–200.
— "Women and Courts in the Maghrib, 1300–1500," in M. Khalid Masud, Rudolf Peters and David S. Powers (eds.), *Dispensing Justice in Muslim Courts: Qadis, Procedures and Judgments* (forthcoming).
— "Women and Divorce in the Islamic West: Three Cases," *Hawwa* 1 (2003), 29–45.
Rabie, H. *The Financial System of Egypt, AH 564–741/1169–1341*. London: Oxford University Press, 1972.
—"Ḥujjat Tamlīk wa-waqf," *Majallat al-Jamʿiyya al-Miṣriyya lil-Dirāsāt al-Taʾrīkhiyya* 12 (1964).
Rāġib, Yūsuf. "Un contrat de mariage sur soie d'Egypte fatimide," *AI* 16 (1980), 31–37.
Rapoport, Yossef. "Divorce and the Elite Household in Late Medieval Cairo," *Continuity and Change* 16/2 (August 2001), 201–18.

— "Ibn Taymiyya on Divorce Oaths," in Levanoni and Winter (eds.), *The Mamluks in Egyptian and Syrian Politics and Society*, 191–217.
— "Legal Diversity in the Age of *Taqlīd*: The Four Chief Qadis under the Mamluks," *ILS* 10/2 (2003), 210–28.
— "Matrimonial Gifts in Early Islamic Egypt," *ILS* 7/1 (2000), 1–37.
Reynolds, Dwight F. *Interpreting the Self. Autobiography in the Arabic Literary Tradition*. Berkeley: University of California Press, 2001.
Richards, D. S. "Mamluk Amirs and their Families and Households," in Phillip and Haarmann (eds.), *The Mamluks in Egyptian Politics and Society*, 32–54.
— "The Qasāma in Mamlūk Society: Some Documents from the Ḥaram Collection in Jerusalem," *AI* 25 (1991), 245–84.
Roded, Ruth. *Women in the Islamic Biographical Dictionaries: From Ibn Saʿd to Who's Who*. Boulder: Lynne Rienner, 1994.
Rowson, E. "Two Homoerotic Narratives from Mamluk Literature: al-Ṣafadī's *Lawʿat al-Shākī* and Ibn Dāniyāl's *Mutayyam*," in J. W. Wright and E. Rowson (eds.), *Homoeroticism in Classical Arabic Literature* (New York: Columbia University Press, 1997), 158–91.
Sabra, A. *Poverty and Charity in Medieval Islam. Mamluk Egypt, 1250–1517*. Cambridge: Cambridge University Press, 2000.
Sadan, J. *Le mobilier au Proche-Orient médiéval*. Leiden: E. J. Brill, 1976.
al-Sajdi, Dana. "Trespassing the Male Domain: The Qaṣīdah of Laylā al-Akhyaliyya," *Journal of Arabic Literature* 31 (2000), 121–46.
Schimmel, A. *My Soul is a Woman: The Feminine in Islam*, trans. Susan H. Ray. New York: Continuum, 1997.
Schmidtke, Sabine. *The Theology of al-ʿAllāma al-Ḥillī (d. 726/1325)*. Berlin: K. Schwarz, 1991.
Schregle, G. *Die Sultanin von Ägypten: Šağarat ad-Durr in der arabischen Geschichtsschreibung und Literatur*. Wiesbaden: Otto Harassowitz, 1961.
Serjeant, R. B. *Islamic Textiles; Material for a History up to the Mongol Conquest*. Beirut: Librairie du Liban, 1972.
Serrano, D. "Legal Practice in an Andalusī–Maghribī Source from the Twelfth Century CE: The *Madhāhib al-Ḥukkām fī Nawāzil al-Aḥkām*," *ILS* 7/2 (2000), 187–234.
Shatzmiller, Maya. *Labour in the Medieval Islamic World*. Leiden: Brill, 1994.
— "Women and Property Rights in al-Andalus and the Maghrib: Social Patterns and Legal Discourse," *ILS* 2 (1995), 219–57.
— "Women and Wage Labour in the Medieval Islamic West," *JESHO* 40 (1997), 174–206.
Shoshan, B. "Exchange-Rate Policies in Fifteenth-Century Egypt," *JESHO* 29 (1986), 28–51.
— "Grain Riots and the 'Moral Economy': Cairo 1350–1517," *Journal of Interdisciplinary History* 10 (1980), 459–78.

Stone, L. *Road to Divorce: England 1530–1987*. Oxford: Clarendon Press, 1990.
Sublet, J. "La folie de la princesse Bint al-Ašraf (un scandale financier sous les mamelouks bahris)," *Bulletin d'études orientales* 27 (1974), 45–50.
Tabbaa, Yasser. *Constructions of Power and Piety in Medieval Aleppo*. University Park: Pennsylvania State University Press, 1997.
Talmon-Heller, Daniella. "The Cited Tales of the Wondrous Doings of the *Shaykhs* of the Holy Land, by Ḍiyā' al-Dīn Abū ʻAbd Allāh Muḥammad b. ʻAbd al-Wāḥid al-Maqdisī (569/1173–643/1245)," *Crusades* 1 (2002), 111–54.
Tapper, Nancy. *Bartered Brides: Politics, Gender and Marriage in an Afghan Tribal Society*. Cambridge: Cambridge University Press, 1991.
Taylor, C. *In the Vicinity of the Righteous: Ziyāra and the Veneration of Muslim Saints in Late Medieval Egypt*. Leiden: Brill, 1998.
Thorau, P. *The Lion of Egypt: Sultan Baybars I and the Near East in the Thirteenth Century*, trans. P. M. Holt. London: Longman, 1992.
Tucker, Judith. *In the House of the Law: Gender and Islamic Law in Ottoman Syria and Palestine*. Berkeley: University of California Press, 1998.
— "Marriage and Family in Nablus, 1720–1856: Towards a History of Arab Marriage," *Journal of Family History* 13 (1988), 165–179.
— "Ties that Bound: Women and Family in Eighteenth and Nineteenth-Century Nablus," in Keddie and Baron (eds.), *Women in Middle Eastern History*, 233–53.
Tyan, E. *Histoire de l'organisation judiciare en pays d'Islam*, 2nd edn. Leiden: E. J. Brill, 1960.
Walker, Bethany J. "Rethinking Mamluk Textiles," *MSR* 4 (2000), 167–95.
Wiesner, Merry. "Spinsters and Seamstresses: Women in Cloth and Clothing Production," in Margaret W. Ferguson, Maureen Quilligan and Nancy J. Vickers (eds.), *Rewriting the Renaissance: The Discourses of Sexual Difference in Early Modern Europe*. Chicago: University of Chicago Press, 1986, 191–205.
Williams, C. "The Mosque of Sitt Ḥadaq," *Muqarnas* 11 (1994), 55–64.
Winter, M. "Mamluks and their Households in Late Mamluk Damascus: A *waqf* Study," in Levanoni and Winter (eds.) *The Mamluks in Egyptian and Syrian Politics and History*, 297–316.
— *Society and Religion in Early Ottoman Egypt: Studies in the Writings of ʻAbd al-Wahhab al-Shaʻrani*. New Brunswick: Transaction Books, 1982.
Zarinebaf-Shahr, F. "Women, Law and Imperial Justice in Ottoman Istanbul in the Late Seventeenth Century," in El-Azhary Sonbol (ed.), *Women, Family and Divorce Laws*, 81–95.
Zilfi, M. "'We Don't Get Along': Women and *Hul* Divorce in the Eighteenth Century," in M. Zilfi (ed.), *Women in the Ottoman Empire: Middle Eastern Women in the Early Modern Era*. Leiden: E. J. Brill, 1997, 264–96.
Zomeño, Amalia. *Dote y matrimonio en al-Andalus y el norte de África. Estudio de la jurisprudencia islámica medieval*. Madrid: Consejo Superior de Investigationes Científicas, 2000.

# Index


abandoned wives 40, 75, 76–77, 80, 87
Abu Lughod, L. 7
Abū Shāma, Shihāb al-Dīn 10, 31–32, 39
adultery 69, 72, 73, 81, 104
ʿĀʾisha al-Bāʿūniyya 11
Aleppo 23, 40
Alif bt. ʿAlam al-Dīn al-Bulqīnī 80
Ānūk b. al-Nāṣir Muḥammad 12
al-Aqfahsī, ʿImād al-Dīn 63
al-Aqṣā Mosque 19, 21
al-Ashraf Shaʿbān (Sultan) 26, 70
Ashtor-Strauss, E. 103
Aswan 56
*awlād al-nās* 21, 26
Ayyubids 22, 40, 41, 70
Azbak al-Ẓāhirī 80

Baghdad 39
Banū al-Munajjā 103
Barqūq, al-Ẓāhir (Sultan) 56
Barsbāy, al-Ashraf (Sultan) 36
bathhouse 33, 41, 47, 61
Baybars, al-Ẓāhir (Sultan) 70, 91, 94
Bedouins 104
Beguines 44
al-Biqāʿī, Ibrāhīm b. ʿUmar 10, 87–88
Black Death 5, 22, 26, 83

chamberlain (*ḥājib*) 79, 80
Chamberlain, M. 103, 109
children
  custody of 66, 69, 73, 87
  and divorce 71, 83
  support of 51, 58, 62, 66, 73, 74, 77, 78
  *see also* marriage

Christians 3, 5
compensation gift (*mutʿa*) 71
concubinage 11, 49, 75; *see also* polygamy; slave-girls
confinement, of women 36, 71, 73, 74, 76, 81, 109
consensual divorce (*khulʿ*) 2, 4, 65, 69–70, 72–73, 79, 84, 85, 87, 95, 98
courts, military (*maẓālim*) 8, 51, 69, 79–82
credit association 25
creditors, women as 24, 62, 80
custody *see* children

David b. Zekharya, Rabbi 62
*dawādār* 79, 80, 81
Ḍayfa Khātūn 23
Ḍayfa bt. ʿUmar (seamstress) 35–36
demography, men–women ratio 18, 45
*dikka* (multipurpose wooden chest) 12, 15
divorce *see* consensual divorce (*khulʿ*); judicial divorce (*faskh*); oath of divorce; rates of divorce; repudiation (*ṭalāq*)
domestic violence 69, 76, 79, 81
dowry (*jihāz*) 6, 44
  of childless wife 17
  converted to cash 26–27
  as heirloom 15, 20
  as inheritance 13, 18–19, 20–22
  among Jews 16–17
  in Latin Europe 111
  as loan 17–18
  in North Africa and al-Andalus 18
  among the poor 15–16
  registration of 20
  revocation of by father 17–18
  as trousseau 6, 12, 13, 15, 61
  value of 12–13, 14–15, 17, 20, 26

# Cambridge Studies in Islamic Civilization

*Other titles in the series*

Mannerism in Arabic Poetry
*A Structural Analysis of Selected Texts*
Stefan Sperl

Popular Culture in Medieval Cairo
Boaz Shoshan

Early Philosophical Shiism
*The Ismaili Neoplatonism of Abū Yaʿqūb al-Sijistāni*
Paul E. Walker

Indian Merchants and Eurasian Trade, 1600–1750
Stephen Frederic Dale

Palestinian Peasants and Ottoman Officials
*Rural Administration around Sixteenth-century Jerusalem*
Amy Singer

Arabic Historical Thought in the Classical Period
Tarif Khalidi

Mongols and Mamluks
*The Mamluk-Īlkhānid War, 1260–1281*
Reuven Amitai-Preiss

Hierarchy and Egalitarianism in Islamic Thought
Louise Marlow

The Politics of Households in Ottoman Egypt
*The Rise of the Qazdağlis*
Jane Hathaway

Commodity and Exchange in the Mongol Empire
*A Cultural History of Islamic Textiles*
Thomas T. Allsen

State and Provincial Society in the Ottoman Empire
*Mosul, 1540–1834*
Dina Rizk Khoury

The Mamluks in Egyptian Politics and Society
Thomas Philipp and Ulrich Haarmann (eds)

The Delhi Sultanate
*A Political and Military History*
Peter Jackson

European and Islamic Trade in the Early Ottoman State
*The Merchants of Genoa and Turkey*
Kate Fleet

Reinterpreting Islamic Historiography
*Harun al-Rashid and the Narrative of the 'Abbāsid Caliphate*
Tayeb El-Hibri

The Ottoman City between East and West
*Aleppo, Izmir, and Istanbul*
Edhem Eldem, Daniel Goffman and Bruce Masters

A Monetary History of the Ottoman Empire
Sevket Pamuk

The Politics of Trade in Safavid Iran
*Silk for Silver, 1600–1730*
Rudolph P. Matthee

The Idea of Idolatry and the Emergence of Islam
*From Polemic to History*
G. R. Hawting

Classical Arabic Biography
*The Heirs of the Prophets in the Age of al-Ma'mūn*
Michael Cooperson

Empire and Elites after the Muslim Conquest
*The Transformation of Northern Mesopotamia*
Chase F. Robinson

Poverty and Charity in Medieval Islam
*Mamluk Egypt*, 1250–1517
Adam Sabra

Christians and Jews in the Ottoman Arab World
*The Roots of Sectarianism*
Bruce Masters

Culture and Conquest in Mongol Eurasia
Thomas T. Allsen

Revival and Reform in Islam
*The Legacy of Muhammad al-Shawkani*
Bernard Haykel

Tolerance and Coercion in Islam
*Interfaith Relations in the Muslim Tradition*
Yohanan Friedmann

Guns for the Sultan
*Military Power and the Weapons Industry in the Ottoman Empire*
Gábor Ágoston

Descartes

l'idée que l'on peut sentir dans le sommeil (dans nos rêves) dans la même façon que l'on sent quand on est éveillé.

Je songe à cette idée bcp en ce moment quand les souvenirs de ce qui m'est arrivé dans mes rêves, de ce que je sentais hier soir ou ce matin) m'apparaît si réel que ce qui m'est arrivé quand j'étais éveillé hier. => Dans quelque façon il n'y sait plus réel en commençant.

CPSIA information can be obtained at www.ICGtesting.com
Printed in the USA
240878LV00003B/7/A

9 780521 045803